THE BEST
OF TIMES

THE BEST OF TIMES

CHALLENGES AND TRIUMPHS IN
BRITISH POLITICS, ECONOMICS AND
FOREIGN AFFAIRS 2013–2015

MARK FIELD MP

Biteback Publishing

First published in Great Britain in 2016 by
Biteback Publishing Ltd
Westminster Tower
3 Albert Embankment
London SE1 7SP
Copyright © Mark Field 2016

Mark Field has asserted his right under the Copyright, Designs
and Patents Act 1988 to be identified as the author of this work.

All rights reserved. No part of this publication may be reproduced,
stored in a retrieval system or transmitted, in any form or by any means,
without the publisher's prior permission in writing.

This book is sold subject to the condition that it shall not, by way
of trade or otherwise, be lent, resold, hired out or otherwise circulated
without the publisher's prior consent in any form of binding or cover other
than that in which it is published and without a similar condition, including
this condition, being imposed on the subsequent purchaser.

Every reasonable effort has been made to trace copyright holders of material
reproduced in this book, but if any have been inadvertently overlooked
the publishers would be glad to hear from them.

ISBN 978-1-78590-073-0

10 9 8 7 6 5 4 3 2 1

A CIP catalogue record for this book is available from the British Library.

Set in Garamond by Adrian McLaughlin

Printed and bound in Great Britain by
CPI Group (UK) Ltd, Croydon CR0 4YY

CONTENTS

FOREWORD

It was in his celebrated novel contrasting the fortunes of the two cities of London and Paris during the French Revolution that Charles Dickens observed, 'It was the best of times, it was the worst of times…'

For these past fifteen years, I have represented in Parliament the two cities of London & Westminster through the booming first half of the 2000s to the financial bust of 2008, and the long road to recovery ever since. My first book, *Between the Crashes*, charted part of that journey by observing the economic calamity that befell the City of London through the telescope of political events in the City of Westminster, where the Labour administration of Gordon Brown was making way for the first coalition government since 1945.

Signing off at the halfway point of the coalition's term in December 2012, my concluding observations in *Between the Crashes* were tempered with some foreboding for the future and a distinct sense that there was more economic pain to come. Some three years on, however, the second crash alluded to in the book's title never came.

Instead, the security blanket thrown over the global economy in the immediate aftermath of the 2008 meltdown – industrial levels of quantitative easing complemented by record low interest rates in the Western world, and colossal Chinese stimulus in the East – remained firmly in place. By 2016, the Bank of England had not budged from the 0.5 per cent emergency interest rate regime first imposed in March 2009. The US Federal Reserve had only recently dared to nudge its base rate up from 0.25 per cent to 0.5 per cent,

and the European Central Bank had announced that eurozone interest rates would be cut to zero in a desperate bid to stimulate growth.

While the pause button may have been pressed on economic policy, politics did not stand still. This, my second book, follows the
increasingly turbulent flow of global affairs as anger with the political establishment and economic elite starts to carve channels of deep
disillusionment into which nationalist, populist and extremist sentiment begins to bubble. Meanwhile, Putin's ever-opportunistic Russia
and agents of chaos in the Middle East and north Africa slip into
the voids created by an increasingly inward-looking United States
and a hapless Europe struggling amidst a tangle of its own problems.

As post-Cold War assumptions on diplomacy, security and the
international order start to crumble, could it be that the years of
2013, 2014 and 2015 come to be considered as *The Best of Times*?

***

Writing these introductory remarks at Easter 2016, I wish to present a snapshot of a mood and a moment in time rather than a
set of predictions that will age poorly before the decade is much
older. Nonetheless, if a lesson in forecasting can be taken from the
pre-crash years of the 2000s, it is that if things seem too good to be
true, they very likely are.

The noughties era of soaring house prices, cheap credit and high
public spending appeared to come at no cost, until suddenly the
clouds of creative finance evaporated and a contagious panic set in.
Similarly, it is surely unthinkable that the post-crisis strategy of rock-
bottom interest rates and quantitative easing will not have to be paid
for with consequences. Most obviously, the menu of monetary policy options when the next downturn comes will be much shorter
now that conventional measures have been stretched to their limits.

Beyond that I make no predictions, but offer in *The Best of Times*
an account of how the political and economic outlook developed
between 2013 and 2015 in the hope that it may add to our understanding of whatever is to come next.

The Best of Times traces the steady march of the anti-elite, anti-establishment sentiment that began first to emerge from the ruins of the 2008 financial crisis. However there has been a distinct shift. The seething anger that was felt towards the banking fraternity in the immediate aftermath of the crash broadens into a much wider debate about the responsibility of big business and wealthy individuals to the nations in which they operate.

I was struck when putting this book together by just how many articles from this period examine the issue of tax avoidance by global corporations and global citizens. Look beyond the headlines on high-profile cases of avoidance and evasion, however, and there lies a deeper conundrum – how, in a world of competing jurisdictions and hypermobility, can a government simultaneously attract the wealth of international business and the super-rich, while ensuring that these groups pay proper regard to the benefits they enjoy from a nation's social capital? I fear the regularity with which tax avoidance clampdowns appear in financial legislation only suggests that it is difficult to make any real headway in this contentious area without a commitment to sweeping tax simplification.

This applies equally to the issue of housing. With persistently low interest rates in developed economies creating a boom in asset prices, *The Best of Times* returns time and again to the generational and transnational divisions cleaved by the ballooning cost of real estate. As even young professionals fear that neither hard work nor talent can assist in their aspirations to the first rung of the property ladder, the system of incentives that lies at the heart of capitalism's success starts to disintegrate and frustration grows towards older home owners and wealthy overseas buyers. Trying to walk the tightrope between an expanding band of the disenchanted and a comfortable class of asset-owners, politicians from all parties offer prescriptions of new taxes, housing schemes and incentives to build, but ultimately are unable by 2016 to resolve this problem.

But it is not only ultra-low interest rates that stoke house prices during this period. The London economy recovers robustly from the crash, acting as the engine for a nascent UK revival that starts really to take hold by 2014/15. Continental stagnation and growing instability abroad make our capital ever more attractive to a global workforce, and debate continues about the desirability of inward migration and foreign investment as pressure is placed upon housing supply and infrastructure. With the government struggling to control the numbers arriving on these shores, demand remains for a restrictive immigration system and I explore in *The Best of Times* some of the unintended consequences as universities and top-end employers fight to attract and retain the world's brightest and best.

It perhaps only underlines the difficulty that successful, developed economies have in these years in acting nimbly and flexibly in response to the forces of globalisation. In an age in which people are able suddenly to communicate, transact and arrange travel using only a mobile phone, mass migratory flows of the lower middle classes in the developing world to the jobs and prospects in Europe and the United States become ever harder to control. Regional instability from Nigeria to Pakistan makes illegal trafficking routes busier, but it is the unrest in Syria and Libya that sparks the flight of hundreds of thousands which, by 2016, has become an unmanageable tide of human misery.

The institutional architecture of the post-war era is increasingly regarded as blunt and clunky in the face of rapidly changing events, particularly in the absence of sustained engagement from the United States. This is a time in which Britain, the EU and the US all struggle to balance the pressing need to engage internationally to solve complex problems with a growing domestic demand to withdraw from the world's worries. The civil war in Syria rages on but attracts even darker forces to the Middle East. A new terror group, ISIS, emerges from the chaos and the Levant becomes the stage for a wider battle between Iran and Saudi Arabia as plunging oil prices and a thaw in Iranian–American relations shifts the regional balance of power. Meanwhile, Russia's President Putin spies an opportunity to enhance his nation's global position by intervening in Syria and fomenting unrest in the Ukraine.

After engagement in a miserable series of intractable conflicts in Iraq and Afghanistan, and caught up by domestic troubles, Western electorates and politicians are in no mood for new wars. *The Best of Times* traces the emergence of a brave new, potentially multipolar, world in which all actors are reassessing their post-Cold War roles and where the policy prescriptions of nations like Turkey, Russia and Iran are as relevant to solving regional tensions as the West's. This is a period in which threats become ever more dynamic, unpredictable and opportunist, creating great uncertainty over Western forces' power to influence events in spite of the dire consequences of inaction.

By 2016, the eurozone crisis remains stubbornly unresolved. In the three years preceding there are flashpoints in Cyprus, Portugal, Spain and, as ever, Greece. In the increasingly bitter battles between economics and politics in keeping the euro afloat, immediate financial imperative continues to win out. This culminates in the signing of a further Greek bailout deal in the summer of 2015 against the explicit mandates of both a snap referendum and general election in Greece. Democracy can be ignored, it seems, for the sake of the single currency – for now.

In Britain, *The Best of Times* follows the steady advance of a referendum on the UK's membership of the European Union, from the Prime Minister's Bloomberg speech in January 2013 announcing a renegotiation of that membership, to the surprise Conservative victory at the May 2015 general election and the promise of a concluding EU summit on the British question by early 2016. But with eurozone woes and the migration crisis occupying the minds of EU leaders, the risk looms large that the prevention of so-called Brexit slips down the priority list.

Perhaps ordinarily, supporters of the UK remaining an EU member could rest easy at the likely outcome of a referendum. However, these years also see the creeping appeal of anti-establishment ideas and movements that creates an air of unpredictability. In Britain, this manifests itself in a strengthened UKIP which sweeps to victory at the 2014 European elections, wins two parliamentary by-elections and commands 12.6 per cent of the vote at the general election. Labour under Ed Miliband starts to move away from the centre-ground of politics with a series of populist policy announcements, and while 'Red Ed' leads his party to crushing defeat in May 2015, in his place comes an astonishing victory for the left-wing Labour leadership contender, Jeremy Corbyn. In Scotland, a fiercely fought independence referendum ultimately leads to a vote for the status quo but entrenches an SNP insurgency north of the border. Meanwhile the Liberal Democrats are punished bitterly for their role in coalition with our Conservative Party.

On the continent, far-left and far-right movements march into the mainstream. Socialist Syriza takes the reins in Greece, Podemos is founded in Spain and a coalition of greens, socialists and communists is able to take power in Portugal. Far-right groups such as Pergida in Germany and the Sweden Democrats are emboldened by grassroots panic over the migration crisis. And in the United States, a battle for the presidential candidacies of both Republican and Democrat parties sees the populist figures of Donald Trump and Bernie Sanders respectively cause upset to the established way of thinking and doing.

By the end of 2015, this appetite for the unordinary has not been so overwhelming as to deliver a crushing blow to the status quo but an appetite for change has started to gnaw.

***

The question for 2016, at least politically, is whether a breakaway from the conventional might be made – by a President Trump, perhaps, or the UK severing ties with the European Union.

The Best of Times signs off at the end of 2015, before the fateful February 2016 EU summit at which our Prime Minister formally concluded the UK's renegotiation and announced a referendum on our EU membership on 23 June. Before long, my contemporary view that we must remain a member of the European Union will be irrelevant and the British people will have spoken. For now, however, I contend that to boil the Leave/Remain decision down simply to one of self-interest would be a dereliction of duty to our fellow Europeans in the course of the continent's present difficulties. Not only that, but today's darkening global economic clouds and the threat of international terrorism indicate how interdependent our interests are with other nations.

I happen to believe passionately that there is an unashamedly emotional case to make for our continued membership of the EU, something too often regarded as the exclusive preserve of those who wish us to leave. We have now enjoyed over seventy years of peace in the heart of this continent; my eight-year-old son will, I trust, be the third generation of Field menfolk who have not had to go to war. Frankly, over the past four or five centuries, it has never been the British way to walk away from international difficulties. Not for us, the road of isolationism or protectionism – crossing the street when international troubles brew. Instead, our national instinct, one I am confident remains present in the hearts of today's generation of Britons, is to play a *full* role on the global stage. We cannot deny the reality that our exit from the EU would precipitate a huge crisis of economic, diplomatic and political confidence across our continent – and the United Kingdom.

With the dawning of 2016, I have also reflected on the similarities between the crises of the 1930s and the era since 2008. In both momentous times, a financial bust that began in the US spread to Europe, resulting in foreclosures in the real economy and then across the global system. The pattern of mass unemployment, beggar-thy-neighbour devaluations and collapsing trade has to some extent been repeated, while the disillusionment with mainstream politics and politicians resulting in nationalism, populism and extremism winning out at the ballot box also shows clear signs of being replicated in the latter half of the 2010s.

Perhaps a fully fledged second crash, at least in the financial sector, will be averted. However, we should be reluctant to take at face value the reassuring official line that bank balance sheets are now fixed. They may be less precariously placed than eight years ago, but in a future financial tsunami too much of the risk remains hopelessly mispriced, and monies owed by households and governments have never been higher. The cost of underwriting the financial sector will be borne by current and future taxpayers, and it seems likely that much of this debt pile will have to be written off one day.

I fear too that there will not be a sustainable recovery until the cost of borrowing returns to some sort of normalcy. Yet for virtually every Briton under the age of thirty the notion of near zero interest rates, and the distortion to risk-taking and asset values that results from this, *is* the new normal. Naturally, this being the United Kingdom, it is in the residential housing market where this distortion is most profound. I also note over the past three years the unwarranted faith that we have placed in the wisdom of central bankers. Once again the parallels with the inter-war years are striking, and as recovery takes hold there is a growing suspicion that the policy responses from the Fed, the ECB and our own Bank of England may be less surefooted than they would have us believe.

After we Conservatives secured an unexpected majority at the May 2015 election, it became increasingly apparent that the tranquil years of coalition stability had given licence for too little government urgency to be expended in the fundamental changes in direction required to repair the profound policy failures and complacency of the Gordon Brown chancellorship. From the turn of the century onwards, expectations of welfare and healthcare entitlements had been systematically ramped up with the commensurate structural uplift in public expenditure that has proved difficult to tame ever since. However, this spending splurge was funded by a windfall in receipts from the financial services industry and a property boom, which Brown & Co regarded as a permanent feature of the economic landscape.

The last Labour administration spent up to and, as we now know, well beyond this illusory expansion in the UK's tax base. When the money ran out, widespread voter expectations about public sector entitlement sadly did not. We are still living with the consequences:

a persistent, dangerously high deficit with its affordability apparently sustained by the maintenance of an emergency interest rates regime. Perhaps even more cause for concern has been the continued difficulty even in the past half-decade of addressing poor UK labour productivity. Thankfully, today's government is trying to address this issue aggressively through infrastructure investment, increases in public service efficiency, projects such as the Northern Powerhouse and the radical education reforms started by Michael Gove. But these policies will take time to bear fruit.

The Chancellor rightly warned of a 'dangerous cocktail of new economic threats' as this year began. Until the end of the period covered by this collection of essays, the conventional wisdom had been that slowly but surely the world economy is on the road to recovery – the financial system has been rescued, the eurozone crisis contained and the overall debt burden steadily dealt with. The parallels with the world of nine decades ago are stark – then, the end of wartime hostilities lulled policymakers of the time into believing that all would now return to 'business as usual'. Is that not, in our hearts, where we might be today?

Fascinating times, certainly. *The Best of Times*? We cannot yet be sure.

I should like to thank Pool Re, and in particular chief executive Julian Enoizi, for sponsoring the publication of this book. We have worked together over the past few years to understand how we can best prepare and protect UK Plc from the economic consequences of any terror attack, and I am glad to continue that work going forward in the arena of cyber-security.

Once again, I am grateful to the fantastic team at Biteback for helping us put this book together with their usual efficiency, professionalism and enthusiasm. Finally, I must thank my chief of staff, Julia Dockerill, for writing this book with me and complementing my views and thoughts with her own valuable insights.

Rt Hon. Mark Field MP
March 2016

2013

The dawning of 2013 represented the halfway mark of the coalition government's five year term. Formed between Conservatives and Liberal Democrats in the wake of 2010's indeterminate general election result, the coalition's avowed raison d'être was to unite at a time of national crisis and shut the UK's gaping budget deficit. In 2009–10, that deficit had stood at 10.2 per cent of GDP – £154 billion in cash terms, the highest in the UK's peacetime history. Government debt, meanwhile, hovered just under £1 trillion.

By the time of Chancellor George Osborne's Autumn Statement in December 2012, however, it was clear that the coalition was being badly blown off course in restoring order to the public finances. Osborne's gloomy report to the Commons revealed that the government was going to miss its debt reduction target, with public debt predicted to balloon to £1.5 trillion in 2016, some 80 per cent of GDP. Meanwhile, growth was proving elusive. After forecasting in June 2010 that real GDP growth between Q1 2010 and Q4 2012 would be 7.4 per cent, instead it had limped in at 3.5 per cent with private consumption, business investment and residential investment all undershooting the projections in the coalition's inaugural Emergency Budget.

The Chancellor was not to mourn the closing of 2012. His downbeat Autumn Statement had followed the so-called Omnishambles Budget in March of that year, which had been sharply criticised for introducing an assortment of relatively modest taxation changes on the less wealthy – with new levies on grannies, pasties, charities and caravans – at the same time that the top rate of tax was dropped for the very highest earners.

While Osborne's reserves of personal political capital were running low as the New Year beckoned, he was nonetheless protected by the continued weakness of his opponents. Labour Leader Ed Miliband and his shadow Chancellor Ed Balls had made some headway in narrowing the credibility gap with the Tories on the question of economic management, developing a new 'One Nation' theme at their October conference. However, there was scant evidence that they had convinced voters of their readiness to retake the reins of government.

Stagnation and crisis continued to plague the eurozone, with 2012 witnessing major bailouts of Greece and Spain and spiralling unemployment rates that suppressed continental demand for British exports and fuelled speculation that a domestic triple-dip recession might be on the cards. Conversely, figures showed that British jobless queues were shrinking but question marks hovered over the quality of the employment opportunities that the UK economy was now providing. Were low wages and high job insecurity the new norm for UK workers? Such anxieties fed the anti-wealth rhetoric that had stalked the nation since the financial crisis, ramping up yet more hostility towards bankers and the political elite. For all the patient and painstaking reform of the financial sector, the banking system remained dangerously fragile as 2013 approached, and the persistent failure of banks to lend to businesses led to frenzied government efforts to get credit flowing by other means.

The broader international outlook stoked the economic pessimism. US President Barack Obama's re-election bid was successful, but Washington remained deadlocked over how to balance the US budget. As 2013 approached, the prospect of America falling off a fiscal cliff to trigger automatic spending cuts and tax rises wove fresh risk into the nascent global recovery. In China, a new era was also beginning as November saw Xi Jinping replace Hu Jintao as the new President. After a decade of jaw-dropping growth, it remained unclear how China might transition to the next stage of its economic development, weaning itself off colossal investment spending towards greater domestic consumption.

Never far from the headlines, the Middle East provided its fair share of dark clouds too as the hope of the Arab Spring chilled to an Arab Winter. The violence of President Assad against his own people showed no sign of abating in what was becoming a state of full-blown civil war in Syria. The Muslim Brotherhood's Mohammed Morsi won the Egyptian Presidential Election, exacerbating tensions between Egypt's secularists and Islamists, and the US Ambassador to Libya was brutally murdered as security deteriorated yet further in that nation.

Meanwhile, coalition relations were souring. A failure to secure House of Lords reform before the summer recess badly damaged Nick Clegg's credibility with his own Liberal Democrat party. He took his revenge on his Conservative coalition partners by instructing his MPs to vote against Boundary Commission recommendations to redraw parliamentary constituencies, destroying cherished Conservative ambitions to reduce Labour's electoral advantage by equalising constituency sizes.

Political pundits were predicting that 2013 would be another difficult year for the coalition partners, although most assumed both parties would struggle on together, if only to avoid a potentially devastating election. With the 2015 general election looming on the horizon, however, the Liberal Democrats would begin a new strategy to differentiate themselves from their coalition partners in order to stem dismal poll ratings and poor by-election performances. It was a risky approach – neither taking full ownership for coalition successes nor seeking to withdraw from the uncomfortable arrangement.

Conservatives had their own electoral worries, fearing the rise in fortunes of the UK Independence Party, which was beginning to make inroads into mainstream politics as disillusion with the Establishment deepened. Such disillusion now extended to the mainstream media, which was itself under the microscope as Lord Leveson issued his report on press freedoms, and lurid allegations about the conduct of Jimmy Savile and the BBC bubbled to the surface. With UKIP entrenching themselves and his own backbenchers baying for blood, Prime Minister David Cameron was under increasing pressure to set out his position on Europe as 2013 dawned.

Nonetheless, a triumphant summer in 2012 for the UK, which had seen the Queen's Diamond Jubilee celebrations and the London Olympics showcase Britain's creativity and cultural vibrancy to the world, had left a feel-good factor hanging over the capital and nation at large.

Such was the backdrop to the fresh year that beckoned and com-
pelled my pen to return to paper to carry on from where my first book,
Between the Crashes, *had left off…*

Corporate tax avoidance, 7 January 2013

The bailout of global banks with taxpayers' money in the wake of 2008's
financial crisis enraged electorates across the Western world. The notion
that the international elite had designed a 'heads I win, tails you lose'
system pervaded public sentiment, and manifested itself most visibly in
the Occupy protest movement whose slogan, 'We are the 99 per cent',
drew attention to the amount of wealth now concentrated among the
world's richest one per cent.

With banks chastened and far less profitable than their pre-crash
incarnations, focus shifted towards the new generation of global cor-
porate giants and their tax arrangements. Anti-austerity group, UK
Uncut, managed to close down Vodafone's Oxford Street store in 2010
when reports surfaced of the company's tax avoidance activities. But
the issue refused to go away and by December 2012, the tax affairs of
Starbucks were in the spotlight after it was revealed that in fourteen
years of trading, the hugely successful coffee chain had paid only £8.6
million in UK corporation tax in spite of sales in 2011 alone of nearly
£400 million. Following public outcry, Starbucks agreed to pay more –
though HMRC pointed out that tax was not voluntary. The story was
much bigger than coffee sales, however. US corporate giants like Google,
Facebook, Amazon and Apple and many others also had their tax con-
tributions brought into question.

The problem of how to react to this tax avoidance phenomenon in
an integrated global economy, where large firms could pick and choose
in which jurisdiction to base themselves, was the subject of a House of
Commons debate to which I made the following contribution:

Mark Field (Cities of London & Westminster) (Con): I am rather
concerned by the strongly anti-business approach to this issue shown
by Members [in this debate].

I have a great deal of sympathy for the leaders of all the political parties in formulating what would be regarded as an adequate response to the hot potato of corporate tax avoidance. In today's 24/7 media world, there is a constant demand on political figures to provide a running commentary on populist media campaigns following high-profile cases, including global businesses such as Google, Amazon and Starbucks.

I can fully understand the temptation to brand this as a moral issue, appealing to corporates' consciences when the legislative framework has failed, but it is a temptation that we in politics should try to avoid. In sparking a debate on morality in relation to the payment of tax, I fear that elite politicians open up a dangerous flank, because it suggests that the government are either impotent or are being disingenuous in their outrage. That applies to governments of all colours. After all, Parliament must ultimately set the rules within which companies operate. The precedent that has now been set, with Starbucks paying an amount of tax that it alone has determined sufficient publicly to salve its conscience, is a very odd one.

I am very concerned about the whole idea of mob rule. We must recognise that we are a democracy and that this is the forum within which the rules should be made. We should not try to inspire mob rule, whether on the payment of tax or for any other purposes within our society.

I have lost count of the number of times that media commentators have remarked that they would be delighted to apply the same approach to their own tax affairs by paying what they feel like rather than what the government demand of them. However, I have a much wider concern – that investors will begin to sense that UK policy on tax and regulation is becoming ever more arbitrary, governed more by sentiment and the news cycle than by the strict rules that should be enforced by HMRC and ultimately by the courts. The UK should be proud of its traditional place as a bastion of commercial certainty attracting investment from every corner of the globe, and will be undermined by high-profile rows such as this.

That is not to say that all is well. As we saw in my own constituency with the protest outside St Paul's Cathedral only a year or so ago, there is deep-seated concern that the rules of capitalism are being skewed. None of us should take this issue lightly, not least – dare I say it? – Conservative Members, as middle-class Tory voters often feel most strongly about it. To focus on arbitrary media campaigns or to invoke mob rule, as several Members have, is entirely the wrong way forward.

Too often, coalition Ministers have conflated the concepts of avoidance and evasion in debating taxation policy. The ideal solution is for aggressive tax avoidance schemes to be stopped in their tracks before they are marketed. That requires constant dialogue and the re-establishment of trust between HMRC and tax intermediaries. As a matter of urgency, therefore, the Treasury needs to promote a much better and more extensive pre-clearance regime to allow companies, individuals and tax advisers to road-test their proposed schemes. HMRC must start investing more time in developing and managing relationships with accountants and tax lawyers.

Meanwhile, the Treasury is committed at the time of the next Finance Bill to introducing general tax anti-avoidance provisions. It is clear that any such general power of anti-avoidance will feature some retrospective taxation. That is wrong in a free society, and it will risk further damaging our nation's reputation as a free, open and transparent place to set up, develop and run businesses.

I represent a central London seat where a lot of big businesses are based and operate. Nothing is more important than encouraging independents, whether they are restaurants, wine bars or bookshops, rather than just relying on big multinationals. No one wants to see all our high streets entirely dominated by large international corporations, many of which may involve themselves in what is currently regarded as aggressive tax avoidance.

The underlying lesson is that the UK tax code and regime remains far too complicated. The godfather of tax avoidance is complexity and uncertainty in the system. When even tax experts find it impossible to understand the workings of the tax code, people begin to question whether everyone is really paying their fair share. This, in turn, creates a sense of greater acceptability in the avoiding and evading of tax. Furthermore, a complicated and opaque tax system will always be vulnerable to misrepresentation, particularly by the media, and that again weakens confidence and encourages further avoidance. People think, 'If Amazon can get away with not paying its fair share, why should I bother to stump up?' I can understand why that is a general sentiment, but it frustrates many of the corporates that have paid in an open and transparent manner and will ultimately undermine their whole business framework.

Government can make piecemeal efforts to address particular instances of avoidance – they can play catch-up to a certain extent – but responses tend to involve making the entire system far more complex, thereby reinforcing the very factors that have driven avoidance in the first place, displacing the activity and giving rise to a whole set of new avoidance techniques. Instead, the government need to take an entirely different and fresh approach. They should look at how they can overhaul the entire system so that avoidance and evasion offer a similar, smaller reward and will therefore be seen as far less acceptable. Fundamentally, that can mean only lower taxes and a radically simplified tax code. For example, a single income tax applicable to income, however it is received, at the same single rate is the best way of stripping out of the system any incentive to avoid income tax. A simpler tax code would also free up HMRC resources to concentrate on tackling the real problem of tax evasion while making transgressions easier to identify.

It has been a pleasure to make a brief contribution to this debate on an important issue to which we must all return. However, I am concerned that too much of the rhetoric coming from this place almost suggests a sense of powerlessness that gives rise to the view that there is an aggressive anti-business approach in this country. We do need to have a thriving business sector. Global businesses can, of course, choose where they locate their business. We should be proud in this country of having a track record of being open to business, but I also accept that we want to ensure that businesses pay their fair share, because we have a huge deficit and a huge debt that has to be paid off if we are not to burden future generations.

I hope that we will look at the whole issue with that in mind, but above all I hope that the Treasury will take on board the idea that HMRC needs to have an approach that is much more open to the pre-clearance I referred to. We must also, as a matter of urgency, look at the complications in our tax code that are allowing some of the high-profile avoidance to take place.

‡

The first skirmish of many?, 21 January 2013

In 2010, I was appointed by the Prime Minister to parliament's Intelligence and Security Committee which scrutinises the work of MI5, MI6 and GCHQ. Fellow committee members included former Labour Cabinet Minister Hazel Blears and former Liberal Democrat leader Sir Menzies Campbell. We were expertly chaired by ex-Foreign Secretary Sir Malcolm Rifkind, and in our five-year term were tasked with examining many of the issues relating to Islamist terrorism and the use of communications data by the security services. My role on the ISC broadened my knowledge and understanding of the politics and security situation in vast tracts of the Middle East and Africa, particularly with regard to the terror groups operating there.

At the beginning of 2013, al-Qaeda-linked militants attacked the In Amenas gas plant in Algeria, close to the border with Libya. A siege began and over 800 staff at the jointly run BP, Statoil and Sonatrach plant were taken hostage. By the time Algerian Special Forces stormed the compound four days later, forty staff and twenty-nine militants had been killed. The demands of the terrorists for an immediate end to French military operations against Islamists in northern Mali woke the world up to the sheer geographical reach of Islamist terrorism, which was now fomenting fear in nations from Nigeria to Indonesia.

Thankfully, few people have to endure the unimaginable terror that beset our nation's hostages and waiting relatives as the In Amenas gas plant siege dragged on last week. In a world of relentlessly

demanding 24/7 media coverage, the frustration of senior government ministers was palpable, as unreliable, piecemeal information
trickled through from Algeria.

While today's attention rightly focuses upon the bereaved, little
time should be lost in developing a diplomatic and intelligence strategy in this region. For we shall hear much more of al-Qaeda in the
Islamic Maghreb (AQIM) and the Nigerian fundamentalist terror
group, Boko Haram, in the months ahead.

The sheer vastness of this part of north Africa is best illustrated by
the fact that Algeria's capital, Algiers, is nearer to London than it is
to that nation's southern-most districts. Indeed the utter remoteness
of the In Amenas complex meant that any plans to engage British,
French or US special services in the hostage rescue were fanciful.
Besides, after a brutal civil war in the 1990s, the Algerian security
forces are highly experienced, albeit uncompromising. Moreover,
the lesson that the Algerian government will have learned from the
West's treatment of one-time ally Colonel Gaddafi in neighbouring Libya is to act ruthlessly in the face of any perceived insurgency.
It understandably fears similar betrayal by France (its old colonial
master) and the West. So any suggestion that the so-called 'Arab
Spring' might have extended to Algeria would have led to Western
military assistance to rebel forces, in which AQIM would almost
certainly have featured. What message would the Algerian government have been sending to its own people over recent days if it
had allowed protracted negotiations over the siege or foreign armed
forces to engage on Algerian soil?

The French decision to commence military action in Mali may
well have brought forward the attack on the Algerian gas refinery,
but its sophistication clearly means such an operation had been long
in the planning. Arguably, the US and Western success in decon-
structing al-Qaeda's strongholds in Pakistan and Afghanistan over
the last decade or so has resulted in its reorientation in both the Arab
Peninsula (particularly Yemen) and more recently in the Maghreb
and Sahel. Inevitably, these developments have stretched further
our military and intelligence resources. To a large extent, reflecting

historical ties in the region, the UK has sub-contracted some of the responsibility for strategic security to the French. However, if, as widely feared, the conflict in Algeria, Mali and Chad extends to Nigeria, then more significant UK commercial interests will be directly threatened. The largely Muslim north of Nigeria is increasingly under the control of the fundamentalist Boko Haram, whose separatist goals have resulted in a refugee crisis and desperate food shortages. This regional instability will require the UK government and our allies, especially the US and France, to embark upon a patient campaign to win hearts and minds. This will require judicious use of our international development budget and an intensification of diplomatic efforts and intelligence gathering and sharing.

Significant numbers of UK nationals live and work in Algeria and neighbouring states. They are by no means exclusively employed in the oil/gas and mineral sectors, whose international importance is likely to increase in the foreseeable future.

This is going to be a long and thankless diplomatic haul requiring boundless patience and a remorseless eye on the long-term. But if we can learn the lessons of our mistakes during the last ten years in Afghanistan, Iraq and Libya, the UK will be safer in the decades ahead.

‡

Bash the banks and global companies if you must, but we need them more than ever, 2 February 2013

January 2013 proved a seminal month in David Cameron's leadership. In a long-awaited speech on Europe, delivered at Bloomberg's City headquarters, the Prime Minister confirmed plans to renegotiate the UK's membership of the European Union before holding an in–out referendum by the end of 2017. With this bold intervention, he hoped to quell the criticism of right-wingers in his own party who were fearful of being outflanked by UKIP in the affections of an increasingly Eurosceptic public. Yet in expressing his own preference to remain in the EU, doubt was cast over just how significant any renegotiation concessions might be.

Receiving acclaim among the British press for his pledge, Cameron simultaneously threw a blanket of uncertainty over the UK economy and international relationships, as well as a fresh spanner in the works of any potential post-2015 coalition. Nonetheless, many pundits speculated that given the electoral mountain Conservatives would have to climb ever to secure a working majority, the Prime Minister may already have calculated he would be unlikely ever have to honour his own promise.

Only days after the Bloomberg speech, Cameron flew to the World Economic Forum in Davos where he committed the UK to leading a global clampdown on tax avoidance, telling global corporations to 'wake up and smell the coffee' and arguing that the G8 needed to cooperate in stopping the 'travelling bandwagon' of accountants and lawyers who assisted firms in exploiting loopholes and moving between favourable tax jurisdictions. Later that evening, it was revealed that the UK economy had gone into reverse by 0.3 per cent in the final quarter of 2012. The Chancellor reminded the public that there was a difficult path ahead.

Berate banks and bankers if you wish.

Slate the tax arrangements of large multinationals, whose contributions in VAT and employers' national insurance remains substantial, even if their corporate tax contributions (thanks to a hopelessly complicated UK tax code) fall short of that demanded by a print media (whose own holding companies are operated by tax-efficient trust).

But for so long as UK governments of any colour remain addicted to spending well beyond our means, then we are in hock to both banks and global corporations. For even as the annual ritual of banker bonus baiting is upon us, it is these institutions that are integral to the market system that feeds the national borrowing and spending addiction.

The harsh truth is that the clamour for ever-greater public expenditure is the biggest roadblock to meaningful reform of our banks.

The government's attempts to kick-start bank activity via the Funding for Lending scheme have delivered some success in the area of subsidised mortgages (albeit largely where borrowers have existing

significant equity holdings). More faltering has been progress at
lending into the real economy.

As bank manager after bank manager has told me, the trouble is
that for all their plans to lend more widely there are relatively few
borrowers in the market place at the moment. Confidence remains
elusive. Meanwhile the twin burdens of tax and fears as to rising
interest rates are dissuading many companies from investing for
the future.

The big retail banks remain fearful of the next toxic legacy of the
boom years of the noughties that will begin to unravel. PFI, LIBOR,
interest rate swaps and other synthetic derivative products will no
doubt be joined by a range of other novel financial products that
were marketed in the past, but with the benefit of 20:20 hindsight
will be regarded as missold. If in future banks are terrified at the
prospect of any sort of innovation, we should not be surprised to
see their profits plummet permanently. The prospect of several new
waves of class action litigation claims arises at the very time we desperately need banks to lend normally. If certainty and stability do
not return to the world of financial services, there is precious little
prospect of the UK enjoying the future economic wellbeing that is
created by growth.

Few would dispute David Cameron's recent proclamation at
Davos that when it comes to paying tax, large multinationals need
to 'smell the coffee'.

However, taking such a political stance has its risks – not that
anyone should be overly concerned at the knee-jerk reaction by
many FTSE 250 communications directors in the immediate aftermath, arguing that UK Plc was being 'talked down'.

A more legitimate concern is the hazard that tax and regulation
becomes arbitrary. One of our nation's greatest assets as a place to
do business is our reputation as predictable, reliable, certain and
underpinned by the rule of law. We undermine that timeless tradition as an open place to trade and prosper at our peril.

If large international corporations are arranging their affairs to
avoid paying their 'fair share' of tax, the government should cease

moralising and get back to legislating such loopholes out of existence. Naturally, the sheer complexity and size of the UK tax code,
now larger even than the once-derided Indian version, has been the
creator of the highly remunerated Guild of Tax Avoiders.

What should worry us most is that once the tax authorities are
empowered to make ethical judgements on the affairs of global corporations, before long they will turn their attention to ordinary
taxpayers who have every right to feel that, once settled, their tax
affairs should not be re-opened on a whim.

This perceived imbalance between the rewards for success and the
risks of failure is the essential roadblock to restoring confidence in
our small, medium-sized and growing business sectors. Without it,
economic recovery will remain tantalisingly elusive.

‡

London under threat from a European banking union?, 5 February 2013

*I was asked by the French Chamber of Commerce to write the follow-
ing article for their magazine, INFO. They were keen for my perspective
as the City's MP on whether London's position as Europe's financial
hub was under threat by the prospect of banking union among eurozone members.*

*As the eurozone crisis had worn on, it had become ever clearer that
the single currency's problems were unlikely to be solved unless there
was greater financial and political integration between its members.
A vicious cycle had developed because of an interdependency between
sovereign credit and bank credit that needed desperately to be broken.
Since one of the key ways of judging a bank's strength was to look at
the likely support the sovereign would provide in the face of imminent
collapse, the fragile banking system was putting enormous strain on
national finances and making credit scarce. In crippling any possibility
of growth in the wider economy, sovereigns were further weakened, re-
infecting banks which held large sums of sovereign debt.*

To break this pattern, the process of banking union was initiated in June 2012 at a euro-member summit, shortly after another Greek election. This summit made way for banking supervisory authority to be centralised within the European Central Bank (ECB), moving most regulatory decision-making for euro-area banks from national to European authorities. The banking union was to be defined by two specific policies – the Single Supervisory Mechanism (SSM) and Single Resolution Mechanism (SRM). The SSM transferred a number of supervisory duties and the power to grant or withdraw banking licences from national authorities to the ECB. The SRM, on the other hand, was intended to centralise authority in dealing with non-viable banks.

By that July, the ECB President, Mario Draghi, declared that the 'ECB is ready to do whatever it takes to preserve the euro'. With markets reassured that this would include buying large amounts of the sovereign bonds of the euro's weakest members, Draghi hoped finally to initiate a positive cycle fuelled by greater market confidence.

Spiralling borrowing costs in Spain and Italy; protests in Greece; questions over French finances; growing German unease about its liability for eurozone debts. All these ingredients contributed to a poisonous cocktail in 2012 of deepening financial uncertainty.

As the UK economy limped through the last twelve months, dire trade figures and weak confidence were blamed largely on that continental uncertainty. It has been of no surprise that the official line in London has been to welcome any moves that might precipitate the end of the eurozone crisis. The break-up of the euro – which would undoubtedly inflict significant short-term pain on the City of London, the UK's famous financial district – remains the British government's greatest immediate fear. Forget triumphalism about the UK staying out of the single currency. Britain's key trading partners remain European. If they suffer, so too does the UK's forlorn hope of export-led growth.

Nevertheless, the greater existential threat to the UK comes from a successful banking and fiscal union among eurozone members. Before the 2008 financial crisis, the City of London drew envious glances from Frankfurt and Paris and was the great success story of the British economy. In spite of all the upheaval that followed the global credit crunch, by 2010 the financial and associated professional services sector was still contributing 14 per cent to the UK's GDP, comprised 7 per cent of total UK employment and contributed £63 billion in tax revenue. To give some idea of the extent of its domination of European financial services, the City is responsible for half of all investment banking on the European continent, with the UK trading twice as many Euros as all the eurozone countries *combined*. In 2011 the UK's financial services trade surplus with the EU totalled £17.6 billion. But it is not at all clear whether this dominance can continue should the eurozone successfully complete its march towards fully fledged banking union.

In December, European member states agreed the shape of the future Single Supervisory Mechanism that will pave the way from 2014 for the European Central Bank to oversee systemically important eurozone credit institutions. The UK, along with the Czech Republic and Sweden, has chosen to opt out of the SSM and has been given firm assurances over the preservation both of the Single Market and non-euro member states' voices over European regulation. Yet the sustainability of this position remains unclear.

These first tentative steps towards banking union do not currently pose an unmanageable threat to the UK's lead in financial services. Nor is the Single Market in immediate danger. Nevertheless, these opening stages represent the start of a process that poses longer-term risks to the City of London, the UK economy and Britain's ongoing membership of the Union.

Since the Single Market is the biggest pull factor of the EU for Britain, the threat of it being undermined by a multi-speed Europe has triggered momentous debate within the UK about whether ever-closer union between our partners pushes Britain inevitably towards the exit door. That debate went up a gear last month when Prime Minister David Cameron announced that he would hold an in/out referendum on UK membership of the EU within five years. The case in favour in the run-up to such a referendum will hold so long as the UK electorate perceives its economic interests to be served by EU membership. The moment that economic case diminishes, we should not be surprised if a clamour for Britain's exit from the EU quickly follows.

In the meantime, British domestic grandstanding risks having a significant impact on diplomatic relations with our fellow member states, potentially spurring a self-fulfilling prophecy as Britain's ability to influence in its favour the outcome of the eurozone crisis and the future direction of the Union declines as a result. The Prime Minister's position has already undermined confidence that the UK is committed to shaping Europe's direction and has a strategy when it comes to maintaining British influence.

The City of London boasts many powerful competitive advantages over its continental counterparts that include a skilled workforce, sophisticated legal system, deeply liquid markets and an international outlook. As a result, many believe that the City has the critical mass to ensure that the UK will play a leading role in global finance for decades to come, no matter what happens on the continent. Nevertheless, since the 2008 crash, the eurozone has understandably demanded greater oversight of its financial infrastructure. Awkward questions have been raised about the ability of London and UK financial services regulators to prevent the system silting up and whether it is sustainable (or desirable) for euro-denominated risk to be cleared offshore in the British capital. In turn, the City has questioned how long it might feasibly avoid being infected by the numerous directives being churned out by the EU to create common financial standards without its global competitiveness being fundamentally damaged. Those question marks only multiply with each step closer to eurozone banking union, putting at risk the City's global status.

History also teaches Britain that economic upheavals are often regarded as too good an opportunity to waste for ambitious European statesmen seeking to impose a wider political agenda. Talk of a transaction tax to be applied throughout the EU would probably represent only the first such salvo. We have already seen too a land grab by the Paris-based European Securities and Markets Authority, which may start sabre-rattling when it comes to the question of which financial entities and products pose systemic risk. To hope that the UK would have any real clout in an EU with fiscally integrated eurozone members would be hopelessly naïve. The City of London is only too aware of the risk of losing business from regulatory arbitrage, having benefited so handsomely in the past from US regulatory clampdowns on Wall Street.

London's position as Europe's leading international financial and business centre is crucial to sustaining jobs and growth – not just in the UK but across the continent. Uncertainty over this relationship with Europe, intensified by the prospect of banking union, risks making the UK less attractive as an international centre across many industries – not just financial and professional services.

As nations in the eurozone push towards closer fiscal and political integration, the need for the UK to have a coherent strategy towards the European Union will only intensify. If Britain does not act now to ensure it has an integral role in European decision-making, the risk that the Single Market will fragment (and with it Britain's incentive to remain a signed-up member of the club) is very real indeed.

‡

This House believes the City is a drain on talent, 21 February 2013

I was asked to speak in a debate at the Oxford Union in opposition to the Motion, 'This House Believes the City is a Drain on Talent'. Joining me for the Noes were Chris Saul of law firm Slaughter and May, James Uffindell of Bright Network and Robin Geffen of Neptune Investment Management. In support spoke Claire Perry MP, Doug Richard, formerly of Dragon's Den, and Sahar Hashemi, Founder of Coffee Republic. It was wonderful to return to Oxford some quarter of a century after I graduated from my college, St Edmund Hall, to make my maiden speech at the Oxford Union.

Madam President,

Rather longer ago than I care to remember, I went down from Teddy Hall convinced that the UK was a place of infinite possibilities. It was 1987. The previous autumn, Prime Minister Margaret Thatcher had introduced the Financial Services Act. It was groundbreaking legislation that took a hammer to the old boys' club of the City of London, smashing established elites and protected industries.

What became known as the 'Big Bang' had an effect on the City, the capital and the wider British economy that was profound. Internationally pre-eminent until the outbreak of the First World War, the City of London was suddenly back in vogue.

By the age of twenty-nine, I had set up my first business, got myself professionally qualified – another City lawyer, I am afraid! – sold my business and set up a second enterprise. All here in Britain.

When my researcher left the 'other place' in 2005, the City was similarly riding high. The economy may have been showing signs of overheating, the Big Bang liberalisations having been combined with loose monetary policy, lax tripartite regulation and a government addicted to spending. Yet London was nevertheless booming as the financial capital of the world.

As a result, graduates in the mid-noughties bemoaned the fact that they were unable to get a foot on the housing ladder as prices whizzed into the stratosphere. But there were still jobs – and plenty of them. Roles in financial services, yes. But also jobs in engineering, public services, creative industries, business. The great question facing graduates was not how to find employment but which career path would give the most personal fulfilment… And if fulfilment was not going to be possible, which would pay the most money!

No such luxury for today's most talented young Britons who graduate in an incredibly tough employment market following 2008's financial crash.

Now I know what many of you are thinking: 'If it wasn't for the City, we wouldn't be in this mess!'

That is a whole other debate, but I ought quickly to address it lest it undermines my case! To blame the bankers for all our current circumstances is a simplistic and superficial analysis. The financial crash was merely the crescendo to a long period of debt accumulation, racked up in response to the West's declining competitiveness but also to our collective desire to expand the remit of the state. Bankers exploited and expedited that debt accumulation, yes. But it was loose government policy that allowed it.

Putting that aside, both my experience and that of mid-noughties graduates show that when the City has boomed, it has not been sucking talent from other industries like some parasite. Far from it. It has given *all* talent possibilities, including possibilities beyond finance.

The City is, in fact, the great talent *retainer* and attractor since it oils the cogs of the wider economy and provides a critical mass of activity that keeps business on UK shores.

Amidst all the fierce debate about the greed of bankers, it is easy to forget what banks actually exist for, what we mean by 'the City'.

Fundamentally, a bank acts as an intermediary between those who seek capital (expanding businesses, governments wishing to fund services) and those who have surpluses that they wish to enlarge (investors, savers, pension funds). In short, banks circulate money to areas of an economy that require it and provide the sense of security so crucial to confidence.

That is why the banks had to be rescued in 2008, because they are the key lubricant that enables other sectors of the economy to work. When those sectors work, the talented thrive.

The City has grown to provide that intermediary role not just for the domestic market, but for the global economy. As a hub for the circulation of money, people want to do business here. When deals are being struck and money lent, people need lawyers and insurers. They require risk analysts, taxation advisers, fund managers, share dealers.

With such a concentration of expertise in a single compact geographical area, companies want to be headquartered here. Those companies need accountants, auditors, management consultants and pension advisers. Not to mention dazzling new buildings requiring innovative architects, engineers and project managers to build.

With legally sound deals, insured trading and access to growth capital, businesses large and small have the confidence to expand. A hub of professionals with money to spend encourages jobs in housing, restaurants, transport, culture, education and domestic services.

And those professionals who leave the City often do so with a chunk of capital that they use to build their own or invest in others' start-ups.

The finance sector also contributes a hefty amount of tax (some £21 billion in PAYE and corporation tax in 2010–11) which governments enjoy spending liberally. That tax is what helps pay for nurses, policemen, teachers. When that flow of money slows, the state must employ fewer people.

So when the City of London went into decline after 2008, there was no great tsunami of talent flooding into engineering, business and the high tech industries. Instead, the economy as a whole was undermined. Our brightest sparks began instead to look beyond the UK *entirely* for the best opportunities – 10 per cent of British graduates from our top universities are now choosing to work away from the UK.

In spite of the tumultuous past few years, the financial services industry remains one of the only world-beating sectors of which the UK can boast. It is also one of the few sectors which has enormous potential to grow as the burgeoning middle classes of China and India, culturally attuned to *invest*, expand their savings and pensions.

Just think of the opportunities. In China, the new rural pension scheme has acquired over 240 million people in only two years – that is more than the number covered by America's *entire* social security scheme. As the Chinese economy matures, there will surely be an ever-greater demand for private pensions and more dynamic investment products.

If the City can grasp that nettle, the UK can retain that unique blend of opportunities that makes the talented want to remain here. If we continue to undermine wealth, bash bankers and scorn success, expect to see talent flow from our nation in double quick time.

I therefore put it to you – the City is no drain on talent. When the City thrives, it acts, in fact, as the UK's greatest talent retainer.

‡

The deeper discontent beneath the mansion tax debate, 23 February 2013

Since 2009, the Liberal Democrats had mooted the idea of a so-called mansion tax, an annual levy on all properties valued at over £1 million. It had attracted a great deal of opposition since the UK property boom, concentrated in London, had made countless people property million-aires without necessarily delivering them the financial means to be able to pay an additional, significant annual tax. Indeed the policy was a deliberate misnomer since many of the properties valued at £1 million were not mansions at all but small flats whose location had pumped up their worth.

Now governing in coalition, the Liberal Democrats' policy proposi-tions caused rather more alarm and became a fresh source of tension between the two parties in power. By autumn 2012, the Lib Dems had revived the idea at their party conference, albeit hiking the threshold of homes that would be affected to those valued over £2 million. When the Labour party declared in February 2013 that it too would introduce a mansion tax if elected to power, pressure shifted to the Conservatives to outline their own policy prescriptions to the growing resentment caused by exceptionally high property prices. In this article, I tried to unpick the reasons for the mansion tax's increasing popularity, delving into the underlying themes of globalisation, wealth inequality and hostility towards capitalism.

'It's like the Harrods sale!' exclaimed Rob Tincknell in January. As chief executive of the Battersea Power Station Development Company, it was no surprise that he greeted the stampede to secure new Battersea homes with elation. More than £600 million worth of prime London properties – three quarters of the 800 homes on site – had been snapped up in a frantic four days. The final tranche of 200 properties is now on a homes 'road show' in Singapore to attract wealthy Far East buyers.

For property-owning Londoners, the Battersea frenzy was no doubt a welcome sign of the continued robust health of the capital's housing market. But I suspect the average renter found the news utterly demoralising. For them, the financial crisis brought great promise of lower house prices. But that never came to pass. Instead, already-stratospheric rents have crept steadily upwards. Mortgage deposit requirements have increased. House prices are climbing and yet still properties are being snapped up in double quick time. When even a Battersea studio costs £343,000, the hope of owning the smallest of homes seems more remote than ever.

Contrast that with the ease with which wealthy foreigners, many of whom will not be resident in the capital, are hoovering up London real estate. Such is their spending power that it is becoming increasingly common for agents to market new London property developments first to overseas buyers whose appetite for homes in the capital, alongside their ability to pay for them, seems not to abate.

An increasing number of Londoners are feeling locked out of their own city. Whatever one's politics, this cannot be desirable – an overcrowded capital in which much of our precious housing stock is being bought by part-time or even absent residents. To many, there is no starker example than the London property market of the growing global divide between the super-rich and everybody else.

***

To me, the greatest attraction of capitalism and globalisation has always been its ability consistently to deliver improved living standards to billions. It held promise that each generation would be better off than the last, with hard work, innovation and talent given just reward. So it had generally been. Yet, in recent years, as wages have stagnated and living costs risen, more and more people have begun to feel that the rules of the game are instead skewed in favour of a growing global elite. This elite seems not only immune from the headwinds battering everyone else but largely uncommitted to and disconnected from the societies that their money influences.

As Chrystia Freeland observed in her recent book about the world's super-rich, *Plutocracy*, the wealthy of today are different to the rich of yesterday. Members of this elite, she concludes, tend now to feel more affinity with one another than their own countrymen. They are, in many ways, not citizens of any one country but belong to a pan-global village in which they can cherry pick the very best that each society has to offer. While they believe in state institutions that permit social mobility and political stability, when it comes to the taxes required to pay for them, enthusiasm can swiftly wane.

It is in London that this phenomenon has become most visible. In 2011, top estate agent Savills published a report, *The World in London*, that documented billions of pounds of foreign money flowing into the capital's prime housing market, 'boosted by the weakness of sterling and the perception of London as a safe haven amidst political and economic uncertainty'. The biggest investors in central London property have been from eastern Europe (15 per cent of the market with an average purchase price of £6.2 million) followed by Middle Eastern and northern African buyers (14 per cent market share with a £4 million average purchase price). Arabian playboys now race supercars along Park Lane, Russian oligarchs buy the capital's football clubs and frequent its auction houses, and glamorous offspring dazzle London boutiques with their family credit cards.

The strength of demand from international cash buyers has only intensified over the past year, with prices in the two boroughs of Kensington & Chelsea and my own City of Westminster rising 15–20 per cent. Such is the scale of transactions in these two areas alone that in 2011–12, they accounted for 13 per cent of all stamp duty collected on house sales nationwide.

It is undeniable that as a collective, this international elite's colossal spending power injects verve into certain sections of the capital's economy. Luxury retailers, restaurateurs, hoteliers, property developers and high-end service providers (private schools and the like) all benefit from the presence of global high rollers. At a time of zero to low growth, Britain can ill afford to drive away those with money to burn.

But there is a more pernicious economic impact as well. As the international enclave expands, more and more central London stock is made unavailable to residents, driving up prices in less central areas as those who would have lived in the city centre are forced out. It is arguable that inflated house prices have, and continue to have, a distortive effect on the competitiveness of the UK economy. In truth, they lead to ever-higher wages, a drain on the benefits budget and diminish available resources for investment and economic innovation. This will become especially acute as the UK tries to thrive in ever more competitive global economic markets. With greater proportions of household budgets consumed by rent and mortgage costs, people have less money to save and to spend. Ironically the high cost of London property also becomes a significant factor in detracting the brightest and the best from abroad from coming here to work or study.

There is an additional problem in London having become a 'safe haven' for international capital flows, a proportion of which has its origins in corruption and rent-seeking activities that would be illegal in the UK. As detailed in Misha Glenny's *McMafia*, laundering the proceeds of such activity in London property is just about the easiest and most secure way of banking a large amount of money. The UK is one of the few countries which combines a unique mix of deep and liquid real estate supported by supply shortages, an open capital account, a foreign banking presence, stable judicial institutions and the rule of law. In running an open capital account without there being a level playing field whereby the UK's benign investment conditions are mimicked elsewhere, there is a net transfer of British assets to a class from developing regions who have obtained money from acts that would be criminal on these shores. It is one thing to have an open border to welcome foreign business people who create employment and contribute to growth and government revenue. It is quite another for the London housing stock to have become an international currency that is traded between foreigners with little connection either to the city or the nation.

This state of affairs has been tolerated as the price for high foreign investment in Britain in the absence of economic growth. But as the living standards of the majority diminish, we are fast reaching a tipping point at which this inequality is so exaggerated as to become intolerable. I am not advocating a return to the class warfare of the 1970s – it was my distaste for the politics of envy during that era that first motivated my aspiration to public life. However, I fear that the capitalist system's safety mechanisms are being undermined by exaggerated wealth.

People work harder if they are incentivised to do so. Witnessing those who have made their money from cartels and monopolies or from risking other people's money in a game of 'heads I win, tails you lose' mocks the ambition of the ordinary man. It creates a sense of impotence – that no matter how hard one works or how talented one is, the simple desire to own a home and afford a family is becoming out of reach. It means that the restoration of growth alone is insufficient to rectify the structural flaws that stand between the 'squeezed middle' and their aspirations. It also explains why there is such anger being directed towards those who apparently dip into our society, enjoy all its benefits and yet pay little tax.

Naturally this disconnect between the super-rich and everyone else is not an exclusively British problem, as we know from the 'We are the 99 per cent' Occupy protests which first took root in New York. Occupy protestors have been criticised for having no coherent alternative plan. Yet it is not up to them to deliver solutions – politicians should recognise them simply as a manifestation of society's outrage. It is our job as political representatives to address that outrage rather than simply to mimic it. The effect in politicians sharing public anger is for governments to look either utterly impotent or disingenuous in that outrage. This must be addressed before the last vestige of faith in our economic and political institutions is undermined.

I believe policymakers must now undertake an objective cost–benefit analysis of the presence of an international super-rich. If the cost is found to be too high, how do governments seek to minimise it? How do politicians design a system that inculcates a sense of societal responsibility within this elite, without driving money, talent and investment to other shores? How can we distinguish between genuine foreign business people who become resident in Britain, create employment and contribute to the UK economy, and those who effectively freeload on the nation's infrastructure?

Passionate domestic debate about the imposition of a 'mansion tax' is now all the rage. In part it is seen as an answer to some of these very questions. My primary concern over such a levy has always been for those who happen to reside in homes whose value has inflated to a level that bears no relation to a household's ability to stump up large cash sums. In other words, the asset rich and cash poor. I suspect a mansion tax would most likely drive greater numbers of Londoners from their homes, vacating even more prime, central property for the delectation of foreign buyers. In short, a mansion tax would exacerbate rather than fix the problem.

In light of this, in recent months I have canvassed interested constituents for alternative solutions. A first suggestion has been to publish data. Only then can the problem fully enter the public consciousness and inform national debate. We need to understand just how much London residential property is owned by non-resident, non-tax-paying foreigners.

Next, it has been suggested that we look at the levying of taxes on non-resident, non-British owners of property through the abolition of the distinction between domicility and residence. Residents would be taxed on their worldwide income and assets, while non-residents would be levied with special holding taxes on passive property assets they hold. In New York, apartments can incur a tax of up to $20,000 if they are left empty – might we look at such a plan here?

Some of my constituents believe these plans could discourage non-resident foreigners from buying real estate assets in the UK, while making the fiscal regime attractive to foreign business people who wish to be resident in the UK. Even just a 5 per cent capital tax would generate sufficient revenues to make a big difference.

Furthermore, a reduction in net capital inflows would reduce the value of sterling and add to our competitiveness.

The government has made a start with stamp duty – a 15 per cent levy on purchases of property over £2 million by non-natural persons and an annual charge on UK residential properties valued over £2 million owned by non-naturals. Undeniably, however, the Conservative Party is nevertheless being left behind in public debate on these issues. If we are to oppose vigorously a mansion tax, we must rapidly come up with an alternative solution before we cede these contentious and important matters to Labour and the Liberal Democrats. It is not difficult to frame this debate in a distinctly 'Conservative' way. The principles that make capitalism work are being warped, and it is for our party to declare that it wishes to address that in order to nourish hard work, aspiration and responsibility. This is not about envious wealth confiscation, rather a government addressing the structural problems that are snuffing out ambition.

Over the past few decades, we have witnessed an unprecedented shift in the ownership structure of central London residential housing stock. The ripple effect has been profound and the inequality of wealth in our capital is now reaching a tipping point. Enough with public hand wringing and moralising. Ultimately, these are issues which politicians are elected to address – we must now change the rules of the game.

‡

Some pre-Budget thoughts, 5 March 2013

On 22 February, credit rating agency Moody's downgraded UK government bond ratings one notch from AAA to AA1 status. They presumed that sluggish growth would now extend into the second half of the decade, posing a challenge to the government's fiscal consolidation programme and reducing the capacity of the government's balance sheet to absorb shocks as government debt increased.

It was the first time Britain had lost its triple A rating since 1978, and the Chancellor's Labour opponents were quick to leap on the news as evidence that his economic plan was not working and that he needed now to spend more to boost growth. Those who followed the figures instead, argued that spending needed to be cut still further, and taxes raised.

I was asked by a global law firm in the City to outline some of the challenges facing the Chancellor in the run-up to the March Budget, and made the following speech:

Whereas in previous run-ups to Budgets and Autumn Statements there has been a clamour for George Osborne to do more to boost growth – tax cuts, big capital investment and so on – there seems now to be a quiet acceptance that the time for boldness has passed.

In these acutely difficult times, the government has virtually no room for manoeuvre. Contrary to what the opposition would have you believe, the Moody's downgrade in our credit rating a week or so ago is not a sign that we need Plan B. Quite the contrary. The rating agency was explicit – the deficit reduction strategy is the right one. We are simply not delivering it.

If we look beyond the rhetoric of 'savage cuts', there lies an uncomfortable truth. The total spend by government by the time this financial year is out is forecast to be some £683 billion, with an expected £120 billion added to the government debt pile. Insofar as it can boast of achievement, the coalition has been able to recalibrate the public finances in such a way that we are now borrowing £1 in every £5 we spend collectively, rather than the £1 in every £4 that UK taxpayers borrowed in 2009. We are simply digging that cumulative debt hole just a little less slowly than in the recent past.

One only needs to read the newspapers to understand the trouble the government is having in enacting its austerity strategy. What appears to amount, at times, to serial incompetence dogs the coalition, with recent unforced errors including the West Coast Main Line fiasco, disappointment on the coalition's apprenticeship initiatives, and difficulties in delivering the much-vaunted Work

Programme. That is aside from broader battles it is rightly and bravely waging over benefits cuts and pay freezes.

With such difficulties in enacting the 'cuts' side of the deficit reduction strategy, there is all the more reason for the coalition to deliver on that strategy's other pillar – growth. In June 2010 it was expected that the UK would achieve compound growth of between 2.7 per cent and 2.9 per cent per annum over the entire course of the parliament. As we all now know, growth over the past year has stalled and predictions for the near and mid-term look similarly downbeat. To the Chancellor's credit, he has resisted the superficially easy option of a 'dash for growth' of the type that his predecessor Anthony Barber unleashed in 1972. The feverish activity brought about by the tax cuts and industry incentives of the Barber boom brought with it an enormous risk of inflation.

Nevertheless, it has been Bank of England policy (presumably with a blind eye from the Treasury) that a little inflation in the system is a risk worth taking to keep interest rates at rock bottom levels – talk last week of negative interest rates suggest this strategy is unlikely to change any time soon. For those of us who believe in 'sound money', inflation is always a mighty dangerous thing, relieving as it does the burden of debtors at the expense of savers. You may have noticed that government is the biggest debtor of them all. Diminishing living standards look set to define the next few years of political debate and it is this, not economic growth, on which Ed Miliband is now focusing. I suspect this will prove to be a far more fruitful angle for the opposition than attacking the Prime Minister on growth undershoots, job stats and borrowing figures.

Meanwhile, the near-universal acceptance of the near-zero interest rate strategy suggests that the government's primary tactic is to hope that something will turn up in time for the 2015 election. Indeed, I suspect the Chancellor's handling of the UK economy owes rather more than he might willingly admit to the Mr Micawber principle. After all, waiting for something to turn up is not always the ill-advised course of action. The accretion of time often does alleviate, and sometimes even solves, what seems an intractably difficult situation. The sobering truth, however, is that these ultra-low interest rates mean that the UK economic patient remains in a government-induced coma, and these historic low returns provide no incentive for prospective investors to take the plunge again in large-scale UK projects.

In spite of our economic difficulties, the new conventional wisdom is that while the economic outlook to 2015 and beyond remains bleak, the politics for the Conservatives are a good deal more encouraging. That may be right; indeed given there is so little to choose between the Chancellor and his shadow, why not stick with coalition economics come the next general election?

But we cannot afford complacency. With our shaky financials, the UK is exceptionally vulnerable to events. I remain unconvinced, for instance, by the bombastic declaration at the beginning of this year by European Commission President, Jose Manuel Barroso, that the eurozone crisis is over. I have long contended that European leaders can decide whatever they wish at summits and conferences. The greatest unknown for us all is the politics. Putting aside fundamental questions about the Union's economic competitiveness and sustainability, the European project requires belief if it is to survive. Belief from markets. Belief from electorates. The question now is whether each can keep pace enough to satisfy the other.

The European Central Bank can provide the bazooka of support. But will the German people accept the liabilities of a continent? Will the electorates of debtor nations accept swingeing austerity and fiscal rectitude as the price of inclusion in the grand European project? Last week's Italian election result suggests not. And could a fiscally integrated core of EU member states be reconciled with a broader and looser Union of twenty-seven member states? The answer to that question, after the Prime Minister's recent promise of an 'in/out' referendum, promises to define the UK's relationship with the EU for some years to come.

The US economy may be turning a corner. Yet political stalemate continues and the next great budget battle looms on the horizon. 2013, I suspect, will not be a year of plain sailing for the global economy.

I apologise for what may seem a gloomy assessment of where we are this afternoon. But I hope my candid summary highlights some of the political and economic dangers of this next period and gives you a sense of the mood here in parliament. We still have much to be thankful for – positive employment figures, low borrowing costs, a host of innovative and dynamic companies. Plus, the UK remains a sophisticated economy which is well placed to take advantage of the new opportunities in the East, where there remains strong demand for our professional services. As a global law firm, rightly focused on the ambitions of fast-developing G20 nations, I look forward to you delivering for the UK's exports figures in professional services in the months and years to come!

‡

What are the odds on government getting out of the banking business? (*Daily Telegraph*), 7 March 2013

In response to the financial crash the Labour government, under the leadership of Prime Minister Gordon Brown and Chancellor Alistair Darling, had launched a bank rescue package that saw large chunks of both Royal Bank of Scotland and Lloyds Banking Group come within public ownership in late 2008 and early 2009. This was never intended to be a long-term arrangement, but the clean-up operation of both the financial system and banks' balance sheets took so long that by early 2013, none of the taxpayers' shares in the ailing institutions had yet been sold off.

After it was revealed that net lending had fallen by £2.4 billion in the final quarter of 2012 compared to the previous three months, Business Secretary Vince Cable mused that fully nationalising RBS or Lloyds was a tempting prospect in order to boost lending to UK businesses. In this article, I examined the politics and economics behind any decision to dispose or keep hold of the public's banking shares.

Selling off the huge near £66 billion stakes that the taxpayer holds in RBS and Lloyds Banking Group seems further away than ever.

As 2011 dawned, the UK government briefly sat on a small profit on the £45 billion and £20 billion that had been spent acquiring 82 per cent of RBS and 43 per cent of Lloyds in those frantic few months after the collapse of Lehman Brothers in September 2008. Those halcyon days seem long-distant as the taxpayers' holdings today are worth around one-quarter less than at the time of acquisition.

The Chancellor's recent declaration that any UK bank failing to adhere to the Vickers safety regime runs the risk of being broken up was an understandably uncompromising response to the Treasury Select Committee's demand for an 'electrified' ring-fence. Similarly, few would criticise the populist insistence that RBS will have to fund LIBOR (and presumably other future mis-selling) penalties from senior executive bonus pools. However, at a stroke, the Treasury has in this way inadvertently imposed a permanent impairment on the value of the UK government's stakes in the banking business.

Small wonder that coalition ministers of Liberal Democrat persuasion periodically have floated the idea that the least controversial way of divesting our collective interests in RBS and Lloyds might be in a share giveaway directly to the public. Whether Vince Cable's most recent foray into this field is practicable is another matter – the real risk is that a break-up or a fully fledged nationalisation of RBS would in effect destroy the business. Nevertheless, the fact that this route continues to be contemplated seriously reflects an increasing despair that the coalition will ever be in a position to sell any part of our huge financial interest at a profit.

Once upon a time, the chief fear of City commentators was that the timetable for selling off our sizeable public share of RBS and especially Lloyds Banking Group would be driven more by the electoral timetable than by the desire to maximise taxpayer value. The squeeze in public spending and, more important still, on household budgets, may yet tempt the coalition to rush for whatever cash it can extract this side of May 2015. However, short of divesting small distinct divisions, if this necessitates selling at a substantial discount, it should be resisted.

In fairness, the Treasury also has to balance some other serious considerations. On the one hand, for so long as two of the Big Four domestic banks remain so substantially in public hands, it will be difficult for the underlying issues in the UK's critical finance sector to be regarded as solved, rather than simply parked. On the other hand, the continued deterioration in the public finances (the Office for Budget Responsibility has already revised the anticipated cumulative deficit for the parliament upwards by £212 billion more than its November 2010 calculation) serves to make it ever more attractive that privatisation takes place sooner rather than later in order that the public coffers are boosted.

As we have seen, the persistent uncertainty surrounding the precise terms of banking reform (will it be a super-charged Vickers ring-fence or a Sword of Damacles threat of total separation for future financial offenders?) almost certainly serves to depress further the value of our collective holdings in RBS/Lloyds. Until recently, the most likely scenario was that the Treasury would seek in the final year or so of this parliament to start an aggressive programme of selling off specific divisions in these banks. No longer. The necessity that any such sale be designed to maximise proceeds all but rules out any 1980s-style privatisation public offering. The lack of public trust in the banks is such that any attempt to recreate the glory days of a 'Sid-style' public campaign would probably bring in considerably less revenue than a part-sale, for example, to a sovereign wealth fund.

What should trouble Conservatives is that five years on from the financial crisis, the UK's largest financial institutions continue to operate in an unholy alliance with government. Even those institutions functioning without official state support have an implied guarantee and inevitability of survival, which gives them a commercial advantage over any new competitors whose entry to the financial services market is effectively barred.

Unfortunately, much of this stems from the deals that were done by the last government back in the autumn of 2008. One of the curiosities of the global bank bailout process since that time has been the consensus that the bailout episode symbolised courageous, decisive government action at its best in providing an essential life-preserving shock to the domestic economy. As I have written before, however, I believe some serious strategic mistakes were made at that time that help to explain why there remains to this day an over-riding sense that the bankers 'got away with it', with the taxpayer picking up the tab.

While the banks undoubtedly presented the government with a crisis on a huge scale, the Treasury was nevertheless in a position of enormous strength (as is any organisation about to spend such colossal sums of money), and should have recognised immediately that the status quo no longer existed. No options for golden good-byes for the most discredited chief executives, no blind acceptance of unrealistic share valuations. Beyond the first priority of prevent-ing systemic risk, Ministers should have asked, 'How much money can we make out of this?' and subsequently struck as good a deal for the taxpayer as possible. Moral hazard might then have been sewn into the heart of the regulatory system, with recapitalisation a deeply unattractive last resort rather than an ultimate backstop and commercial advantage.

With the government driving a hard bargain, the fear of bailout would have served as a far better regulator of behaviour than reams of new laws and fresh bodies in place to police the system. If a better deal had been secured for the taxpayer, with year-by-year forecasts on the value of its stake, the debate on the future of banking might have been shaped entirely differently. Instead, there has been a sense that the biggest risk takers extricated themselves from the crisis scot-free, dumping taxpayers with rotten husks which appear to serve the needs of executives before taxpayers. In their impotence, politi-cians have tried to placate the public with a damaging PR campaign against the financial services sector and its employees, grandstand-ing on bonuses, cash/share splits and tax.

Nothing can change the original terms negotiated during those 2008 bailouts, but they really must hold lessons, both for now and the future. Beware the vested interests or entrenched mindset of the expert. Be sure to exact terms in line with the risks taken. More important still, robustly and continually define the strategic objective in the general national interest.

As time – and new regulation – passes on, we should not be surprised that RBS and Lloyds will now expend their energies keeping their political paymasters happy rather than reaching out to their consumers. This should not be the signal for a loss of nerve by the government; far from it – it should redouble its efforts to maximise taxpayer value.

‡

Financial Services (Banking Reform) Bill, 11 March 2013

The Financial Services (Banking Reform) Bill formed a key plank of the coalition's strategy to create a functioning, competitive banking system that would support the economy without leaving taxpayers the bill for any future failures. It received Royal Assent in December 2013, becoming the Banking Reform Act, and implemented many of the recommendations of the Independent Commission on Banking, chaired by Sir John Vickers, as well as those made by the Parliamentary Commission on Banking Standards.

The legislation led to the requirement for UK banks to separate their everyday retail banking activities from their investment banking operations – the so-called Vickers ring-fence. However, many of the details on how the ring-fence would work, as well as precise rules on banking standards and conduct, were left unfinalised.

I spoke at the Bill's Second Reading to express some of my concerns about the principle and application of any ring-fence.

No one could accuse the Treasury or the coalition of rushing into banking reform; nor, to their credit, has there been anything other than the most comprehensive consultation with – and without – the banking industry here in the UK. I shall not repeat the timeline that colleagues have referred to, save to say that I accept the concerns expressed that the Bill will not be considered directly in tandem with the report of the Parliamentary Commission on Banking Standards.

Above all, we all need to face up to our complacency. The conventional wisdom of the day, to which I fully signed up in the first half of the last decade, was that financial services would thrive best with light-touch regulation. What a difference half a decade makes! It was also during that period that the present Chancellor fatefully nailed his colours to the mast. Despite clear evidence that we were collectively living well beyond our means during the previous administration, and amidst growing public and private debt, he decided to stick to the outgoing Labour government's spending plans and characterise our fiscal aspiration as 'sharing the proceeds of growth'. I regret the fact that as a result, when the crisis hit home, my party was unable to make the orthodox Conservative case that the seeds of that financial destruction had been profligacy and the leverage that was referred to earlier. Instead, the established view was, and continues to be, that regulatory failings – of which there were undisputedly many – and reckless actions by the bankers were the primary, if not the sole, cause of the financial calamity. Hence the persistent demand for more extensive and punitive regulation of the banks, and the constant chatter of hostility towards bankers and all that they do.

My contention remains that the core issue we need to tackle is global imbalances, many of which are still worryingly in place after a half decade of near stagnation economically. Alongside this, a generation of Britons – as well as Americans and continental Europeans – have lived and continue to live miles beyond their individual and collective means. We are still mortgaging the future of our children and grandchildren.

The Chancellor's recent declaration that any UK bank failing to adhere to the Vickers safety regime would run the risk of being broken up was an understandably uncompromising response to the Treasury Committee's demand for an electrified ring-fence. Similarly, few could criticise the populist insistence that RBS would have to fund LIBOR – and, presumably, other future mis-selling – penalties from senior executive bonus pools. At a stroke, however, the Treasury has inadvertently imposed a permanent impairment on the value of the UK government's still huge stakes in the banking business. Our £66 billion investment in RBS and Lloyds is currently worth two thirds of what we paid for it. Nothing in the Bill will bring forward the date on which we, as taxpayers, will be compensated.

It is often claimed that the banking lobby, here and on Wall Street, has used its considerable muscle to water down, undermine or even cast aside moves by politicians and public interest groups to rein in the banking system. Ironically, much of the criticism comes from the self-same media outlets that have placed intense pressure on elite politicians to dismantle the proposals for their own industry, as set out in the Leveson report. As a matter of fact, the banks have taken much of what has been proposed on the chin. Many have privately expressed great concern to me about the wisdom and practical application of ring-fencing, but they feel that they have no choice but to accept Vickers virtually in its entirety.

Ironically, existing financial services players could reap the unanticipated benefit that comes from erecting ever more onerous barriers to entry for potential new banks. Sadly, the zest of competition has been largely ignored in an effort to make banking safe and to punish banks for their past wrongdoing.

The City of London's size and global reach continues to make the UK economy especially vulnerable to turbulence in the financial markets. The centrepiece of the Bill's reforms – the plan to ring-fence domiciled banks' retail arms from their investment ones – is based on the notion that the less risky retail operations require protection from the so-called casino excesses of investment banking. The aim to reduce the burden on the British taxpayer in the event of banking failure is, of course, a laudable one. Many in the financial fraternity are simply glad that the reforms fell short of a return to a full-blown plan along the lines of Glass-Steagall. That was the US legislation that separated commercial and investment banking for almost seven decades until 1999. In addition, the big banks will now need to raise capital and loans equivalent to 20 per cent of the part of their balance sheet for which UK taxpayers would be liable in a crisis.

The coalition government were swift to accept the Vickers recommendations almost without reservation, giving British banks until 2019 to install their ring-fence. However, I fear that the question of the separation of banks' retail and investment arms has still not been successfully settled here in the UK. Fears have been raised that the Vickers reforms will tie up billions of pounds in additional capital and impose on banks a requirement to overhaul compliance and corporate affairs – a burden that will, I am afraid, have to be met by our constituents, the general public, in higher interest rates and in the sharply reduced amounts that banks are willing to lend.

One of the causes of this paralysing uncertainty that has enveloped the UK's big banks is the mixed messages coming from the Treasury on the one hand and the central bank on the other over the dual requirements to recapitalise and thus reduce the risks of future taxpayer bailouts, while also being ready to lend to credit-starved UK Plc as if it were 2006 or 2007 all over again.

Meanwhile, at EU level, the Liikanen report has recommended to the European Commission a similar, Vickers-style ring-fencing of retail banking from investment banking. This has given a small crumb of comfort that the UK might not be going down this path alone. However, I fear that the Liikanen proposals are sufficiently different from the Vickers proposals to heap further uncertainty on financial services here in the City.

Since there is likely to be precious little consensus between the EU, the UK and the US authorities any time soon as to whether the structure of banking is best under Liikanen, Vickers or indeed Volcker, how should banks realistically now prepare? Once again, I fear that the cost of all that uncertainty will be borne by the consumer and the wider economy, not to mention heavy job losses throughout the financial services industry. In this regard, it is important to nail the understandable public misconception, also heard here tonight, that it has been 'business as-usual' in the City since 2008. It would be fair to say that particularly over the past two years, volumes of business have collapsed, state financial support has been largely withdrawn and there has been and will continue to be a huge jobs cull. If we couple that with falling salaries and bonuses for the vast majority of workers, it means bad news all round, as Treasury receipts from financial services have plunged to what I suspect will be a new norm for the future.

Aside from the issue of commercial uncertainty, there are, I believe, question marks over whether the ring-fence will actually work. The Bill's template is based on a somewhat simplistic and outdated division between what amounts to wholesale and retail banking. There are numerous transmission mechanisms between the two that make a hard-and-fast split between high-street and casino investment banking very difficult to achieve.

Historically, the City of London has repeatedly benefited from arbitrage with Wall Street, from the withholding tax under President Kennedy over fifty years ago, which precipitated the creation of the eurodollar and eurobond markets, right through to the 'Big Bang' in the mid-1980s and the effects of Sarbanes-Oxley in 2002 in the aftermath of the Enron and WorldCom collapses. If the UK is to prevent its competitors from benefiting from unilateral action along the lines set out by Vickers, it must continue to press for international agreement on the future landscape of the financial services world.

There is, in my view, a danger that the UK and EU regulators will somehow look at the Bill's ring-fencing as a panacea, and will sell it as such to the general public. Instead, in light of the pitfalls of the ring-fence options, it might prove more effective to look at an alternative dual system when it comes to ordinary deposit accounts. This would allow those who desire a risk-free place to store their money to place it in savings banks, while those happier to take a risk – unprotected, of course, by any government guarantee – could have an account with a fractional reserve bank, as used to be the case in the UK until the mid-1980s.

Tighter regulation, new-fangled restrictions and imploring banks to behave ethically as set out in this Bill and future legislation will no doubt do little to restore the City's reputation for integrity. I fear that the spate of mis-selling scandals still has a hell of a long way to run, especially as, in fairness, 20:20 hindsight now deems that almost any novel financial product created and marketed by our banks since 2000 will be regarded as being mis-sold against consumers' interests.

If governments of any political colour continue to take ultimate responsibility when consumers purchase products from our banks, a whole set of unhealthy and perverse incentives will continue to plague our financial services industry. It is imperative to remember that regulation is often the sworn enemy of competition – one of the other avowed goals in the Bill. Public confidence and ethical foundations will slowly and surely be restored in financial services only when the landscape becomes far more competitive. That means, in my view – whether we like it or not – that consumers of financial products need to take a far greater level of responsibility. No amount of banking reform or new regulation will otherwise create the conditions for free-flowing capital to build the successful businesses of the future, let alone restore the reputation of our nation's most important invisible export, which is and remains financial and business services.

‡

What the Cypriot haircut means for the eurozone, 18 March 2013

In common with countries across Europe, Cyprus was badly affected by the global financial crisis of 2008, which had pushed the island's economy into recession. With a large offshore banking industry, however, Cyprus was particularly exposed to bad debt on its banks' balance sheets – in the good times, Cypriot banks had lent Greek borrowers the equivalent of 160 per cent of the island's GDP. As Greece went into economic meltdown, Cyprus' financial sector struggled to keep its head above water. Without the means to launch a rescue bid of its own banks, the Cypriot government was forced to ask the European Union for a bailout.

A deal was agreed in Brussels late-night on Friday 15 March that would see a one-off 10 per cent savings levy forced upon Cypriot depositors the following Tuesday as part of an emergency €10 billion bailout

– the first time such a measure had been included in any rescue package. Panic swept across the island and people rushed to withdraw their savings only to find that banks had been closed. I wrote this article after that tumultuous weekend.

Just when the markets were being lulled into complacency, this weekend's dramatic news from Cyprus has acted as a timely reminder that, at best, the problems of the eurozone have been parked, rather than solved.

Unsurprisingly, the markets have taken fright and it is by no means certain that the Cypriot government will be able to force through its plan to sequestrate funds directly from bank depositors' accounts.

As the eurozone crisis moves into fresh territory, there are four quick observations I would make on this fast-moving story:

1. Philosophically, not to mention economically, the European Central Bank's decision to insist that its bailout be conditional upon depositors taking a levy of 9.9 per cent for deposits over €100,000 and 6.75 per cent for those under €100,000 (although there is now talk of a backtrack on taxing small deposit holders, leading to a potential uplift in the 9.9 per cent levy) is ground-breaking in its perversity. Not least as once again, bondholders get off scot-free. The rationale in 2008 to exempt bondholders was made on pragmatic grounds that there was an overwhelming risk of contagion given the interconnectedness within financial markets.

   By contrast, bondholders who have lent to Cyprus over the past few years have done so in an environment where the risk of 'haircuts' has been ever-present. They have also done so at generous interest rates; presumably as a fulsome reflection of inherently greater risk. Yet, once again, the risk:reward ratio has been utterly ignored by regulators.

2. While the UK Treasury has understandably and swiftly sought to protect the 3,500 UK servicemen and civil servants out in Cyprus from taking losses from the levy, it begs the question: should the

other 55,000 or so UK nationals with deposits in Cyprus not also demand or expect special treatment? This will get messy, especially as many account holders live, run businesses and are electors here in the UK. Many reside in key London marginal constituencies and their political influence is likely to outweigh their number. This will also reopen domestic debates about the British government's lack of involvement and clout in eurozone governance.

3. I believe the risk of contagion may have been rather overstated. But with confidence still at rock bottom levels, it is not difficult to see that events in Cyprus may yet precipitate bank runs in more sizeable, struggling eurozone nations such as Italy and Spain. Any suggestion of further bailouts being required anywhere in the eurozone will almost certainly lead to intense speculation that similar strings will be attached by the ECB. A febrile economic atmosphere risks being brought to a calamitous state in several EU states at some point in the months ahead.

4. As ever, we should not discount the role that raw politics has played in the ongoing eurozone saga. We are now less than six months away from a German Federal Election. Distaste and impatience from German politicians (coupled with the recent upsurge in support for a domestic Eurosceptic party) has led to a demand that 'southern Europeans' should take a hit when financial bailouts are agreed.

The other unspoken issue is that the entire Cypriot banking system has only been saved from collapse over the past few years by the influx of Russian money. While this hot cash has helped underwrite Cyprus's banks and financial institutions, there have been growing doubts about its providence. The suggestion that laundered Russian money has been used to prop up an EU economy has troubled eurozone regulators and politicians alike. Their argument today is that Cypriot banks have for some time been essentially insolvent, and the relatively small contribution being demanded by depositors is equitable in the circumstances.

‡

Budget 2013, 19 March 2013

I previewed the March 2013 Budget for prominent political blog, ConservativeHome, suggesting that the Chancellor's room to manoeuvre would be limited by the poor state of the public finances. In the event, he was able to hike the personal allowance to £10,000 from 2014, a year earlier than planned, and reduce corporation tax, alongside popular measures to scrap planned increases in fuel and beer duties. However, these announcements were once again overshadowed by the figures. Forecast at 1.2 per cent in December, predicted growth for 2013 was revised down to 0.6 per cent, with debt as a share of GDP increasing from 75.9 per cent in 2013 to 85.6 per cent in 2016–17.

We should neither expect, nor want, fireworks on Wednesday.

There is no doubt that the Chancellor's room to manoeuvre is incredibly limited. Much of this, of course, can be attributed to global events – we only need to look at the weekend's dramatic news from Cyprus to know that the eurozone crisis is far from over. However, it has also become ever clearer that in the coalition's first Budget in June 2010, the government was complacent about growth.

The short pre-election boom following 2009's VAT reduction and the large, early rounds of quantitative easing, lulled the coalition on assuming office into believing that the growth baked into the system would somehow do the heavy lifting when it came to deficit reduction. The coalition's plan to eliminate the structural deficit required the gap between revenue and expenditure to be narrowed by £159 billion in 2014/15. Tax rises were expected to contribute £31 billion and spending cuts £44 billion to this total.

Unfortunately, however, the coalition ended up with the worst of all worlds. It has received relentless criticism for harsh austerity measures when, in reality, too often it has lacked the political will and necessary competence to execute the levels of savings required. The fact is, for all the rhetoric, we are still overspending by some £300 million each and every day and thus needing to borrow to the tune of £120 billion year-on-year. In 2010 we should have looked the electorate in the eye and been quite clear about the magnitude of the task that lay ahead to rectify the public finances. Early U-turns on school sports, forestry and book-reading schemes augured ill for the government's ability to push through some of the more important and wide-ranging savings.

But we are where we are.

I personally take the view that talk of radical tax cuts as the vital shot in the arm following this Budget is unrealistic. As a former businessman myself, of course I want to see taxes down as low as possible. However, I fear confidence is so low at the moment that until it is restored, almost any tax giveaways are more likely to be squirrelled away as savings either for businesses or individuals than pumped back into the economy. We would also run the serious risk of the markets losing faith in the event that we played faster and looser with public borrowing than we are already doing. In spite of the recent loss of our triple A rating from Moody's, the Chancellor's great achievement – and this really should not be underestimated – is that we are still able to borrow at such low interest rates. The lesson of both 1931 and 1976 is that once the markets turn, all is lost.

Similarly, we probably have to get real about the likelihood of the coalition being able to enact further, significant public spending cuts in advance of the 2015 election, in addition to those already planned in years four and five of this parliament. That is not to say that in an ideal world we should not try. We are, after all, continuing to live well beyond our means. But the notion that anything we do now, with only two years to go until the general election, will have a sufficiently significant impact on the economy is probably unrealistic.

So anticipate a bland Budget.

Since it is hard to see in the short term how we can bridge the sizeable gap in the national finances, my main hope for this Budget is that the coalition takes some of the long-term decisions that the British economy requires. I think there will be some targeted additional borrowing for some of the shovel-ready projects like house-building and science parks, and in areas like the technology sector. Ideally, we would also try to give businesses certainty on some of the key long-term issues facing the British economy, particularly over aviation and energy. We cannot let these political footballs be kicked into the next parliament once again.

I should also like to see the Chancellor put some light at the end of the long tunnel the British economy is currently travelling through. The magnitude of Britain's difficulties is intimidating and I am not implying the government has an easy job – the legacy it inherited was a grisly one and a crucial part of building an environment favourable to enterprise involves unravelling that legacy. Nevertheless, for our nation to be successful and for our party to enjoy popular electoral support, it must first level *properly* with the public when it comes to just how serious is the state of the public finances (no juvenile name calling, no blaming the 'last government', no partisan political dividing lines).

After that, however, it must tell a positive story, recognising that in today's global race, successful countries will be those in which ideas and dynamism are captured and retained. That translates as an immigration system open to the highly skilled from across the globe so that innovative and creative people can gather to exchange and develop ideas. It means governments creating certain and stable environments that breed confidence when it comes to borrowing and lending. Places where infrastructure is targeted so that hubs like the Silicon Roundabout growing around Old Street are linked into transport, supply and high-speed broadband networks. Regulatory environments in which taking on staff is not perceived as too costly or high risk. Places where universities and schools provide the market with employees who are well equipped and eager, with an appreciation of what they need to do rather than what they are owed. Where governments are much more consumer-focused and able to adapt to change themselves.

Is our government currently providing such an environment? Well, usually it is getting the rhetoric right. I very much support, for instance, the high-profile business delegations to India and the focus on high-speed visa processing for business people looking to come to the UK. But there are two things that worry me: first, the gap between the government's rhetoric and its success at following through, and second, the anti-success narrative that seems to be developing in our nation.

Entrepreneurial enterprise, of which we need more so desperately, has always required a degree of risk-taking. But nowadays the risks seem greater because, in spite of what the government says, there are still hefty taxes to pay, the cost of living is stubbornly high, banks remain reluctant to lend and it is still too costly to take people on. Furthermore, tax law seems much less certain and the general population far more receptive to the bashing of the wealthy, wealth-creators and capitalism than has until recently been the case. I speak to people in businesses large and small in my constituency and I talk to leaders in the City – not, I hasten to add, exclusively in the banking profession. Suddenly, for the first time *ever*, global corporations are beginning to consider the almost unthinkable prospect of political risk being attached to the UK. Small wonder few will expand so rapidly anytime soon. Politicians of all colours cannot keep stoking up the hue and cry towards big corporations.

If there is one thing the Chancellor can do, it is to forget about pressure for quick fixes and transient boosts and focus relentlessly on *delivery* as well as longer-term measures to make our nation a more tempting prospect. If we are not to get breathtaking growth before the 2015 election, let's at least get some credibility for doing the right thing for Britain in the long term and give people some sense of hope for the future.

‡

Whatever happened to that export-led growth?, 14 April 2013

One of the criticisms levelled at the pre-2008 UK economy was that it was far too reliant on services, particularly financial services, weighted too heavily towards London and the south-east and neglectful of the manufacturing sector, creating a gaping trade deficit. The coalition trumpeted its determination to address these apparent weaknesses head-on by 'rebalancing' the economy and boosting exports. Three years into its term, I questioned how much progress had been made.

In a fast-changing world, the truth is the global race has been under-way for some time.

The past half-decade ought to have been the best of times for UK exporters. After all, in the immediate aftermath of the financial crisis, sterling dropped in value by over 20 per cent against the cur-rencies of both our biggest export markets. The pound's fall against the US dollar (nearer 30 per cent) and the euro, in an era before enforced austerity within the eurozone, happened when consump-tion remained relatively high.

Since the financial crash, our floating currency has remained remarkably stable against these competitor currencies, the slight gains in 2009–12 only being cancelled out by downward movement in recent months. Worryingly, however, despite the devaluation, UK companies appear to have missed this opportunity to boost export sales, and the UK's healthy surplus in services exports continues to be undermined by a stubbornly high goods deficit.

The government's avowed strategy of rebalancing the economy towards trade and manufacturing, where the UK is currently the elev-enth largest goods exporter worldwide (in 1990 the UK stood proudly in fifth place), and away from financial and professional services where we rank at number two, is part of the issue. We might rightly have expected a manufacturing renaissance to compensate for weaker ser-vices exports in the aftermath of the financial crisis. Yet, as the pound was falling after 2008, so were British manufacturing exports – by some 8 per cent. In expanding, non-EU markets, the export of goods has fallen by over 4 per cent year-on-year, with the much vaunted car industry witnessing a slump of 23 per cent from its January 2012 peak.

Our performance in the emerging markets remains weak – indeed, the weakest of any G8 nation for the period 2000–2011, an era when emerging markets were regarded as the key route to expansion. The Germans exported nearly twice as much in goods to India in 2011 as their UK counterparts, while the Belgians similarly continue to dwarf our own exports to that vast nation. Indeed, when it comes to the Indian market, Britain is taking a mere 1.5 per cent slice of the cake, and ranks nineteenth in the 2012 league table of exporters. Given the historical UK–India ties of Empire and Commonwealth, let alone the benefits of common language and culture, this is little short of a national disgrace.

Similarly, Spain and Portugal, while under the weight of stiff ECB-sponsored austerity programmes, have cleansed much of their non-performing business, and in recovery mode have put in better export performances than the UK, where our 0.3 per cent decline indicates a fall in global market share. This applies even in our traditionally strong market sectors, where the coalition is supposed to have focused the UK's rebalancing efforts. In high tech/high value added manufacturing, our export record has been disappointing, declining to less than 11 per cent of GDP, two thirds of the EU average which we matched less than twenty years ago.

To be fair, both David Cameron and Boris Johnson have led high-profile trade missions to the Indian subcontinent in particular, in order to kick-start a fresh wave of trade deals. The appointment in recent months of eight trade envoys to specific overseas territories is designed to pay dividends in the future and the new same-day visa for Indian businessmen, alongside the lifting of restrictions on Indian students, sends precisely the right message about Britain being open for business.

These envoys, working closely with UK Trade and Investment and overseas embassies/High Commissions, should regard their roles not as propagandists for UK companies, but as providing long-term intelligence about the 'go-to people' on the ground in territories for prospective exporters, especially in the SME sector.

In truth, however, the developing world still has an overwhelming appetite for mid-market manufactured goods, rather than the services that make up the UK's competitive advantage. Even in China and India, the most mature of the emerging markets, demand for services is at a relatively immature stage in the growth curve. However, we forget at our peril that the cultural propensity of the fast-growing Asian middle class to save means that before long they will assuredly be prime targets for our financial, consulting and professional services exports.

In most other countries coping with financial crises, the export boost from devaluation has been the great sweetener leading those economies back to growth. Take South Korea, for example; a country whose currency dropped in the aftermath of the 1997 Asian financial crisis to a similar degree as ours post-2008. In its wake came a 15 per cent increase in manufacturing exports. The mysterious failure of the UK similarly to capitalise on the back of a weakened pound suggests our problems run deeper – we have a productivity issue.

Demographically the UK faces a double whammy. On the one hand, the proportion of the overall population in work continues to decline (not, it should be said, as precipitately as many of our European neighbours). On the other, we face a huge challenge in respect of the quality of our labour market. Complacently, the UK has prided itself on having a highly skilled, inventive and productive workforce. Yet the functional illiteracy, innumeracy and chaotic lifestyles of a worryingly high proportion of UK adults have rendered them unfit for the modern-day service industry workplace. Witness the huge numbers of foreigners employed in hospitality at a time of high indigenous unemployment. While in a bygone era many of the unskilled might find employment in traditional industry, such jobs have disappeared.

The abandonment of the UK's science and technology edge has resulted in a near terminal decline in our manufacturing capacity. Nowhere is this more apparent than in London. In the half century between 1960 and 2010, the capital's industrial base contracted precipitously. At the start of this period, manufacturing accounted for virtually one-third of London's wealth; it is now reduced to just 7 per cent and with it three quarters of industrial jobs have been lost. Truly, there is no way back.

For sure Chinese companies are able to manufacture mass-market goods more cheaply, but the lack of UK commitments in enhancing graduate and apprentice level skills in IT, science and engineering has served ill our chances of expanding exports in this most perilous of decades. In 2008, China had 3.7 million engineering students and produced fourteen times as many engineers as the UK. If a half-century ago top UK engineering companies still attracted many of the best graduates, the decline in the appeal of this discipline (even for those with an academic and practical training) has been marked. The services industries – banking, the media, law, management consulting – attracted many more of those entering the workplace in the 1980s and 1990s, with the even more specialist financial service outlets of private equity and hedge funds appealing until the crash of 2008.

Sadly, the UK probably now lacks the critical mass in technical graduate engineering skills or a home manufacturing base to recover, even if banking and professional services were to remain (relatively) in the doldrums for years to come. Furthermore, Britain's small and medium sized businesses (SMEs) appear stubbornly reluctant to export, with only 20 per cent of the UK's 200,000 SMEs doing so.

UK Trade and Investment is determinedly trying to address that by helping such firms spot export opportunities. Other than appointing envoys, SME assistance and the liberalising of immigration rules, what else can government do to rebuild the UK's trade performance? The Export Guarantee initiatives are welcome but invariably take time to bear fruit. They are the lifeblood for mid-sized enterprises breaking into new emerging markets. The UK needs to exploit supply chain finance within the eurozone and recognise the strengths of its position as a distribution hub. To be frank, we are well behind the French and German governments, which are often accused by British prospective exporters of unfairly promoting their own national exporters in new markets in Asia, Africa and South America.

Now is not the time for orthodoxy and timidity in the export guarantee field: we need to integrate policies in this area and aggressively market that diminishing but still highly respected UK expertise at the top end of the value chain in the manufacturing sector. Inevitably some export guarantees will go sour, but that is the price any government must pay if we are to exploit the new export markets that will invigorate the UK's traditional role as a global trading nation in the century that lies ahead.

Beyond that, however, the UK requires serious long-term thinking that identifies future growth industries and links them to new infrastructure projects, targets them for R&D subsidies and equips the workforce with the skills to operate in the growth areas of tomorrow.

It is unrealistic to expect a speedy turnaround of our trading fortunes in emerging markets, but the marketing of UK manufactured goods and services abroad needs to be reinvigorated before the UK economy can claim an export renaissance. We still have a great deal to offer, not least as the goods we do manufacture have a reputation for quality. But our export needs to be far wider and deeper than professional services and high end goods if we are to close the gaping British trade deficit.

‡

Between the Crashes, 24 April 2013

On 8 April 2013, the former Prime Minister, Baroness Thatcher, died peacefully in her sleep at the Ritz Hotel in my central London constituency. She had been the political titan of my generation and a towering figure in the modern Conservative Party, acting as Life Patron of my own Cities of London & Westminster Conservative Association.

Margaret Thatcher became Prime Minister when I was fourteen and left office when I was twenty-six. I was a grammar schoolboy in the 1970s when selective education was under threat and had been repelled by the politics of envy and class-war rhetoric commonplace at that time. From then on, I held dear the ideas she personified and articulated of choice and individual responsibility. By the time I left university, Mrs Thatcher had firmly stamped her mark on our nation and I was convinced that the UK was a place of infinite possibilities. Mrs Thatcher championed liberty at home and abroad and broke down orthodoxies. She gave people the opportunity to shape their own destinies through merit and hard work, independent of the state. She told people to have confidence in themselves – and in Britain.

If there was one thing that Mrs Thatcher had in spades, it was authenticity. People knew what she stood for and were able to respect that, even if grudgingly. It was this authenticity, alongside her enduring qualities of leadership and conviction, that I reflected upon as she was laid to rest.

Lady Thatcher received a state funeral on 17 April, with her hearse driven through the streets of London from the Houses of Parliament to St Paul's Cathedral. One week later, my first book, Between the Crashes, *was published and I include the speech I made at its launch since it provides a useful reminder of the mood of the times, and the roots of many of the themes within* The Best of Times.

If there was one group of people protesting on the sidelines at Margaret Thatcher's funeral, it was not those who had lived through her prime ministership, but a band of disenchanted young voters who needed to find someone at whom they could lash out. Thankfully, their protests were overshadowed by the countless ordinary Londoners who were able to recall from their own memories the extent to which she gave them and the nation a renewed sense of self-belief.

Nearly five years ago, the global financial system was sucked into a spiral of crisis. Since my election in 2001, I had represented the City of London at the peak of its reputation. Suddenly, it was being blamed for economic calamity, the focus of national disdain.

The conversations I had with politicians, financiers and constituents in the feverish months and years that followed inspired a series of articles and speeches, brought together for the first time in *Between the Crashes*.

In book form, they tell the story of a country in crisis. Mired in debt. Battling against international headwinds. Caught up in institutional scandal… and falling behind in the global race.

They also provide – perhaps for the first time – a timeline of these seismic political and economic events as they were being played out, alongside a robust, distinctly Conservative analysis of the challenges facing Britain today.

Between the Crashes serves up some constructive suggestions and positive ideas on how we can best harness the assets of our great nation in the twenty-first century. But ultimately I hope it serves as a warning to future generations of the mistakes ours has made.

In putting the book together, some consistent themes have struck me:

- Generational division.
- The fundamental shift of power away from the West and towards the East.
- The poisonous amalgam of apathy and anger towards capitalism, business and markets.
- The failure by Western leaders to level with the public about the pain ahead.

All, I believe, are set to define the decade ahead. All are inextricably linked to the debt that clings like fat round the arteries of the British economy, a festering testimony to our collective dodge of difficult decisions.

How did we get to this point?

In the late nineties and noughties, we Britons indulged ourselves with an ever-expanding welfare state, cheap goods, never-ending lines of credit, and inflated house prices. But we were racking up colossal problems for generations to come.

Instead of courageously confronting these issues, politicians from ALL parties instead told people what they wanted to hear. Just as Blair attempted to mimic Thatcher, my own Conservative Party had formally adopted the language of Chancellor Brown by making, in 2007, a fateful commitment to 'stick to Labour's spending plans' and 'share the proceeds of growth'.

The Lehmans' collapse of 2008 ought to have signalled the moment when Britain came to terms with a new reality, a reality where our declining competitiveness and unaffordable spending habits could be cloaked by borrowing no longer.

Instead, scapegoats were sought. What followed was a global economic downturn; a banker-induced crash; Labour mismanagement;

Thatcher's Big Bang legacy. Absent was any collective admission that we had been living well beyond our means long before the crisis.

As a result, by the 2010 general election, we Britons had still not been prepared for the new reality. Which is why the three main political parties at that time were satisfied to confine debate only to a narrow choice – when best to cut £6 billion in public expenditure, a sum we were in fact borrowing every fortnight.

By the time the coalition was formed, it lacked any explicit mandate for the cuts to expenditure that the state of the public finances dictated. Since then, the country has struggled to wean itself off the drip of borrowed money, with £120 billion added to the UK's debt pile every year. Indeed, by the time its term ends, the coalition will have added more to the public debt than any previous administration.

With the blame for our travails pinned firmly on bankers, the debates over the future of financial services in this period have been similarly characterised by a lack of honesty. I have never been an apologist for the banking fraternity but *Between the Crashes* charts the endless populist battles, mixed messages and spasms of banker-bashing that have defined the past few years. Frequently running entirely counter to the national interest, these episodes have coated Britain in an anti-business, anti-wealth, anti-success rhetoric at odds with the UK's pressing need for economic growth.

Between the Crashes also makes plain the scale of the economic challenges facing this government, crediting the coalition for some of the difficult work it has begun. The road is being built for a leaner and fairer welfare system. Vital reforms of the education system are underway. Much of our rhetoric on growth is spot on, and the Prime Minister is absolutely right when he talks of Britain competing in a global race.

But all too frequently, we have fallen short on delivery, our coalition partners often a convenient alibi for an absence of resolve. As we edge closer towards the 2015 election, I believe the coalition is ever more vulnerable to mission drift.

Last Wednesday, the nation laid to rest one of the towering figures of twentieth-century politics. Inevitably, debate has raged over

Mrs Thatcher's legacy and how the Iron Lady might have steered our nation through today's tricky waters.

She led the nation at a different time. Undoubtedly 21st-century Britain requires fresh solutions, driven forward by its own actors.

Nevertheless, I reflected that Mrs Thatcher brought to her role three qualities which modern Britain requires if it is to tackle the generational divide, the draining of economic power and the loss of faith in politics that *Between the Crashes* highlights as the legacy of our indebtedness.

When she took the reins, Mrs Thatcher led the country with passion. She brought with her a sense of mission. But more than anything, she came with an overriding sense of urgency.

Today, low interest rates and quantitative easing have lulled us into a false sense of security. Yet they are merely an indicator that the British economy remains on life support. Britain's circumstances require action, not promises of what will be done after 2015. We are in government NOW. We need decisions NOW – on energy supply, aviation policy and skilled immigration, to name but three.

Between the Crashes is designed to be a crushingly honest and independent Conservative take on a time in our nation of great change. For observers of economics and politics, this has been a fascinating era, whose ups and downs I hope have been captured in this book.

But it must not become an era of wasted opportunity.

In 2045, when all of us here (I hope) come to look back at a century of post-war Britain, my greatest fear is that Mrs Thatcher's time will be seen as a golden blip… in an otherwise consistent decline in British economic and diplomatic influence.

I hope *Between the Crashes* reminds future generations of the mistakes ours has made in getting here. But most of all, I hope it triggers debate. In all crises, time heals some of our problems. But our nation requires political determination, resolve and a sense of urgency if we are to restore the sense of pride and strength that will ensure Britain seizes the twenty-first century rather than becomes consumed by it.

‡

The mispricing of risk, 11 May 2013

'Is there more to come?' It was with this question in mind that I gave my first book the provocative title, *Between the Crashes*.

Launched last month with the support of ConservativeHome, *Between the Crashes* provides a timeline of the momentous political and economic events that followed the collapse of Lehman Brothers in 2008. As I came to write the book's conclusion in December, I was struck by a sense of how a crisis which began half a decade ago may still have much further to unwind.

This fear was only compounded by a seminar I attended some months back at Gresham College, '*The City's Great Financial Scandals, Past and Future*', which was rounded off with a compelling lecture by a banker with over forty years' front-line experience. There are two types of financial scandal or disaster, he suggested. The first might cause great pain to those closely linked to the failed institution(s) but have no wider impact on society; the second, a collapse of such magnitude that financial calamity leads to social discord. This might be characterised as the difference between the failure of Equitable Life, which caused considerable pain to policy-holders but had little wider impact, and the implosion of Lehman Brothers, which was the catalyst that exposed the unsustainable nature of the West's debt bubble and whose consequences we are still dealing with today.

On this basis, our lecturer feared we might well be in the throes of the latter type of crisis by the decade's end. Why? Because in the current climate, when all the normal market signals have disappeared under a mountain of cheap money, it remains nigh-on impossible to make a rational investment decision. Risk is always and everywhere mispriced.

The classic role of economists, governments and central banks is to promote a stable monetary and legal framework that lubricates the economy with trust, the most crucial ingredient in any economic transaction. In the absence of such a framework, any asset related to a central bank agency is not capable of being properly priced; as a consequence, no rational risk assessment can be made of it.

So how are today's central banks doing when it comes to providing such a framework? Not all that well, if we look at their current aims. The US Fed has accepted an employment target around which to frame its interest rate policy; the Bank of England aims to achieve a nominal GDP; the European Central Bank does whatever it takes to save the single currency. None of these goals has the maintenance of trust at their heart. The misguided manipulation of the price of money via interest and exchange rates, added to the printing bonanza of quantitative easing (£375 billion and counting from the Bank of England), has stolen from the market its ability to signal to investors what is risky and what is not.

How might these seeds grow into financial disaster? As ever, we need to follow the money. Since the beginning of 2008, investors have parked over $1.1 trillion into the supposedly safe haven of bond mutual funds and exchange-traded funds. To give some comparison, that is thirty-three times more than went into equity funds during that period. Earlier this month, yields on ten-year UK gilts fell close to their lowest level since August. It is a similar story for German and US gilts. Indeed, if you look at any long-run analysis of interest rates on UK government debt (say, fifteen-year term bonds) – whether examining the 300-odd years since bonds were introduced or even the period since the Second World War – the mean average interest rate is 5 per cent to 6 per cent, versus the 2 per cent today. Are we really saying that the risk of buying bonds is at its lowest level for 300 years? Moreover, do today's prices remotely reflect worth?

Over the past few decades, bonds have been seen as virtually 'risk-free', fixed-income investments. It was perhaps entirely understandable, therefore, that in the volatile, post-Lehman world, investors would take fright at unpredictable share markets and turn instead to unexciting, stable bonds as a safe means of preserving capital and getting a guaranteed return. Nevertheless, when coupled with a new world of ultra-low interest rates and active bond-purchasing by central banks, bonds began to give equity-like returns, leading to a boom in post-2008 bond sales that drove prices up.

Such investments have *not* been risk-free, however. In fact, their over-valuation leaves purchasers vulnerable to clear, specific risks – most of all, the risk of inflation. When consumer prices rise, the fixed interest from the bond loses some of its real purchasing power. If yields are high enough, those price rises can be accommodated without losing an investment's initial value. If not, the bond is actively destroying that value. Inflation also increases the likelihood of central banks hiking interest rates, making other investment comparably more attractive. The ostensible security offered by fixed-income bonds can soon evaporate away.

An end to ultra low interest rates and bond yields would of course be indicative of a return to some sort of economic normality. But if such things came to pass, one fund manager predicts that it is quite possible bondholders could lose up to 40 per cent of their money. 'So what?', we may be inclined to ask. Well, it should be noted that typically, bondholders are not simply banks and insurers. They are just as often institutional pension funds (funds which reportedly now own more bonds than equities). The mispricing of bond risk, caused in large part by the manipulation of the money supply by central banks, could potentially lead to the destruction of savers' capital on a massive and unprecedented scale.

If interest rates were simply to revert to their long-run mean average, a portfolio held in such bonds would devalue by between 35 per cent and 44 per cent, even if inflation stayed at the roughly 3 per cent it is at today. If inflation took off as well, there could be a devastation of bond values. Yet pension funds, insurance companies and banks have all been encouraged to hold ever more of these supposedly 'safe assets'. It is vital that governments cease pushing through legislation based on Basel III and Solvency III that force the holding of these bonds on pension funds, insurance companies and banks. Beyond that, it is imperative that investors be made aware of the risks – and *fast*. It is interesting to see this week that the portfolio managers of a number of US university endowments have drastically reduced their exposure to US government bonds from as much as 30 per cent in 2008–09 to near zero in many cases.

Nobody wants to be last in line should this be the start of a head-long rush out of the market.

The crisis kicked off by the Lehmans' collapse was brought about by an irrational exuberance, most obviously in the housing market, that made it difficult for investors to make rational risk/reward investment decisions. The next 'crash', if it came about in our bond markets, would instead be as a result of deliberate government economic policy.

But would such an outcome lead to social calamity? We can only hope not. Yet history is littered with periods where the debasement of money (hyperinflation) – and therefore the debasement of trust – has gone on to undermine social cohesion, not least as it has first wiped out an aspirational middle class. A widescale destruction in the value of pension funds triggered by a bond crash would coincide with the erosion of debtors' liabilities by inflation. This would likely trigger a deep sense of injustice as savers and the responsible in society lose out to the profligate.

Worryingly, the Bank of England is now controlling the supply, demand and price of bonds in the UK. It seems unthinkable that this is a prescription without consequence. The fear that we remain 'between the crashes' still looms all too large.

‡

The OBR – it seemed such a good idea at the time, 30 May 2013

The Office for Budget Responsibility was created by the coalition in June 2010 to produce independent economic and fiscal forecasts for the UK. Such forecasts had previously been produced by Treasury, calling into question their independence from political meddling. However, in its first three years, the OBR had consistently got it wrong on growth. While the OBR had predicted that the UK economy would expand by 2.7 per cent by 2013, in reality it had grown by only half that figure. Headed up by Robert Chote, former head of the Institute for Fiscal Studies, the

OBR's credibility was thrown into doubt by its apparent support for Treasury optimism.

This year's Budget continued a hapless, unparalleled record of forecasting failure for the OBR.

Sadly, what has so undermined City commentators' confidence is that the OBR's independent analysis has invariably veered in the direction of robust support for the Treasury's economic projections. At each succeeding Autumn Statement and Budget since June 2010, the OBR has been forced to downgrade growth outturns, while continuing to hold optimistically to the notion that the public finances will be transformed by robust growth starting earnestly in two years' time. It all seems so reminiscent of the Brown Chancellorship's discredited financial projections that persuaded global investors to allow Britain to borrow well beyond its means with such disastrous consequences in the noughties.

Few doubt that economic forecasting is an especially dismal science, not least in these turbulent times. However, the OBR's intervention at last December's Autumn Statement proved essential in buying the Chancellor welcome breathing space (which he has certainly exploited, as the economic corner appears to have been turned since). With most commentators assuming that the coalition's plan to reduce the deficit year-on-year had been flunked, their figures were a timely political fillip. What now appears to critics a sleight-of-hand gave Mr Osborne an easy ride with the press in the aftermath of the Autumn Statement, but set the scene for cynicism and deep disappointment as a mere fourteen weeks later, aggregate borrowing for the next four years was projected at an eye-watering £49 billion higher.

The Treasury's decision to bring back onto the public balance sheet some £37 billion as the profit, or 'coupon' in the jargon, of quantitative easing interest payments, was not without critics at the time. Indeed if QE is eventually to be a success in its own terms, its unravelling will require a markedly larger sum eventually to be returned from the public accounts. Naturally, this will be at some future date, well beyond the next general election. While this was an accounting device, it also allowed the Treasury at the time of the Autumn Statement to reduce substantially the headline figures of public borrowing. More controversially, despite the 4G licence sale not having by then taken place, its estimated receipts were included in the borrowing calculations. In fairness, the sale proceeded during the 2012–13 tax year – however, the auction brought in barely two thirds of what had been accounted for (£2.3 billion as opposed to £3.5 billion).

Moreover, the much vaunted Swiss tax repatriation agreement, still subject to a referendum approval, was taken account of to the tune of £330 million. Small beer, perhaps, but critical in making the case for overall borrowing falling in 2012–13. The OBR sanctioned this being included in the Autumn Statement, although not a penny has yet reached the public coffers. Indeed, the projected receipts from the entire Swiss repatriation programme of £5.5 billion over the next two years is almost universally – at least outside the hallowed halls of the OBR – regarded as wildly optimistic. Even the mighty EU economic powerhouse, Germany, for example, reckons it will only repatriate £2 billion in this way.

This was the backdrop to the OBR's strong reaction to the Prime Minister's speech in early March over growth (when he had referred to their figures to support his case). Subsequently, Robert Chote (the OBR's chairman) reasserted his institution's independence. Perhaps more serious still than accusations that the OBR is insufficiently at arm's length from the government of the day, is the increasing realisation that the Office for Budget Responsibility has, in its methodology, consistently failed to understand the new reality of the squeezed private sector budgets in an era of continued public sector profligacy.

Meanwhile the proudly unfettered Institute for Fiscal Studies (Mr Chote's former employer) was unimpressed at the way the Treasury appeared to have given 'every indication that [spending commitments] had been carefully managed with a close eye on the headline borrowing figures for this year' by the wheeze of 'exceptional inter-period flexibility' (a practice which, in plain English, entails pushing payments into the next financial year rather than spending the money now). Indeed like-for-like comparison had the deficit *rising* to £123.2 billion in 2012–13, not falling from £121.0 billion (2011–12) to £120.9 billion as published. If Gordon Brown had done this we would rightly be berating him for 'fiddling the figures'.

Almost comically, every single Brown Budget between 2001 and 2007 forecast that the public finances would move back into surplus in a tantalising three or four years' time. As time wore on, the debt and annual deficit rose inexorably as the Treasury employed smoke and mirrors to conjure the illusion of fiscal stability. Those rosy forecasts belatedly attracted ridicule from our party and played their part in making it easy for Britain to borrow money during the past decade. And borrow we did, even in the good times – we all now know the disastrous consequences.

Indeed it was this salutary experience which provided the genesis of the idea for an Office for Budget Responsibility, which the Chancellor proposed in late 2008 when he was the shadow. While the principle of the OBR at that time seemed admirable, I expressed concern about problems of practice. Surely, I suggested, the real strains and potential limitations of any OBR would come at the point in the economic cycle when we most needed prescient and instinctive judgement? At such times of crisis in any economic phase, we would require a robust willingness to stand up against the conventional wisdom of the day.

Do we really believe that in the run-up to 2008's financial crisis, the OBR, contrary to every forecasting organisation, would not only have seen the crash coming but have had the mettle to contradict the optimistic forecasts of other bodies and suggest to the previous government that we were living well beyond our means? Equally, might the perceived infallibility of a conventional OBR forecast have restricted the ability of a Chancellor to act against common wisdom at that time, had he have possessed the wherewithal to express concerns about our direction of travel?

When the interim OBR was eventually introduced after the 2010 election, it produced predictions for growth that appeared far too optimistic. So it has proved, partly because of some unavoidable conflicts in its operation. Organisational independence was always vital to the OBR's credibility but it has had necessarily to rely upon a close relationship with the Treasury in order to understand its methods and have access to its data. Yet without the trust that stems from the OBR's autonomy, the organisation is nothing.

I also suggested back in 2011 that part of the OBR's continuing role ought to be constantly to remind us all of its own fallibility and advise on a range of possible outcomes, pointing out to politicians and financial markets the longer term threats to our economy in the event that the markets prove too forgiving. Instead, it has served to entrench rather than challenge conventional wisdom.

The restoration of confidence to our economy was always going to depend largely on rebuilding trust. The establishment of the OBR should have marked an important milestone in encouraging us to place our faith once again in the financial and political systems of our nation. The Bank of England's notional independence already stands in question – for some forty consecutive months now, its inflation target has been surpassed. Yet the near-zero interest rate policy first employed over four years ago by the erstwhile Labour administration and continued with gusto since the coalition came into office has been adopted by political complicity between the Bank and the Treasury. The economic case for this can be robustly made, but it flies in the face of an 'independent' Bank of England.

Unfortunately, the OBR has also appeared to have become part of Britain's national economic furniture, widely perceived as a tool of the Chancellor of the day, rather than an impartial challenger of facts, figures and strategy. This perception is one the OBR must urgently counter if it is to prove a genuinely valuable part of the UK financial landscape.

‡

Anti-avoidance and the slippery slope to tax tyranny (*City AM*), 4 June 2013

The Chancellor's March Budget once again promised a clampdown on tax avoidance, the hot topic of the moment following a fresh batch of scandals over the tax arrangements of famous celebrities, as well as the usual stories about the likes of Amazon and Starbucks. Nearly three years after it had first been drafted, a General Anti-Abuse Rule (GAAR) was introduced in the Finance Bill 2013, designed to catch out any taxpayers using schemes specifically designed to produce a tax advantage, as judged by a new eleven-strong advisory panel. In addition, Disclosure of Tax Avoidance Schemes (DOTAS) legislation was to be updated such that HMRC would be able to request client lists from companies suspected of operating abusive schemes, and an information-sharing deal was entered into with US tax authorities. I had serious concerns about the impact of some of these measures on legitimate business and wrote the following article for City AM *outlining my thoughts.*

What's not to like about cracking down hard on tax avoidance?

As the Finance Bill meanders through its customary summertime parliamentary scrutiny, the flagship policy designed to rid the UK economy of the scourge of tax avoidance takes centre-stage.

The imposition of a General Anti-Abuse Rule (GAAR) comes as a response to ever-intense public focus upon large corporations failing to 'pay their fair share of tax'. It also builds on the erstwhile Labour administration's first foray (via s58 of the 2008 Act) into retrospective taxation, aimed firmly at that time towards individual non-payers.

What's good enough for aggressive and abusive tax-avoiding citizens should apply equally to Google, Starbucks and Amazon. Or should it?

The Treasury has neglected to provide a firm definition on what counts as tax abuse, falling back on a standard 'just and reasonable' test. This risks creating an unprecedented transfer of power from parliament to the hands of HMRC. So our executive agency of the State will now be empowered not simply to apply the law, but to rewrite it as it – or perhaps a tenacious, campaigning press – would wish it had been written. Imagine the outcry from civil liberties groups if such a power was bestowed on the police over criminal justice legislation! Would anyone stand idly by if the police could happily arrest people for doing something that was not a legal offence, but where senior officers (maybe similarly in response to a relentless media hue and cry) wished it had been a criminal offence?

In the meantime, let's return to the proposed GAAR. I fear this initiative may end up creating more problems for HMRC (which itself has sadly become a watchword for incompetence in recent years) than it solves. In truth, more of its fire is likely to be directed not at the likes of Google and Starbucks, or even multi-millionaires with complex tax arrangements, but at ordinary taxpayers. Such constituents are already writing to me, fearful that the extension of retrospection will lead to established HMRC rules being changed under their feet alongside the never-ending uncertainty.

As part of its crackdown on avoidance, the Treasury recently heralded the hiring of 2,500 more tax inspectors. Surely it is not a mere fanciful concern that this will result in even more interpretations of what is 'fair', 'aggressive' or 'abusive', enriching litigators but acting to the detriment of the hapless individual taxpayer.

HMRC's arbitrary approach also runs counter to everything in UK mercantile tradition and risks further damaging the coalition's aim to make Britain 'open for business'. Alarm bells are already ringing at the casual interchanging of the terms 'avoidance' and 'evasion' by senior coalition figures, not to mention the emergence of the concept of 'aggressive avoidance'. This is not simply of concern to the tax advisory community. In a free society, individuals and businesses *should* be entitled to organise their affairs in such a way as to minimise their tax liability.

One would have more sympathy with a beleaguered Treasury, as it constantly tries to play catch-up with the creation of new loopholes, if it put its own house in order. A simpler and more certain tax code (faithfully promised by our party when in opposition) would be the surest way to minimise tax avoidance. The once-derided size of the Indian tax code has now been exceeded by our own government.

Indeed, if we are to adopt a GAAR (and further entrench retrospection in our tax system), I have long argued that it must go hand-in-glove with the creation of a comprehensive pre-clearance regime. This would enable companies and their tax advisers to road-test their proposed taxation schemes with senior HMRC officials.

Ideally, if this were to work efficiently, no new scheme would be permitted to be marketed until approved.

The UK will only attract new jobs, investment and growth if we can remain attractive to multinational businesses. We need to hear less from our elite political class about morality and witness a greater commitment to a simpler, more certain tax regime.

‡

Forget the British Empire – Syria's fate is not ours to determine (*Daily Telegraph*), 5 June 2013

It is hard to recall that in the summer of 2013, as politicians discussed what to do about the rapidly deteriorating situation in Syria, terror group ISIS was not even a blip on the national consciousness. Instead, Prime Minister David Cameron had started to believe that the time was ripe to begin arming groups opposed to the Syrian dictator, Bashar al-Assad, who had been using brutal violence against his own people after protests first broke out against his rule in March 2011.

Under pressure to stop the murderous Assad, President Obama had made clear in 2012 that if chemical weapons began to be moved around the country or used in any way, it would be akin to Assad crossing a red line that would trigger 'enormous consequences' from the United States. As evidence began to stack up that Assad had indeed used sarin gas, the case for Western action – likely in the form of military support to rebel groups – got stronger.

I remained unconvinced that a decision to arm such groups would not come back to haunt us, and wrote the following piece setting out my case for the Daily Telegraph. *Later that summer, after a suspected chemical attack on the outskirts of Damascus killed hundreds, MPs were asked to approve a British military response. The coalition lost the parliamentary vote that would have paved the way for action.*

Anyone listening to recent reports on the alleged use of chemical weapons by the Assad government in Syria would no doubt have uttered to themselves that familiar conclusion: 'Something must be done'.

As tales from Syria get bloodier and more barbaric, as more women and children get caught up in the fighting, and as the displaced swell Jordanian, Lebanese and Turkish refugee camps, it is an understandable and powerful sentiment.

But the compulsion to 'do something' is a dangerous one. For a start, it is tainted by unintentional arrogance often underpinned by misguided echoes of the British Empire. An opinion piece in last week's *Evening Standard*, was a case in point. 'Cameron could not allow Syria to be a failed state,' the headline declared, as if that nation's future lies firmly in our Prime Minister's hands. It does not.

While a 'do nothing' mentality often appears to infect the entire UK political class when it comes to tackling a host of long-term domestic issues, one might be forgiven for thinking that our medium-sized European nation is omnipotent when it comes to foreign affairs. Perhaps the starker truth is that Syria's fate was never in our hands. In reality, the fortunes of foreign nations are rarely dictated by UK intervention. That is not to say that Britain has no influence in such matters. In some instances, as Libya proved, our intervention can be decisive in facilitating regime change. But our ability to control what happens next is far less certain, particularly in a complex situation like Syria. To take such a view does not amount to defeatism or Britain turning a blind eye to suffering. It is a practical acceptance of our considerable diplomatic and military limitations.

Second, let us look at the realities of any intervention. Huge question marks would surely linger over the extent of any UK commitment to the Syrian crisis. British intervention in Afghanistan was aided not only by a far higher degree of domestic financial and political support than can be garnered for Syria, but was driven by the political will and economic clout of the United States, the world's unchallenged superpower at that time. In spite of that commitment, we have remained in Afghanistan for over a decade with a dubious record of success. What hope for a Syrian intervention

– whether military or humanitarian? The UK government is not advocating involvement on anywhere like as large a scale, but even its limited actions thus far have lacked the explicit support either of the British public or the US government. Without clear backing from these quarters, it is very difficult to see how our government can provide the sort of long-term commitment required for any meaningful solution.

Third, and most importantly in the case of Syria, in 'doing something' just who are we supporting? And with what objective in mind? The vast majority of correspondents among my electors are utterly opposed to the UK becoming engaged in yet another Middle Eastern military adventure. In a nutshell, the main worry is that we are gradually being sucked into a civil war that will rapidly escalate along Sunni/Shia dividing lines throughout the region. Last week's EU declaration lifting the arms embargo to the Syrian opposition has prepared the ground to aid and arm some pretty unsavoury folk who, if they were living in the UK, would almost certainly be subject to a TPIM and 24-hour police surveillance.

Many constituents have expressed concern that in assisting the disparate and disunited Syrian opposition, we are also inadvertently arming those who seek to drive out the Christian communities in that nation, who currently feel safer under the Assad regime. The near unspeakable truth now is that the sizeable Christian communities in war-torn Syria are at greater threat from their ancestral homes than has been the case for generations – often at the hands of the self-styled freedom fighters so feted by the Western press.

Syria is an emotive issue. The notion that we are abandoning the vulnerable and allowing a government to kill its own people naturally sits incredibly uneasily with all of us. But the urge to 'do something' is not reason enough to intervene in such an ethnically complex and rapidly evolving situation. As Syria descends into a darker spiral of violence, I am not convinced that its people's fate is any longer within our capacity to determine.

I support the coalition government in examining all our options carefully and meticulously. I accept that the Foreign Office has worked tirelessly to find common ground within the international community. But to arm rebel factions is to take things to a radically new level. We must be incredibly clear about what we are trying to achieve here. Nobody wishes to see rent-a-mob Jihadists, with no real stake in the affairs of Damascus, as our next set of Middle Eastern allies. The people of the UK, via their parliamentary representatives, will understandably demand that they have their say before our involvement in Syria escalates.

‡

Yet again the City is under attack
(*Daily Telegraph*), 19 June 2013

I was asked by the Daily Telegraph *to give my initial reaction to the release of the Parliamentary Commission on Banking Standards' final report, which included a recommendation to make 'reckless misconduct in the management of a bank' a new criminal offence that would carry a custodial sentence.*

The recommendation in today's Banking Commission report that reckless bankers should face jail sentences in future was designed to grab the headlines. How this will enhance trust, stability and profitability in the financial services sector is far more difficult to see.

The stark truth is that in the decade or so before the 2008 crash, bankers behaved rationally given the excessively low interest rates and credit conditions in the West. This came about as a result of catastrophic policy misjudgements by central bankers, policymakers and politicians alike. Here in the UK, for example, Gordon Brown was running an annual deficit of up to £40 billion, even during the boom.

Similarly, Brown's policy of putting public pension liabilities, vast scale PFI building programmes and the re-nationalised Network Rail off balance sheet – as a means of disguising the true state of the UK's public finances – has played as large a part in the huge debt pile being passed on to future generations as the collapse of the financial system.

The fact that we are still collectively living massively beyond our means to the extent that the government is borrowing £1 in every £5 that we spend is the clearest indication that banks, bankers and the City are not alone in being responsible for our economic plight.

UK business and the economy as a whole desperately need a thriving financial services sector. The Banking Commission's report – amidst some strong recommendations – risks relegating our banking industry to an inefficient, bureaucratic, public utility. This cannot be in the national interest.

‡

The eurozone's shadow still hangs over us, 23 June 2013

Some three months have now passed since the dramatic Cypriot bailout. In virtually equal measure, there were hopes and fears that March's developments in one of the eurozone's smallest nations would be the catalyst for the endgame to the eurozone's travails. Rumours abounded then that Slovenia would be next in line to default.

Characteristically, however, the Cypriot skirmish appears to have been yet another storm before the lull. Economic realities have once again been relegated to their improper place as the electoral clock ticks incessantly towards late September's Bundestag elections.

The Cypriot crisis was arguably brought to a head only because of German political imperatives. The recent emergence there of a fledgling Eurosceptic party, *Alternative für Deutschland* (whose channel of communication with Tory MEPs has caused diplomatic flutters between Berlin and Downing Street), led the ever-canny Angela Merkel to shore up her right flank.

Cyprus's economy, until very recently with its Icelandic-scale financial services imbalance propped up by Russian money, was sacrificed as collateral damage in these political manoeuvres. As the attention of the financial world moves on, make no mistake: the Cypriot economy is about to plunge into tailspin. The capital controls that have been imposed on Cyprus have resulted in the evaporation of trade, business activity and growth; this in a micro-economy already absurdly overloaded with household and business debt. Almost inevitably, its brightest young and middle-aged people, in a nation respected for its education system and language skills, will vote with their feet. Indeed, the fanciful threat that Cyprus might soon be forced to leave both the eurozone and the EU will only accelerate this process.

While it is fashionable to blame the European Central Bank (and its German paymasters) for the crisis, this tells only a fraction of the story. For sure it monumentally mishandled the Cypriot crisis, insisting first on an unmanageable bailout and then a revised deal that was accompanied with a sense of menace against a eurozone member widely judged as too small to bring down the whole edifice. However, amidst the chaos, some sound principles were being entrenched. Once the initial plan to seize even insured deposits was shelved, the ECB rightly imposed penalties instead on bondholders.

They have been forced to bail themselves into the rescue by a bonds-for-equity swap. While in Cyprus this was insufficient to properly recapitalise its two big banks, it has set a positive precedent in the increasingly likely event that other eurozone countries return cap-in-hand to the ECB for more assistance. If – and remember this also applies to the UK – we can begin to wean failing banks off their implicit taxpayer guarantees it will prove a very good thing indeed. The brutal truth is that even here in Britain we may soon need to follow this Cypriot precedent.

The eurozone remains appallingly mired in debt with unsustainably large public sectors, labour-market inflexibility and excessive tax rates, all of which hinder any real chance of sustained economic growth. The enforced dragging down of labour costs in Spain, Italy and Portugal have in the immediate term helped exports. Hereby those countries have started down the road towards more competitive economies, but at the short-term price of precipitate collapse in domestic consumption, a further factor undermining any hope of their economies returning to growth any time soon.

Meanwhile, the financial markets have until now been supportive of the notion of the UK as a 'safe haven' amidst all this continental turmoil. Yet there is *no* room for complacency – deeper crises elsewhere are unlikely to distract investors from some of the fundamental weaknesses in the British economy for ever. Foreign investors' demand for gilts, a driver of the pound's relative strength during the height of the financial crisis, peaked in November 2011. But there are some nagging fears about the UK's progress in cutting the deficit, alongside concern about the overall state of the national debt, sluggish productivity, stagnant growth and a banking system that still seems unable to direct cash to the parts of the economy that require it. Our low interest rates and quantitative easing, by depressing the pound's value, have also made sterling a less attractive prospect for potential currency purchasers.

In fairness, there is a keen sense that the UK economy has now turned the corner, albeit steadily. Nevertheless, the continued dark clouds hovering over the UK's single biggest export market, the eurozone, may yet prove debilitating in the future to domestic business confidence. Even the Treasury/Foreign Office aggressive manoeuvres at export-led growth elsewhere are paradoxically being undermined – or undercut might perhaps be the better word – by those eurozone nations being forced by extreme austerity measures to slash labour costs.

So on balance it may be unwise to give too much credence to short-term equity markets' strength. Indeed the continued upward movement in both the FTSE 100 and Dow Jones index over the past year probably reflects only a relative upturn in business confidence rather than the general health of the UK and US corporate sector. However, the value of sterling, notwithstanding its 'safe haven' status, should be a warning sign of how interconnected the UK's economic fortunes are with the travails of the eurozone.

In such a situation, it is unquestionably difficult for the coalition government to determine the wisest, most consistent course of policy. Since it will be some time before we are able to step from the eurozone's shadow, this makes it all the more important to keep prospective investors in the UK happy by addressing our own vulnerabilities. In short, the Chancellor must ignore those critics demanding a change in outlook – we must press relentlessly on towards the goal of deficit reduction.

‡

Governor Carney – a new broom on QE and interest rates?, 1 July 2013

On 30 June, suave Canadian central banker Mark Carney took over as the new Governor of the Bank of England after a decade with Sir Mervyn King at the helm. Carney was to be the first foreigner ever to hold the top job in British banking, and it was hoped that he would help lead the institution out of a period of record low interest rates and quantitative easing – emergency measures imposed to deal with the aftermath of the financial crisis.

Few central bankers have stepped foot in Threadneedle Street accompanied with such high expectations as Mark Carney.

The subdued image of Montagu Norman, whose tenure as Governor of the Bank of England extended virtually throughout the inter-war years, stands in stark contrast. Naturally that was a different era, but Mr Carney (as he now is) arrives with a reputation – not to mention salary and transfer fee – akin to that of a star centre-forward moving on from an unfashionable provincial club into the Premier League.

As European economies continue to stall, the real risk is that too much hope and expectation has been placed on Carney's arrival in the six months since his appointment was announced. Predictably, much of the coverage over his Treasury Select Committee appearance in February focused upon his bumper salary package – expect this to continue, especially if there is no sustained upturn in our economic fortunes.

I suspect in the key areas of interest rate policy and quantitative easing, the Carney regime will reflect a faithful continuation of the monetary policy we have had over the past few years rather than any change of pace as has been widely anticipated.

Indeed, George Osborne was probably most attracted by the prospect of an incoming Governor prepared to maintain the ultra-low interest rates we have had over the past four and a half years along with a willingness to print more money as the main tool of monetary stimulus.

I have argued before that the notional independence of the Bank of England already stands open to question. For over forty con-secutive months now, its inflation target has been surpassed – this has come to pass as a consequence of political complicity between the Treasury (both pre- and post-May 2010) and the Bank. While the economic case favouring this cause of action can be robustly made, it clearly flies in the face of an 'independent' Bank of England. This continues to damage its credibility.

However, as we approach the pre-election season, I can only imagine this complicity continuing. With the date of destiny with the voters soon upon us and growth at best spluttering, brave would be the governor who resists political pressure for a fillip timed for spring of 2015. With the Chancellor making clear that there will be no shift in fiscal policy, all rests on the Bank's monetary arsenal – or what is left of it – to deliver the goods.

Yet, while a combination of loose monetary and tight fiscal pol-icy has usually seemed enough to jump-start the British economy in past recessions, in the near five years since the financial crisis, a turbo-charged version of that strategy has merely kept us in a state of suspended animation. GDP still remains 2.5 per cent below what it was immediately prior to the crash. Cheap mortgage credit seems to be the only uplift from the Funding for Lending initiative and will now be reinforced by Help to Buy, which surely risks re-inflating the property bubble. In spite of a plunge in the value of sterling, our trade deficit is stubbornly high.

Unfortunately, cheap money acts only to delay the sort of reform needed to address Britain's flagging competitiveness. Both the private and public sectors remain hugely over-leveraged, with that debt the main driver of continued caution from businesses and households when it comes to spending and taking on fresh liabilities. Ideally, Mr Carney would start sketching out an exit strategy that might tackle the structural roots of our economic sickness. However, since (perhaps understandably) there is neither the commercial appetite nor political nerve to allow the bankruptcies and repossessions that would help wipe the economy's slate clean, passive restructuring (otherwise known as inflation) will be the order of the day. While two decades ago, Carney's native Canada and Sweden were able to turn around banking crises within three years, that was in an era of rapid global growth. Such expansion is highly unlikely to assist this time.

Which is why I suspect kick-starting growth is unlikely to be the central challenge of Mr Carney's tenure. Instead, it will be the prospect of diminished living standards as wages continue to stall and 'gentle' inflation continues to be used as a means of effective debt reduction. No wonder the Chancellor is encouraging the Bank to take on a broader remit beyond inflation-targeting, with new powers to target unemployment and aid growth. Mr Carney has also indicated that he wants to provide businesses and consumers with much better long-term signals or 'forward guidance' about the economy, including how long low interest rates are likely to last (I suspect we can expect silence on the latter front this side of May 2015).

So as we look ahead at what a Carney governorship may bring, it would be safe to bet that we have not yet reached the road with monetary activism, always assuming that the recent turmoil in the bond markets is not a signal that the central bankers' room for this sort of manoeuvre has come to an end. Furthermore, events at both RBS and the Co-op bank in recent weeks have shown that interference by the Bank of England and the Treasury, even in the affairs of notionally independent institutions, is endemic – a situation that will only intensify as the general election approaches.

Anticipate a looser still position on interest rates and quantitative easing in a bid to ease further the value of the pound if growth continues to stall. Expect clearer communication and a more informal style masquerading as transparency from Threadneedle Street, and

perhaps in the coming months a flirtation with additional, uncon-
ventional ways of stimulating the economy. The Bank will certainly
continue to neglect to keep the lid on inflation. But if there is one
thing that we should neither ask nor expect from the new man at
Threadneedle Street, it is miracles.

‡

Will hugging close to coalition plans help Labour make progress on economic competence?, 15 July 2013

*In spite of the troubles it had in squeezing growth out of the economy,
and its difficulty in meeting deficit reduction and borrowing forecasts,
the coalition enjoyed one significant blessing: continued public distrust
in the economic policy of the Labour Party. The notion that the coalition
had a firm plan to which it was determined to stick led to it being consistently favoured over the alternative offered by Eds Miliband and
Balls – two political figures still closely associated with Gordon Brown's
rocky reign at No. 10. No matter the gap between rhetoric and delivery, it seemed the public had finally been convinced of the pressing need
to get public spending under control. Labour would have a tough time
overturning that advantage in time for the May 2015 general election,
I mused in this essay for ConservativeHome.*

Recent weeks have confirmed that politics can be a strange and
unpredictable trade.

Barely three years ago, the coalition came into office pledging
to eliminate the UK's structural deficit within a five-year term.
Cumulative public sector net borrowing between 2011–12 and
2015–16 was forecast at £322 billion. The voters were warned in
terrifying terms that any larger a deficit would result in explosively
higher long-term interest rates. As a consequence, Labour's plans to
borrow an additional £50 billion over the course of the parliament
were derided by coalition ministers as irresponsible and potentially
ruinous to our economic health.

The outcome of near stagnant growth since then means that, according to the OBR's own projections, five-year borrowing will come in at £539.4 billion, almost £220 billion more than planned. Yet what would have been regarded as reckless over-borrowing only three years ago has had negligible impact on interest rates (for now at least...).

By rights, this might have been seen as a glorious vindication of Labour's consistent contention that the UK government could, and should, have borrowed more in classic Keynesian style since 2010. By contrast, this grisly outturn in deficit reduction plans has instead persuaded the opposition that it should stick firmly to the coalition's spending proposals for 2015–16.

George Osborne's tactical gambit some weeks back of announcing a single year Spending Review so early for the first year of the next parliament was reasonably transparent. It was clearly designed to put Labour on the spot – should it show some leg now or hold back, lying low and not committing itself to its own plans on spending and, more toxically, welfare, until the run-up to May 2015?

So by sticking to the government's proposals to trim £11.5 billion from departmental budgets in the tax year that commences with the next election and folding so early in the game, has Labour walked into a trap? After all, you only stick to your predecessor's plans or course of action if you wish to *neutralise* an issue, and fight the forthcoming election on what you perceive is more favourable ground.

In 1996–97, Tony Blair largely blunted the constant Tory refrain that the economy was thriving by matching the then government's policies. Similarly, David Cameron between 2006 and 2010 relentlessly sought to reassure the electorate that his administration had no plan to reorganise the NHS and would ring-fence real expenditure on healthcare. Ironically the parking of that issue may yet make it harder for Conservatives to derive any political benefit in the aftermath of the appalling Mid-Staffs and Care Quality Commission scandals. While both assuredly happened on Labour's watch, the nightmare scenario is that voters may see these examples of mismanagement as failings that have come to light during a time of austerity, and blame the Conservatives in spite of the near decade-long political truce on the NHS. It is certainly encouraging that Jeremy Hunt is so firmly on the front foot as the patients' champion – he deserves the party's strong support.

In spite of Labour's clear failings here, it may yet provide the opposition with a more familiar and comfortable line of attack in its May 2015 campaign (a reprise from 1997 of 'twenty-four hours to save the NHS' perhaps?).

What has also become evident in the political shadow-boxing of the past month is a deep-seated lack of confidence that Ed Miliband has in being able to sell to voters his sincerely held view that the legacy of the financial crash is that the political facts of life are becoming more social democratic. Arguably, he would be better advised to have spent the next two years painstakingly putting some meat onto the bones of his novel economic thinking, although perhaps he is less convinced by 'pre-distribution' these days!

Instead, I reckon in his and Ed Balls' response to the Spending Review, Labour has signalled clearly that despite the coalition's lack of progress in deficit reduction and its failure to oversee growth, the economy cannot be a potentially winning card for Labour in 2015.

To take just one example: on welfare, the opposition team are congenitally incapable of renouncing the ruinously expensive impact of working tax credits. When instituted in 1997, Chancellor Brown faithfully promised his next-door neighbour that its cost would not rise above £600 million per annum. The true impact of working tax credits has been to delay the urgent case for radically improving the UK's skills base, while simultaneously enabling employers to drive down headline wages at a time of ever-higher immigration. This disastrous vehicle of social engineering has cost the UK taxpayer an average of £7.2 billion in each of the past three years, as part of a tax credits bill now exceeding £30 billion per annum.

However anaemic the state of the UK economy by election time, Mr Miliband has conceded the veracity of the Conservatives' assertion that voters will be reluctant to hand the keys back to those responsible for crashing the car.

‡

The complexity of locating Britain's national interest in the Middle East, 27 August 2013

There was no let-up in the gloomy news coming from the Middle East over the summer of 2013. Alongside the apparent march to war in Syria, the politics of Egypt were aflame. The euphoria of the Arab Spring had encouraged eighteen days of protest on the streets of Cairo that had brought a swift close to the 29-year rule of President Hosni Mubarak in February 2011. Parliamentary and presidential elections eventually followed, which swept Mohamed Morsi to power. Morsi was a member of the Muslim Brotherhood, a political organisation that had been banned under Mubarak's rule, and efforts were soon underway to remove him from office as a result. Mass protests broke out in reaction to the economic upheaval and political unrest that had dogged Morsi's leadership from the start, and in July 2013, the Egyptian Army intervened to depose him.

Former Prime Minister Tony Blair wrote an article in The Times *to warn against the West ostracising the new military leadership in Egypt, and to make the case for military action against the Syrian President, Bashar al-Assad. 'It is time we took a side,' he proclaimed, 'the side of the people who want what we want; who see our societies for all their faults as something to admire; who know that they should not be faced with a choice between tyranny and theocracy.' I remained unconvinced, and set out some of my own thoughts on the regional quagmire.*

The West's tacit support of the military overthrow in early July of Egypt's first Islamist president will have stark implications in the years ahead for our diplomatic relationships within the Middle East and beyond.

The UK's own Foreign Office still talks up the 'Arab Spring' when, in truth, the idealistic enthusiasm of early 2011 that representative democracy might take hold in the region should be consigned to history. Similarly, the Obama administration's policy of selective non-intervention in the troubled Arab world has resulted in it standing on the brink of a military strike unsanctioned by the United

Nations, following hot on the heels of its refusal to condemn the usurping of democracy in Egypt.

Surely this will only feed the sense of historical grievance by the Muslim Brotherhood, Shia Muslims and their fellow travellers. Would there have been a similarly sanguine US response to a military junta deposing a newly elected secular government in Egypt? Will the West's apparent support of the Sunnis in Syria not now elicit a furious response from radicalised elements of the large Shia communities living in Europe?

More worryingly, this sends out the clearest message imaginable to anyone winning a free, democratic election in the Middle East. Namely, at all costs and in double quick time, win over the military and police (as Mohamed Morsi so spectacularly failed to do) and clamp down on the activities of any political opposition. In truth, this lesson has already been well understood by one of the shrewdest political figures in the region, Recep Tayyip Erdogan, the Turkish premier. His coalition includes, of electoral necessity, an influential Islamist faction, whose insistence on a clampdown on civil rights – as understood in Europe – has led to unrest in Istanbul. These activities have to date been contained, as Erdogan exercises ruthless control over the police and armed forces by appointing supporters to senior roles and prosecuting 'dissident' elements in the army.

For all the hope of the flowering of an era of democracy in the region, I suspect this will prove as good as it gets.

The palpable impotence of the United Nations as the carnage in Syria and Egypt continues unabated will not be without consequence either. Diplomacy as the UK has known it since the end of the Second World War, with its quaintly dated institutions and deference to the US 'special relationship', is changing fast in the connected world of the internet. With Russia and China ever willing to exercise their veto against unified international action, I suspect the status of a UN Security Council with its five permanent members is about to reach the end of its shelf-life. This will have a profound impact on the UK's reputation in the international community, for we would no longer sit at the diplomatic top table.

We should not underestimate the impact such a diminution in the UK's world standing would have on the population at large (and especially the more Conservative inclined Britons). So the expedient political decisions over the past decade to extend spending (and borrowing) on welfare and healthcare while continually paring back the UK defence budget have come at a price – in a generation's time, our standing in global affairs may be similar to that of the Netherlands today.

As President Assad holds firm in Syria and ex-President Morsi faces criminal charges (however trumped-up) under the new Egyptian regime, it may also be time for a hard-nosed reassessment of the impact of the International Criminal Court's jurisdiction. In the aftermath of the Balkan conflicts and a series of African civil wars, it seemed a pragmatic, civilised idea to institute a permanent seat in the Hague to bring former murderous dictators to justice. In practice, however, the absence of any method of graceful exit for Heads of State that the international community fervently wish to see ousted means that such individuals have little incentive other than fight to the bitter end with horrific humanitarian consequences.

Meanwhile, a consensus has swiftly developed over the weekend that a quick, surgical strike against the Assad regime will help precipitate the end of the Syrian crisis. A quick rap over the knuckles for the Syrian dictator is not even designed to dislodge him or bring hostilities to a more rapid conclusion. It would simply draw in the West as an additional player in a complex web of conflicting interests, without any clear goal or exit strategy.

Even Tony Blair has now weighed into this debate, imploring British action. We should be reminded that he views all conflict in the Middle East through the prism of his passionately held thesis that we are in the midst of a clash of civilisations that can be won only if clear moral standards are set out and adhered to. He is one of many people mistakenly trying to distil what is happening in Syria into a battle of good and evil, right and wrong, tolerable and intolerable. Yet surely the complexity of the regional situation defies such neat categorisation.

As global TV beams pictures from Syria of victims of chemical weapons into our living rooms, it may seem immoral to put the British national interest front and centre in this debate. But it is what David Cameron must now do. There is no convincing route available to him that can stem the humanitarian disaster that is unfolding in the Middle East. There is no clear benefit to the UK of involving ourselves further in this bloody quagmire.

‡

The need to realign ethics with self-interest, 25 September 2013

On 20 September, Sir Richard Lambert, former Director General of the Confederation of British Industry, began a formal assessment on whether to establish a new professional banking standards body, as requested by the Chairmen of the UK's seven largest banks and building societies. The idea had originated from the Parliamentary Commission on Banking Standards as a means of restoring trust in the banking industry after the financial crisis. In this article, written to coincide with Sir Richard's new work, I reflected on the pressing need for professional ethics to be sewn into the heart of the financial services industry.

Sir Richard went on to launch the Banking Standards Review Council in May 2014, to which the seven largest lenders would report annually in a collective effort to raise standards. The body would identify good practices and challenge banks to pursue them, but would not act as a regulatory body.

'How much do ethics count in the City of London?' This was the question the former editor of the *Financial Times*, Richard Lambert, strived to answer as he gave the Securities Institute's Annual Lecture in 2002.

Lambert (now Sir Richard and about to head a new banking standards body) spoke at a time when the dust seemed finally to be settling on the City after the scrum of self-interest that had followed

1986's Big Bang. The financial deregulation heralded by the Thatcher government had summoned momentous change such that traditional City values, codes of conduct and the 'Old Boys' network' had been turned on their head. The traditional partnership structure, where employees shared an interest in their firm's reputation, prosperity and trading losses, was replaced by something less personal, far more aggressive and potentially ruinous to shareholders and guarantors. The scale of financial activity increased dramatically as a result and a great deal of direct human contact was removed from the art of financial trading. The lines between different types of business became blurred, relationships weakened and the chances of making bigger money increased.

The regulatory system could not keep up. Suddenly, ethical behaviour and self-interest, having previously been aligned, were out of kilter. Few would seriously suggest that individuals working within the City were more ethical before the Big Bang, or that the City was scandal-free until that point. But the environment in which it formerly operated was more conducive to ethical behaviour.

Nevertheless, from a vantage point only eleven years ago, Lambert revealed what now seems a quaint optimism that this was all about to change, citing six reasons why integrity over the next decade was likely to become a competitive advantage. The first was cyclical. As economist John Galbraith observed of the 1929 crash, in a bull market (as the City was experiencing in 2002), people are trusting and willing to involve themselves in dodgier deals. But when the bad times come, commercial morality drastically improves since money is watched with a suspicious eye. Second, the City was entering a period of consolidation following the upheaval of Big Bang. In a more stable environment, firms pay attention to the development of a cohesive corporate culture. Similarly, the new regulatory system was bedding down, the Financial Services Authority making clear that industry leaders would be made accountable for the behaviour of their employees.

Thirdly, ethical behaviour would be born out of practical necessity. From a minimalist regulatory structure based on values, a written-rule culture had emerged. But with new rulebooks running to thousands of pages, regulators would soon realise that a return to a values system was the only practical option.

Lambert also felt intuitively at that point that the returns going forward would not be as high as they had been and offering bucket loads of cash would regardless be insufficient to attract the best talent. Recruits would instead be drawn to firms that they could respect. Fifthly, citizens were increasingly having to take responsibility for their financial futures and would therefore be much savvier. Trust would be the new competitive advantage. Finally, the risks of not behaving ethically were increasing, with Enron acting as the game-changer.

'Once a financial bubble comes to an end,' Lambert concluded, 'it becomes clear that ethical behaviour is not just an optional extra. It's the glue that holds businesses together'.

Rereading his lecture in 2013, Lambert's words seem, oddly, to be both prescient and completely wide of the mark. The elusive ethical turning point he spoke of never came. Instead, we experienced a violent financial crash in 2008, whose consequences, for all the talk of 'turning a corner', we are *still* grappling with. If you ask the man in the street how much ethics count in the City, I suspect most would say, 'Not a lot'. Yet the approach of aligning self-interest with ethics is assuredly needed now more than ever. The question we need to answer today is not whether ethics count or not, but how do we *make* them count.

I have observed many times since 2008 that one of the most damaging costs of the financial crisis has been invisible – the loss of trust. Trust in the system is the crucial lubricant that oils economic transaction, and the integrity of the City of London has for years been fundamental to its commercial offering. I have always felt that the key to restoring that trust and realigning self-interest with ethical behaviour lies in sewing transparency, personal responsibility, fear of failure and lively competition into the heart of the system.

How well have we done so far in that realignment? In some ways, very well. In August, *City AM* reported that according to the

Financial Stability Board, the UK is storming ahead of all its global rivals when it comes to openness and transparency in financial services. A raft of practical changes has been brought in following the work of the Vickers Commission on banking and the Parliamentary Commission on Banking Standards. The financial reward structure is changing – in some institutions, undeserved bonuses awarded in the past are being clawed back. Meanwhile, current bonus funds are being used to pay off fines for scandals such as LIBOR – and greater conditionality is being attached to any short term rewards. Penalties for poor conduct are beginning to outweigh the financial incentives.

Good ethics is about action taken when nobody is looking, acting within the spirit of rules, not just their letter. Britain's bankers are beginning publicly to acknowledge that. Bob Diamond's successor at Barclays, Antony Jenkins, has told his staff to sign up to a new ethics code at the bank or leave, in a bid to reconnect Barclays with its Quaker roots. There has been endless national discussion on the restoration of ethics to the financial services, with even religious leaders weighing in.

Yet in other ways, I am not so optimistic. The financial crisis was seen as the death of light-touch regulation. I am certainly not advocating its return. But in its place has come a government that guarantees against financial failure. There has been ever more meddling in banks' operations, and enormously complex and regularly changing regulation has been coming thick and fast from the UK authorities and Brussels. Immoral conduct thrives in the absence of clarity, with history showing that tougher regulation in the banking sector is a driver for new, innovative and riskier off-balance-sheet vehicles – indeed the explosive expansion of such vehicles over the past decade came about in the aftermath of imposing new regulatory measures following the collapse of Enron and WorldCom.

The weight of complex and confused new regulation is also crowding out one of the most effective ways of aligning ethics with self-interest – competition. By this, I mean the type that is remorselessly skewed towards the interest of the consumer, not competition between investment bankers as to who can pay the highest salaries.

The recent decision by the Co-operative to quit retail banking in the UK augured ill, and although this month's changes to the account-switching process may make it easier for new players to enter the market, there is still much work to be done. Furthermore, British banks still operate with an implicit government guarantee that anaes-thetises them from the fear of failure. Similarly, if customers and creditors are guaranteed, they are less concerned about scandal, less likely to view excessive risk-taking dimly and press banks for change.

The restoration of trust in the banking industry and the realign-ment of self-interest with ethical conduct will be a lengthy process, and one in which we all must actively engage. Governments must create an environment conducive to ethical conduct, ensuring banks are insulated from neither the risk of failure nor competition, and making clear that regulation cannot eliminate risk or act as a sub-stitute for ethical behaviour. Every operator in the financial services should seek to build a corporate culture that helps maintain the integrity and trust of the City at large. Consumers must be demand-ing, alert and appreciative that engagement with the financial system always involves a degree of risk, no matter how small.

Sir Richard, who shortly embarks upon a new role to raise bank-ing standards, was not wrong in his insights eleven years ago. But his aspiration that economic nature would take its course proved misplaced. Ensuring ethics count is an ongoing project whose progress must be watched vigilantly.

‡

Leave Labour to its tactics, there is a better alternative (*Daily Telegraph*), 30 September 2013

With consistently poor approval ratings on economic competence, the Labour Party needed to up its game at its 2013 Party Conference. Instead, its week in Brighton was dominated by grim revelations from the mem-oirs of ex-spin doctor Damian McBride about the culture of smears and distortions that had grown up around Gordon Brown and his regime.

*With continued question marks over his competence to lead, Ed
Miliband needed to up the ante, and duly did so with what was deemed
his best conference speech, delivered entirely from memory and dominated by a 'Britain can do better' theme. Economic growth needed
now to deliver for ordinary people, he suggested, and a Labour government would deliver an energy price freeze, a million new homes, tax
cuts for small businesses, a hike in the minimum wage and more childcare support.*

I was asked by the Daily Telegraph *to outline how I thought
the Conservatives should respond to Miliband's speech at our own
conference, being held that year in Manchester.*

As Conservatives back in Westminster watched Ed Miliband's speech
to the Labour conference last week, a sense of quiet satisfaction
descended. With each economically illiterate policy the Labour
leader revealed, the clearer the dividing lines for the 2015 election.
In vacating the centre ground that New Labour had so effectively
occupied under Tony Blair, Red Ed's foolhardy pledge to cap energy
prices beckoned the return of the 1970s, and will surely fall apart
well before voters go to the polls. Tories can now properly contrast
Labour's costly socialist fantasy with a grown-up policy prescription
that deals with the world as it is, not as some would wish it to be.

Unfortunately, I am not sure we can be so dismissive. The price
freezing promise has been roundly panned by the media, and yet
Miliband has not back-pedalled. Instead, he has aggressively confronted his doubters. This is significant, not for the headache it
presents to the energy companies, but for the defiant challenge the
Labour leader is issuing to the status quo. It is a challenge which
may resonate with more voters than we would care to admit.

In truth, it is not just the usual suspects on the anarchistic left
of politics, but increasingly a lot of middle class, traditionally Tory-
minded people who feel that the system works not for them, but for
an overpaid and ineffectual elite. Despite having a good education
and working hard, these voters are beginning to view themselves as
losers under the globalised, capitalist system. Miliband has tapped

into this by exploiting the everyday pinch points of their unease – spiralling energy bills, unaffordable housing and stagnant wages.

Meanwhile, this group is daily bombarded with examples of the insulated establishment. As the ordinary feel the squeeze, news stories abound of richly rewarded rail chiefs, media executives, bankers and public service managers, many of whom have presided over scandal and failure. Last Tuesday, Ed Miliband sought to present David Cameron not as leader of the country, but as Chairman of this Establishment, Chief Champion of the Status Quo and Lord Protector of Vested Interests.

The Labour leader is, of course, a gross hypocrite. Ed Miliband, with his childhood among the north London intelligentsia and an adulthood cosseted by the corridors of power, is as much a member of the privileged elite as the Prime Minister. Similarly, the energy costs he laments have his fingerprints all over them – when he was Energy Secretary, he at least had the political courage to admit his green policies would substantially hike prices.

Nevertheless, he has presented a tricky challenge to Conservatives, planting Labour in the same populist space that has proved so successful for UKIP. Knowing that the Tories would pin the label on him anyway, Miliband is now wearing his Red Ed badge with pride. It has become a hallmark of his mission to champion the ordinary man.

How can Conservatives best respond to that unashamed populism without pandering to an anti-wealth narrative and without alienating the voters to whom Labour's message appeals?

While dismissing Miliband, I suspect the Tory leadership may be tempted this week to fight fire with fire. After all, the coalition has form. The government is not averse to a bit of market rigging itself (what is 'Help to Buy' if not a state-backed fiddle of the housing market?). Ministers have at times failed to resist banker-bashing. And the Treasury has already tinkered with fuel and beer prices. Yet it would be a mistake to indulge Miliband's economic illiteracy by mimicking his tactics.

What no mainstream party seems truly to have grasped in recent years is that voters respond to authenticity. The Tory revolution of the 1980s was conducted not via the guidance focus groups but instead came from a confidence in what we were doing. Of all the themes the Prime Minister has developed in the course of his leadership, his idea of the 'global race' is the one he seems most comfortable articulating. It also best reflects the space which the modern Conservative Party should occupy in today's Britain – the notion of the UK as a forward-thinking, diverse nation pursuing high standards in education, modernising welfare and liberating businesses in a fiercely competitive world. Unlike the Labour price freeze promise, the rewards of this approach will not be instantaneous. But voters may respond to its realistic yet positive message, respecting the Prime Minister's honesty and leadership.

In contrast to Mr Miliband, that will involve Mr Cameron becoming unashamedly pro-business by making some unpopular decisions. In today's global race, successful countries will be those in which ideas and dynamism are captured and retained. That translates as immigration systems open to the highly skilled so that innovative and creative people can gather to exchange and develop ideas – the government may have to admit that it got aspects of its visa policy wrong.

It means building certain and stable environments that breed confidence when it comes to borrowing, lending and investing. So enough now with the threat of retrospective taxation and media-driven witch hunts. Such a nation also requires targeted infrastructure so that hubs are linked into transport, supply and high-speed broadband networks. Let's please, therefore, get a decision on aviation before the election and give energy firms some long-term political certainty on new investments.

We shall need to build regulatory environments in which the taking on of staff is not perceived as too costly or high risk. Places where schools and universities provide the market with employees who are well-equipped and eager, with an appreciation of what they need to do rather than what they are owed. Finally, where governments are much more customer-focused and able to adapt to change themselves, recognising the necessity of open competition as the ultimate safeguard of consumer interests.

Rather than sneeringly dismiss Ed Miliband's approach, Conservatives must now calmly, carefully and firmly dismantle his ideas. For our nation to be successful and for my party to enjoy popular electoral support, it must ensure that it creates a society which liberates and incentivises people to pursue new ideas and cast aside defunct ones, not where the group of disaffected and fearful losers expands. We have a bold alternative message that combines optimism with realism, ambition and modernity. Let's have the courage to spread it.

‡

The case against the mansion tax, 17 October 2013

Conference season once again threw up a range of policy proposals designed to sate the apparent public appetite for banker-bashing. Naturally, this included a fresh assault against property owners, chiefly in London and the south-east, via a so-called mansion tax. In this essay for ConservativeHome, I once again set out the case against any such levy.

In this throwback to an era of envy politics and wealth-bashing, every policy pledge from our political opponents appears to be funded either by a hike in the trusty bank levy or a tax raid on stately homes and penthouses.

Passionate debate about the imposition of a 'mansion tax' in particular is now all the rage. Both Labour and the Lib Dems made clear at their respective conferences that they favour such a levy on any properties valued at over £2 million. The annual £2 billion that this will apparently raise is to be redirected from the ample clutches of the 'rich' to the innocent palms of our poorest.

Let's deconstruct this policy. First, we need to knock squarely on the head this idea that the well-off do not already contribute significantly to the public purse. According to HMRC data released last year, the top 1 per cent of earners pays over a quarter of all income tax. The top 10 per cent pay well over half. Add the impact of sales tax and existing property levies and it is clear that the wealthiest Britons already pay plenty.

Now let's look at the terminology. Just as the 'bedroom tax' is in fact a reduction in benefits rather than a bill from HMRC, so the 'mansion tax' is a deliberate misnomer. It is shamelessly devised to conjure in voters' minds a land of the wealthy, whose domestic palaces insulate them from reality and whose bottomless bank accounts can single-handedly fund Britain's public services.

Truth is, there are more homes valued at over £2 million with one bedroom than ten bedrooms. A quick online property search in my own central London constituency found that £2 million will typically get you a two bedroom flat, three if you're lucky – hardly property of mansion-like proportions. If Labour and the Lib Dems wish to play divide and rule on this, then it should be made clear that they are drawing a line not between rich and poor but between London and the Home Counties, where property values have sky-rocketed, and the rest of the country.

South-easterners already make a disproportionate contribution to the national tax take while living in cramped conditions, incurring ever more expensive commuting costs and generally experiencing a lesser quality of life than those living in other regions of the UK. As David Cameron has often said, we need to look to General Well Being rather than simply financial assets.

Who is going to be paying this tax? Not landlords or property developers with a clutch of properties worth £1.9 million. It will instead be applied to someone who has lived in their central London home for thirty-odd years and seen its notional value rise to astronomic levels. Many of those who live in such properties (a considerable proportion of whom are my constituents) are asset rich but income poor. Indeed for many, their main – or only – asset is the property in which they live. An annual charge of 1 per cent would be ruinously expensive for many of these so-called 'super-rich'. The envious might retort that these long-term residents should simply sell up. Yet this would merely result in ever more of central London being hollowed out, with a stable residential community replaced by the part-time global super-rich.

How would such a mansion tax work? Before a rapacious government can extract any money, it would require a valuation team to ascertain whether a property is worth over £2 million. Yet accurate valuations are notoriously difficult to determine. Many owners will be tempted deliberately to try to suppress or even reduce the value of their property by allowing it to fall into a state of disrepair. Others would try to challenge HMRC's valuation, tying officers up in endless, costly appeals – the huge backlog of business rates appeals at the Valuation Office Agency looks set to get even longer. A number of independent analysts suggest that the cost of administering the tax would likely reduce substantially any sum HMRC might raise, making it likelier to bring in £1.25 billion – frankly a drop in the Treasury ocean.

There are very real problems in the London housing market. Tenants are being squeezed by ever-higher rates. Not even a professional salary can get you on the housing ladder. Central London is being hollowed out, as prime property is hoovered up by the global super-rich – those from the Middle East, China and the Mediterranean, for example, who take advantage of free capital flows to the UK as they seek a safe haven and hedge against political uncertainty. I have written at length about those issues, suggesting some potential policy prescriptions.

I believe, for instance, that policymakers must now undertake an objective cost–benefit analysis of the presence of an international super-rich in a bid best to distinguish between genuine foreign business people who become resident in Britain, create employment and contribute to the UK economy, and those who effectively freeload on the nation's infrastructure. That might include the levying of taxes on non-resident, non-British owners of property through the abolition of the distinction between domicility and residence. Residents would be taxed on their worldwide income and assets while non-residents would be levied with special holding taxes on passive property assets they hold. In New York, for example, apartments can incur a tax of up to $20,000 if they are left empty.

However, a crude mansion tax is not, and never can be, the solution to any of the substantial problems in the south-eastern property market. As Conservatives, we must vigorously oppose Labour and Liberal Democrat plans for such a new levy by countering their politics of envy and having our own prescriptions to frame the debate in a more Conservative way.

‡

Banking competition – why we need a common platform, 7 November 2013

Open, vibrant competition has always been the ultimate safeguard of consumer interests. But it is an ingredient that has proved stubbornly elusive in the UK's retail banking sector.

Ours is one of the most concentrated such markets in the developed world. In spite of a number of independent commission reports since 2000 which have sought to increase competition, just four players (Lloyds TSB, RBS, Barclays and HSBC) accounted for a 65 per cent market share before 2008's financial crisis. That situation was compounded when, in the midst of the crash, the government negotiated the rescue of HBOS through the creation of Lloyds Banking Group, taking the Big Four's share to 75 per cent of the retail market.

In the aftermath of the crisis, genuine competition has been craved more than ever, not just in the interests of the consumer but as the most effective means of protecting the taxpayer from institutions deemed too big or interconnected to fail. Yet breaking the banking oligopoly has proved a tantalisingly tough task, with the risk of market entry to new players still far outweighing potential rewards.

In September, a new era of choice in British retail banking was heralded when an account-switching guarantee was brought in, allowing the UK's 49 million current account holders to change to a new provider in seven days. In principle this is a very promising development, which will hopefully shake some life into a stagnant market. But we must ensure it does not become another false dawn.

Formidable barriers remain for established smaller players and new market entrants alike, which will require radical action to counter.

Perversely, one of the greatest barriers to entry is customer satisfaction. Regardless of the antipathy towards the banking fraternity in recent years, customer research undertaken by reputable, independent research agencies typically shows good levels of customer satisfaction, which make it difficult for smaller players to tempt customers away. An existing provider's advantage is entrenched by the fact that two out of every three business start-ups choose their main *personal* bank for their business account. In addition, more than 90 per cent of business customers use a single bank for all their needs – savings, current account, overdraft, debit card and loan. Since most business banking customers still use branch services – around 85 per cent go into a branch to open their account – those operators with extensive branch networks have a major entrenched advantage.

Starting an SME bank is expensive, complex and a regulatory maze, even for an organisation providing personal banking. An account system, internet banking, payment systems, ATM connectivity, branches, finance systems – they all require substantial investment before the spiralling costs of regulation and compliance advice are even considered. In order to encourage new players, action will therefore need to cut the cost and complexity involved in market entry, reduce risk and make it easier to open an account.

I believe the cost of market entry might be much reduced if it were possible to link into a banking system that has already been built for, and implemented in, the UK market. The ability to buy or pay to use a proven system would mean that the cost to a new entrant would no longer include major IT development. While it is already possible to buy generic banking systems such as SAP, the cost of customisation in the UK remains high.

The time may be ripe, therefore, to copy the approach taken in the rail and utilities sectors by creating a common platform – a business that runs the infrastructure on behalf of all those offering banking services. RBS already provides partitioned computer systems that allow RBS, NatWest, Coutts and Ulster Bank to share the costs of IT infrastructure. Might we look at whether RBS, still 81 per cent taxpayer owned, could be split into a bank and an infrastructure company that could offer services to other UK financial institutions? This principle could be extended to use RBS's branches, or perhaps those of the Post Office, which could allow shared use of facilities for deposits and withdrawals.

Beyond that, I would propose that we examine making account activity data more accessible so that new entrants may better assess the risk of credit loss. A similar approach might be taken to the sharing of fraud information. Inter-bank fora do exist that share this type of knowledge, but they tend not to involve the sharing of data or predictive models. Similarly, we might look at encouraging banks to exchange information on identity checks. One of the barriers to new accounts being set up online is the problem of fraud. This again favours operators with extensive branch networks, where a customer's identity documents can be checked in person. Perhaps we could even compel banks to share with new providers any previous anti-money-laundering (AML) checks they have conducted on customers. The jewel in the crown of such a shared technology platform would be to make the customers' transfer of accounts from one bank to another virtually automatic.

Previous attempts to inject greater competition into the market have failed to crack Britain's banking oligopoly. With the taxpayer still owning such a significant stake in two of the Big Four, the government inevitably also faces a major conflict of interest in encouraging competition while maintaining the value of that stake. But in the long term, it is firmly in the interests of both consumer and taxpayer that we get a much livelier retail banking market. The scale of that challenge and the disappointment of past competition initiatives dictates that fresh, inventive ideas may now be required – shared IT infrastructure, data and branches must be put squarely on the table.

‡

RBS – back to square one?, 7 November 2013

As autumn set in, the government moved to privatise Royal Mail to help stem its declining competitiveness and raise money to fill the public coffers. When shares went on sale on 15 October, demand was stratospheric with £27 billion of investors' money chasing shares priced at £1.7 billion. This quickly led to questions about whether the government had bungled the privatisation by selling the public asset too cheaply. It also turned minds once again to taxpayers' sizeable shares in RBS and Lloyds Banking Group – was it now time to start selling? I wrote the following article for City AM, *suggesting that we were still a long way from contemplating an RBS sell-off.*

Perhaps it is a little premature to suggest that privatisation fever is back to 1980s' levels.

But the unexpectedly enthusiastic reception to the Royal Mail share offer will have given the Treasury some timely food for thought as it ponders what to do with the public stakes in Lloyds and RBS.

The controversy over the pricing of Royal Mail shares is unlikely to concern the Treasury too much in this regard. It is impossible truly to grasp market interest in a product until it is so tested, which is why privatisation pricing is such an inexact science. If there is a lesson to be learned from the recent share offer, it is that smaller shareholders and individual investors must in future get a proper slice of the action, even when they are seeking large numbers of shares. The government should instead now consider reducing the allocation set aside for large, institutional investors in any future sell-offs.

Amidst all the euphoria, it is also worth stressing that, while enthusiasm from everyday retail investors is clearly back with a vengeance, the public stakes in the part-nationalised banks are of a different magnitude to the £1.7 billion Royal Mail deal.

Nevertheless, the fact that Royal Mail was seven times oversubscribed will encourage the cash-strapped Treasury to pursue a programme of share sales in the run-up to the May 2015 general election. We still own 32.7 per cent of Lloyds Banking Group (valued at £17.7 billion on today's share price). I reckon that by the time of the Autumn Statement of 4 December, George Osborne will be in a position to set out a timetable stretching towards the end of the decade for selling off taxpayers' stake. Some of its discrete divisions will be divested in public offerings; others in deals directly with sovereign wealth funds. Significantly, I suspect that up to half of what the taxpayer currently holds will have been flogged off this side of May 2015. Understandably, the Chancellor will be keen to keep up the momentum of economic good times right until Election Day.

That brings us to RBS, in which we retain an 81 per cent stake. Well, here we are probably back to square one. I should be very surprised if the imminent Rothschild report does not echo the Parliamentary Commission on Banking's recommendation that RBS be split into a 'good' and 'bad' bank. Expect the Treasury to endorse this without delay, to minimise uncertainty. But if Stephen Hester's work over the past few years is to be written off, so too is any foreseeable prospect of the taxpayer being able to exit RBS.

I guess if we knew at the end of 2008 what we know now, the temptation would have been to impose full nationalisation on RBS. Then rather than taking Vince Cable's tortuous path towards the creation of a separate Business Bank, we might have used RBS as the vehicle for an aggressive industrial policy, not least as it has 40 per cent of the struggling SME market. The execution and delivery skills contained in RBS would have allowed for an aggressive road to economic growth.

That is what might have been. While an outbreak of political consensus may be the order of the day when RBS is formally split, I reckon the Chancellor will seek to make political capital over the fate of RBS over the next twelve months or so. He will contrast rapid progress in exiting public ownership of Lloyds with the residual RBS mess ('still clearing up after the people who crashed the car'). It will be politics, not economics, that will underpin the government's programme of privatisation in our banks. On the one hand, 'getting back' the taxpayers' money from Lloyds – on the other, reminding the public of how deep-seated the UK's economic problems remain as RBS continues to languish under a public guarantee.

‡

Britain must lead calls for simpler, more certain tax regimes (*Daily Telegraph*), 3 December 2013

Following my work on the issue of tax avoidance, I was asked to write an opinion piece for the Daily Telegraph's *Business pages to make the case for tax simplicity.*

One would be easily forgiven for believing that, in recent years, tax competition has acquired pariah status in the global economy.

The much-vaunted crackdown on multinational tax avoidance, the fresh attempt to regulate corporate transfer payments and the likely impact of the rolling out of the Foreign Account Tax Compliance Act genuinely means that those who wish to evade their obligations by arbitraging the complex labyrinth of global tax networks will find life much more difficult in the future. The spirit of the age is for national governments to side with 'the little people' against the lobbying power of global banks, and corporate and tax havens.

However, amidst all the furore, we need to recognise that it is competition, and competition alone, that acts to bear down on the overall tax burden afflicting individuals and small businesses alike.

In truth, nowhere has there been a more inconsistent approach to this issue than from the UK coalition government. For once, this owes little to any ideological splits between its Conservative and Liberal Democrat elements.

Instead, having proudly placed multinational tax avoidance 'at the heart of the G8 agenda' last June in Northern Ireland and earlier in the year at Davos by lecturing the likes of Amazon, Starbucks and Google over their highly publicised arrangements, the Prime Minister has simultaneously been making a robust case for favourable tax competition to benefit UK Plc. He is right to do so.

Take the persistent and consistent reduction in UK corporation tax, now down to an eye-catching 20 per cent. This has been expressly designed to enhance our relative competitiveness and attract (in the case of WPP, luring the firm back from Ireland) leading international corporations to domicile themselves here. The 'patent box', an explicit intellectual property tax break, has been aggressively targeting research and development investment to these shores... expressly at others' expense. Next came George Osborne's now fabled trip to China. Standing among the skyscrapers of Pudong (the sparkling new financial district of Shanghai, a kind of Canary Wharf on steroids) he announced a drive to allow the City of London to become the hub for Chinese financial investment, even daring to utter the words 'light-touch' in describing the regulatory burden he intends to impose upon newcomers.

This is all exciting stuff.

It is also an implicit recognition that a sustainable, lasting economic recovery cannot be built upon continued cheap credit and a renewed fillip in the housing market. The only way to encourage investment into the UK economy is to provide incentives and open the door to genuine competition in an intensely globalised corporate environment.

The trouble is that tax competition is the unique selling point of the offshore financial centres that, in its rhetoric, the coalition has done so much to condemn. The danger amidst the pragmatic approach to these matters is that the Prime Minister and Chancellor have laid themselves open to accusations of adopting a duplicitous policy when it comes to global tax affairs. We may still need friends close to home on the international stage, so while perfidious Albion holds sway among the future global economic powerhouses, the UK needs to watch its back closer to home.

Just as Ireland's low corporation tax rates attracted the jealous gaze of Brussels bureaucrats during that nation's EU bank bailout, so Britain walks a tightrope in keeping our tax regime competitive without provoking hostile moves from our European partners. As the EU knows, ultimately the UK remains vulnerable to legislative penalty from the continent. While they may be willing to make some concessions to the UK on financial services in light of its over-weening importance to our economy, there remains considerable antagonism towards the City. The current legal battle over the EU directive to cap bankers' bonuses could prove an early battle in a longer war if the UK continues to push the envelope on tax policy.

So the government needs to be clever and it needs to be care-ful. The move towards lower taxes and the crackdown on so-called aggressive avoidance need not be mutually exclusive. In fact, they can easily be made complementary. Corporation tax is an imper-fect levy that adds significant complexity to the system, since it triggers endless dispute over what counts as profit. Armies of law-yers and accountants seek to bend definitions to lower tax liabilities. Loopholes are found and exploited. Governments end up intro-ducing innumerable reliefs to aid particular sectors. And so the tax manual expands.

As a result, governments berate companies for following legisla-tion that they themselves have created. Once the media has cottoned on to the avoidance activities of high-profile corporations, the path is cleared for arbitrary and retrospective taxation that casts a damaging veil of uncertainty over all business activity.

Several recent studies have indicated that the real cost of cor-poration tax tends to be shouldered primarily by employees (such that countries with lower rates of the levy end up with higher wages and, as a corollary, higher income tax receipts). As such, the case for reducing, reforming or even removing this tax only increases.

We need to hear less from our political class about morality and see instead Britain leading calls for greater international commit-ment to simpler, more certain tax regimes as the key to solving the wide-scale anti-avoidance issue. In actively reducing business levies, the UK's choice should be presented as an implicit recog-nition that, in today's globalised economy, corporation tax is no longer fit for purpose.

2014

'Our long-term economic plan is working'

With 2013 drawing to a close, the Chancellor delivered his Autumn Statement on 5 December in far happier circumstances than those of only twelve months earlier. The OBR had ridden to his rescue with a raft of helpful forecasts and figures that usefully dispelled some of the doubts cast over his control of the public finances.

Growth forecasts were revised up, with 2014 predicted to witness as much as 2.4 per cent growth rather than the 1.8 per cent previously suggested. Meanwhile the deficit was revised down to 6.8 per cent in 2013, dropping to 5.6 per cent in the coming year with a predicted cash surplus in 2018–19, while public debt was £18 billion lower than forecast only eight months earlier at the March Budget. The jobs boom was starting to gather pace with 1.4 million private sector jobs created since the first quarter of 2010, pushing employment to its highest-ever level.

Most importantly, however, new figures revealed that the financial crisis had bitten into the UK's GDP even more savagely than anyone had realised. In 2008–09, GDP had declined not by 6.3 per cent as previously thought, but by 7.2 per cent – equivalent to £112 billion. In short, the coalition had inherited such a mess that, the Chancellor could credibly contend, the road to recovery was always going to be rocky.

Now able to claim that in spite of it all, he was presiding over the West's fastest-growing economy, Osborne could look forward in 2014 to laying the foundations of his own political recovery. Look a little closer, however, and the substance of the OBR's report showed an uptick in

private consumption and housing investment, but continued disappoint-
ment on business investment and net trade, pointing once again to a
typically British recovery based on property and shopping. Nevertheless,
while Ed Balls had every right to crow about continued colossal bor-
rowing, the fact that Labour itself argued for still-higher borrowing
neutralised the Chancellor's vulnerabilities. As 2014 dawned, specu-
lation grew over Balls's own future, with a possible return to the front
benches mooted for Alistair Darling.

'For the moment at least,' concluded the Telegraph's *Ben Brogan,*
'George Osborne has an inkling of being a Chancellor who is master
of all he surveys'.

2013 had witnessed the deaths of two towering political figures in
Margaret Thatcher and Nelson Mandela, and as David Cameron looked
ahead to 2014, he must have pondered his own potential legacy. With a
referendum on Scottish independence now set for September and a draft
bill also published for a referendum on EU membership by 2017, the very
real prospect loomed that history might record him as the Prime Minister
who presided over the break-up of the United Kingdom and paved the
way for Brexit. No doubt another twelve months of tensions beckoned
with his own backbenchers, many of whom had still not forgiven him
for the 2013 legislation legalising gay marriage and the failure to secure
parliamentary endorsement for intervention in Syria. Ed Miliband was
dealing with his own party management crises. After a messy selection
battle for the Falkirk by-election, he was looking to implement sweep-
ing reforms of Labour party membership rules in 2014.

In Europe, September 2013 had seen Angela Merkel secure her best-
ever result in the German Bundestag elections, though it took nearly
three months to cobble together a Grand Coalition between Christian
Democrats and Social Democrats. The United States had hit fresh tur-
moil as 800,000 government workers were forced in June to take unpaid
leave after a shutdown of the federal government caused by another
budget crisis. Further fiery disagreements broke out too over a deal
struck with Iran to ease economic sanctions in return for a curbing of
its nuclear programme. The Islamic extremist terror threat remained at
the forefront of everyone's minds, with fresh attacks in 2013 at the Boston

*marathon and by the Somali terror group, al-Shabaab, in a Nairobi
shopping mall.*

The nuts and bolts of tackling tax avoidance
(*City AM*), 7 January 2014

*In the summer of 2011, Chancellor George Osborne had announced an
agreement with the Swiss tax authorities to recover lost revenue from
wealthy UK tax evaders. An estimated £125 billion had been stowed in
secretive Swiss accounts, and in May 2013, any UK accounts held in the
Alpine nation would be subject to a one-off levy of as much as 34 per
cent. The Swiss authorities would then implement a withholding tax on
any British-owned accounts that had failed to be declared to HMRC.
Total revenues from the deal were expected to hit £5 billion by 2015,
with an initial windfall of £400 million in 2013. Eyebrows began to be
raised, however, as it became clear that the agreement looked unlikely
to raise anything like the level of revenue the Treasury had confidently
predicted. I wrote the following article for* City AM *to unpick what
had happened.*

Well, perhaps there isn't as much money squirrelled away in Swiss
bank accounts as we all thought!

At the 2012 Autumn Statement, the Office of Budget Responsibility faithfully assured us that £3.1 billion would be raised from
the Treasury's much heralded deal with the Swiss authorities. This
projected windfall not only highlighted the UK's avowed intention
to lead the way internationally by getting tough with tax evaders,
but also enabled the OBR to post lower projected borrowing figures
for 2012–13 than in the previous tax year.

The timely and welcome return to economic growth has made
these contentions rather less important, but how exactly did HMRC
end up almost £2.5 billion out of pocket?

In truth, far less money held in Swiss bank accounts was found
to be non-compliant than had been anticipated when the UK and
Swiss authorities signed up for this deal twelve months ago.

Naturally, the conspiracy theorists, including Parliament's own Public Accounts Committee, have eagerly claimed that this reflects only the ease and speed with which money can be – and has been – moved out of secretive Switzerland's banking system once this initiative was announced with such a fanfare. Before we all renew a frenzy of banker-bashing, it is worth looking at a series of more mundane explanations.

What seems evident is that many people with assets in Swiss accounts have adopted the disclosure route as opposed to paying the withholding tax anticipated by the UK authorities. In time this will generate overall revenues, but not in the way HMRC envisaged. The general spirit of the age towards openness and transparency has been a key driver here.

Secondly, the proportion of non-domiciled individuals banking in Switzerland is probably much higher than was thought when these arrangements were drawn up. Non-doms living in the UK are subject to specific tax rules. Those rules apply no matter whether the assets are held in the UK or in Switzerland. For this reason, non-doms are not subject to additional UK tax under this treaty. As Andrew Tyrie, the exquisitely independent-minded chairman of the Treasury Select Committee, reported as long ago as February, the UK has massively 'overstated its assumptions'.

The Anglo-Swiss agreement had four main elements: a one-off levy applied to existing Swiss assets owned by UK residents (this was supposed to bring in the substantial windfall for 2013–14), a withholding tax on future income and gains (arguably to bring in around £300 million per annum), a 40 per cent inheritance levy and a duty for enhanced exchange of information.

The fact that the Swiss bilateral treaty is bringing in less revenue than HMRC envisaged does not mean that the deal should be interpreted as a failure. The deal is set to raise much more than was envisaged by its detractors. It is also raising much more than the alternatives. While the Swiss agreement will yield around £800 million for the UK Exchequer in 2013, this compares with £12 million raised under the EU Savings Tax Directive in 2010.

Nor should the lower-than-expected tax yield to our own Exchequer be regarded as a reflection on the lack of compliance or cooperation of the Swiss banking fraternity. The Swiss authorities have been making major efforts to address the issue of untaxed wealth sitting in Swiss bank accounts. In fact, huge strides in adopting new transparency protocols have been made globally over the past couple of years, for which the UK government should rightly take credit. The ongoing drive to full and open exchange of information, designed to ensure that the global super-rich do not evade paying tax in any of the jurisdictions in which they have financial interests, continues apace.

For all the negative press headlines, this initiative has proved a genuine policy success story for the UK Treasury.

‡

2014 – The Tory equivalent of Brown's missed opportunity?, 18 January 2014

Gordon Brown's premiership in 2007 began auspiciously. From two domestic crises, he managed to fashion a honeymoon. It is easy to forget now, but the new Prime Minister's surefooted handling of a terror alert and severe floods helped project him as a strong, national leader. This translated into soaring poll leads in the summer of 2007 when contrasted with his young, less experienced Tory opposite, David Cameron.

Such was Brown's unexpected popularity that by the time party conference season rolled round, he was widely expected to call a snap autumn general election to secure a personal mandate.

As we all know, it was a decision he famously flunked. Rather than go to the polls that year, 'Bottler Brown' postponed his date of destiny with the electorate. Northern Rock rumbled on and by mid-2008 Britain had been set alight by a financial crisis whose fires were still burning by May 2010, the very last moment at which Brown could call an election. However the indecisive result of that 2010 poll was interpreted, one sentiment was clear – the nation wanted rid of the ailing Prime Minister. 2007 would for ever be perceived as Gordon Brown's Great Missed Opportunity.

According to Matthew D'Ancona's new book, *In It Together*, when the coalition government was formed, it was George Osborne who pushed most vigorously for five-year, fixed-term parliaments. Given the experimental nature of the new government, it seemed to make sense to lock its partners together, snuff out endless electoral speculation and provide as much time as possible to get the economy back on track. The date of the next general election was firmly set for May 2015.

Yet in a rather delicious irony, polling day probably cannot now come too soon for the Chancellor. He had hoped that by 2015, the structural deficit would have been eliminated, the economy would be in full recovery mode and the Conservatives would be rewarded with re-election in their own right. But the task of repair has been far harder than expected. Collectively, we are set to borrow £190 billion more during the course of this parliament than planned at the time of the June 2010 Emergency Budget. The structural deficit remains stubbornly high. Cuts to public expenditure will have to continue beyond 2015. Growth remains fragile, the cost of living persistently high.

Perversely, it is in these circumstances that the Chancellor may have found 2014 a more agreeable time to fight an election. In a keynote speech earlier this month, George Osborne solidified a narrative with which he rightly feels comfortable. We are finally getting some growth in the system – at December's Autumn Statement, the Chancellor was able to revise forecasts upwards and some City economists even believe that growth could hit 4 per cent over the coming year. Osborne makes the case that this optimism is a direct result of his calm and careful stewardship of the economy and his willingness to make the 'tough choices'. The compelling message for 2014 is that steady progress has been made in unpicking Labour's mess, but there is more – much more – to be done.

There are now sixteen tricky months to navigate until the general election, during which this message will be hard to sustain consistently. If powerful economic growth persists, the Chancellor will find himself under increasing pressure to cut taxes, encourage a hike in interest rates and protect existing benefits or restore old ones as polling day nears – all things which jeopardise the project to get the public finances on a stable footing. If, however, the chunky recovery stalls, questions will be asked about whether the upturn was in fact an unsustainable illusion based on cheap credit and an unhealthy boom in the housing market.

Ironically enough, had the coalition not locked itself into a fixed term, its Conservative wing may well have seen 2014 as a golden opportunity to secure a full mandate from the country. As ever, the great charm of politics is its sheer unpredictability.

‡

Ultra-low interest rates carry a cost and it's beginning to rack up (*Daily Telegraph*), 19 January 2014

Reflecting on the forthcoming five-year anniversary since a 0.5 per cent interest rate had been introduced by the Bank of England, I wrote the following article for the Daily Telegraph *pondering the real cost of rock-bottom rates.*

No one ever said it would be easy. But it is fair to raise two cheers at least to George Osborne (and Alistair Darling before him), successive Chancellors who have sought to cushion the shock of the banking crisis and economic turmoil since 2008.

As in the 1930s, and once more in stark contrast to many of our European neighbours, we in the UK have been able to withstand recent shocks to the capitalist system with an air of relative stability.

This has come at a price, however, albeit one that is perhaps only slowly dawning on the electorate.

While eight decades ago the industrial areas of central Scotland, south Wales and the north bore the brunt of the collapse in global trade that followed the great stock market crash of 1929, today it is the young and middle-class savers who are being significantly impoverished by Treasury policies designed to maintain order in an era of crisis.

Since the financial collapse of 2008, UK government policy has been driven by an overwhelming desire to minimise the impact of the economic shock. The generation that enjoyed an expanded welfare state, cheap goods, never-ending lines of credit and inflated house prices has been broadly protected, notably by rock-bottom interest rates.

Less consideration has been afforded to those excluded from this influential and sizeable cohort – today's young people who grapple with sky-high rents and house prices, a less secure employment market and increasing personal debt.

I suspect the friction between the old structure's beneficiaries and its hapless young inheritors will define the West's story for some time. Nevertheless, David Cameron's recent hint that both the pension 'triple lock' and raft of pensioner benefits will be protected beyond the next election indicates that there will be no radical change to the status quo any time soon.

The coalition's primary stated objective on taking office was the elimination of the UK's structural deficit within a five-year term. In this it has palpably failed. Collectively, we are set to borrow £190 billion more during the course of this parliament than planned at the time of the June 2010 Emergency Budget.

Paradoxically, however, the international capital markets have maintained their confidence in George Osborne and his economic plan. Fears that excessive borrowing on this scale would lead to vastly higher borrowing rates have proved unfounded. Osborne's broad-brush, combative confidence and chutzpah may grate on occasion, but, during times of crisis, political leadership requires the self-assured skills of an illusionist rather than a mastery of detail.

Yet history indicates that policies designed to insulate from short-term shock often come with long-term consequence.

The impact of the 1930s Depression was cushioned by restrictive practices and cartels in British industry (which had been subject to widespread consolidation after the First World War) and the then National Government driving through tariff reform. The latter resulted in a 10 per cent levy on imports, designed to insulate domestic manufacturers from international competition. This helped accelerate a move away from global trade towards a policy of Imperial preference. These captive Empire markets feather-bedded UK business in difficult times, but did lasting damage to Britain's longer-term competitiveness, as became evident from the 1950s onwards, since domestic companies had little incentive to modernise and innovate.

Today's ultra-low interest rates have similarly provided UK business and individuals alike with breathing space. Nevertheless, the real question that should be foremost in the minds of policymakers after five straight years of emergency monetary stimulus, is at what cost to the nation's long-term economic interests?

Persisting with near zero rates of interest has retarded the essential cleansing mechanism of capitalism. Countless so-called 'zombie companies' remain in existence, as lending banks have no need to pull the plug on non-performers.

This tying up of capital and labour in non-productive activity has engendered a false sense of security and boosted short-term employment levels, but it augurs ill in the teeth of fierce global competition in the decades ahead.

Similarly, George Osborne has continued the distorting impact of in-work benefits (working tax credits), first introduced in 1997 by then-chancellor Gordon Brown, who had faithfully assured his Downing Street neighbour that their annual cost would never exceed £600 million (on average the Treasury has spent over £8 billion per annum since 2010).

Recent talk of a substantial hike in the minimum wage will only compound the problem. The risk now is that the relatively unskilled will find employers who will regard the enhanced wage as a maximum to be paid. Once employers are confident that any shortfall between a statutory minimum wages entitlement and the wage level required to be 'better off in work' will be covered by the State, where is the incentive to pay more… or to ensure a properly skilled workforce for the rigours of the twenty-first century?

Once again, current policy designed to promote social cohesion kicks into the longer grass the need to make tough decisions. All of this harms the future competitiveness of the UK economy in the global race.

A sustainable household recovery cannot feasibly emerge from a diet of never-ending cheap credit and a new housing boom. While it may be politically canny to shower more future public spending on pensioners in preference to investing in younger voters, it is not the route towards a more competitive economy. Indeed, it has been a long-held fear of mine that the most talented of our younger generation will react to their raw deal simply by leaving these shores, probably never to return.

A price cannot be put on the relative social harmony we have enjoyed since the financial crisis took hold. Extra borrowing and low interest rates have unquestionably staved off considerable personal misery for many and bought politicians time to shore up a rapidly sinking ship. But it should never have been part of the plan to get addicted to this medicine. In the immediate aftermath of the 2008 financial crisis, the lessons of the 1930s were constantly evoked by reference to Keynesian pump-priming. For stage two, that decade offers equally valuable lessons.

Just as the tariff wall of 1932 condemned British industry to years of uncompetitive mediocrity, so today's near-zero interest rates are beginning to rack up their own, considerable cost.

‡

A Miliband government really might take us back to the '60s, 5 February 2014

With just over a year to go until the 2015 general election, all three mainstream political parties had begun to think carefully about which policy themes to develop with the electorate. In January, Ed Miliband summoned the media to the University of London to outline his views on the future of British banking. Building on his perceived energy policy success at Labour's autumn conference, in which he had pitted 'the little guy' against monopolistic firms, he now suggested too much power

*in the banking system was concentrated in too few hands. A Labour
government would break up the banks, forcing branch sell-offs, creating
substantial new institutions and boosting lending to small businesses.
'Under a Labour government,' he promised, 'you will no longer be serving the banks. Instead, the banks will be serving you.' In this article, I
suggested Miliband's 'cost of living' narrative may have wider appeal
than many Tories would give him credit.*

Perhaps predictably as election fever hots up, keynote speeches by
party leaders are now commonplace. However, last month's offering
from Ed Miliband on reform of the banking system may yet herald
a more radical restructuring.

Perhaps we should be thankful that little more has been heard of
his grand theory of 'pre-distribution' since its first outing in 2011. Yet,
in fairness to the Leader of the Opposition, he has started to tap into
a deep sense of unease that there is a 'broken economy'. Nowhere has
this been more evident than among middle class Tory-inclined electors, who increasingly since the 2008 financial crisis have had cause
to view capitalism as being increasingly skewed against their traditional values of thrift, industry and individual responsibility.

As a former small businessman instinctively supporting open,
free markets, I watch these developments with deep foreboding.
Nevertheless, it is clear that Miliband has gradually been able to put
flesh on the bones of his brand of neo-corporatism. We should not
entirely rule out the possibility that he will be proved right – namely
that the financial crisis will in time herald a new economic paradigm.

I suspect the key to this in the short term will be the extent to
which he (or UKIP) proves able to incorporate the support of that
potentially sizeable group of voters disillusioned by the breakdown
in the decades-long historic bargain as understood by the British
middle class.

Standing up for the 'little man' against Big Global Business could
prove a fruitful vein for Labour in the months ahead. In tapping
it, Miliband may be hoping to echo the success of US President
Theodore Roosevelt at the outset of the twentieth century. In the era

of Rockefeller, JP Morgan and US Steel, Roosevelt led an unflinching crusade against the powerful, vested interests of large corporations. As a centre-right President, he instinctively understood that the construction of a populist, robust competition policy was the very best restraint on the type of unbridled capitalism that was generating for business titans monopolistic profits in virtually unlimited quantity. Britain's own centre-right has been rather neglectful in failing to lasso the great Republican's legacy, leaving this fertile territory open for Miliband to conquer.

Even the much ridiculed announcement by the shadow Chancellor that the top rate of income tax under a future Labour government would be raised to 50 per cent may resonate more strongly than we might like with a British public angry with the rich. 'FTSE 100 chiefs slam 50 per cent rate', screamed the headlines – depressingly, this was probably met with cheers by Labour's high command. The economics may stink, but quiet political support for this move, however detrimental to the national interest, may work to Miliband's favour.

I wonder whether the Labour leader's next move may then be to follow in Harold Wilson's footsteps on attaining office in 1964 by breaking up the all-powerful Treasury. Dividing the traditional Whitehall powerhouse once more into a Finance Ministry and an unabashed strategic, long-termist Ministry of Economic Affairs plays to Miliband's spirit of revolutionary fervour and near Ivory Towers, academic approach to government.

At a more base political level, such a plan also helps square the circle over the 'Ed Balls problem'. It potentially allows voters to be pacified that 'the man who crashed the car' will *not* be given sole control of the economic keys going forward. Tantalisingly, such a break-up also leaves open the option, in the event of a coalition, for a leading Liberal Democrat to take the helm in the front line of strategic economic activity. Many on the centre-left might feel this is the proper role for Vince Cable. However, who would sensibly bet against the current Chief Secretary, Danny Alexander, becoming the near-indispensable Hans-Dietrich Genscher of 21st-century Britain if coalition politics is here to stay?

‡

Families have a right to keep finances private
(*Sunday Telegraph*), 25 February 2014

I wrote the following piece for the Sunday Telegraph *to draw attention to legislation being debated in Brussels that could force UK citizens to disclose on a public register substantial amounts of private financial information. The aim of the proposed EU law was to prevent corporate money-laundering, but the legislation was widened to include private trusts.*

The spirit of our age favours transparency. Whether light is being shone on the previously dark corners of intelligence, executive pay, MPs' expenses or overall tax take from global corporations, an insatiable quest for information is rooting out bad practice. But when does this drive for openness morph into an invasion of privacy?

In a bid to beef up EU anti-money-laundering laws, pressure is fast growing on the Treasury to introduce a publicly accessible register of family trusts. And why not? After all, many people assume that trusts in the UK are used almost exclusively by wealthy families, often as a means of avoiding tax. But this is a misconception which, unless challenged, risks exposing to public view the private financial affairs of countless ordinary British families.

Far from being the preserve of the elite, trusts are in fact part of everyday life in the UK – so much so that we often do not even notice them. Though they may not realise it, any couple that owns a home, has a will and life assurance will probably have several trusts.

The result is that while the concept of trusts is almost unknown across much of the EU – reflecting a different civilian legal tradition – there are millions in existence here. Most are very low risk from a money-laundering point of view. Furthermore, UK trusts are rarely used for tax avoidance – indeed they are often taxed at high rates.

The bureaucracy and sheer cost of establishing from scratch a comprehensive trust register, which will have to record millions of such family trusts, should give any government committed to cutting red tape pause for thought. Disproportionate cost, however, is not the only worry. Crucially, a family's right to keep their affairs confidential is also under threat. Among trust funds that have taxable income, HMRC research indicates that about one in four has been established because one or another of the beneficiaries is considered vulnerable in some way. If parents or grandparents wish to set aside some money to help a vulnerable child, should this arrangement be paraded on a compulsory public register?

David Cameron has already personally intervened in the debate in Brussels, arguing that while he is an advocate of greater transparency for companies, trusts are different. He is right. The principle of transparency is a good thing, but in the case of family trusts, there are very strong arguments for maintaining the status quo. The EU Parliament nevertheless continues to press ahead with registry plans.

Substantial damage could be done if we allow the rest of the EU to push the UK into establishing a public trust register. Continental bureaucrats championing this legislation have little or no experience of trusts and we risk an unhelpful precedent being set unless we robustly defend the uniqueness of our system.

A register would be costly, cumbersome and, most seriously of all, intrusive. The invisible line between openness and privacy is about to be crossed.

‡

The Transatlantic Trade and Investment Partnership, 25 February 2014

The European Union and United States together accounted for nearly a third of world trade and half of global GDP, but ambitious politicians on both sides of the Atlantic had long hoped that trade and investment between the two could substantially increase if lower barriers could be negotiated. Talks to secure a Transatlantic Trade and Investment Partnership (better known by its acronym, TTIP) began in June 2013 at the Lough Erne G8 summit with the aim of aligning regulations and standards, improving protections for overseas investors, reducing tariffs and boosting access to services and markets.

However, TTIP was also highly controversial. While the UK government claimed the deal could boost the British economy by up to £10 billion annually, others argued that the benefits of the deal were being overblown and that there were risks to British people's interests. One of the biggest bones of contention was a provision making way for an Investor State Dispute Settlement, which TTIP critics claimed would undermine institutions like the NHS by allowing foreign investors to sue the British government.

I made the following contribution to a parliamentary debate on the TTIP negotiations.

In the aftermath of 2008's financial crisis, politicians the world over were at great pains to avoid the policy mistakes that had followed the banking collapse of the 1930s. Conventional Keynesian pump-priming was continually invoked as the means of preventing a recession turning into a depression. Depressingly, however, rather less interest seemed to be given to the equally important lessons that the 1929–33 era taught us about protectionism.

The Smoot-Hawley Tariff Act of 1930 raised tariffs drastically on goods imported into the United States in a bid to protect American jobs from foreign competition. That Act sparked a domino effect among America's trading partners, who predictably imposed similar measures to protect their own economies. The result was a slump in world trade that devastated economic growth and caused unemployment to soar. It took a World War to reboot the global economy.

In 2010, as growth remained elusive, I wrote of my deep concern that we might see a new wave of protectionist measures put in place by politicians under pressure to protect domestic markets. The House may recall, for instance, the defensive, almost nationalistic tone of debate as Kraft's hostile takeover of Cadbury was going through. I called at that time for political leadership to make a robust case for the massive benefits of free trade, and break down remaining barriers.

It is within this context that I am heartened, four years on, by the enthusiasm with which the Transatlantic Trade and Investment Partnership (TTIP) has been embraced by policymakers. At least on this side of the Atlantic. The main aims of the partnership, whose formal negotiations began last July, are to increase trade and investment between the US and EU by reducing tariffs (particularly on agricultural products), aligning regulations and standards, improving protection for overseas investors, and increasing access to services and government procurement markets by foreign providers.

The prize is potentially enormous and the TTIP is highly ambitious as a result. The US is the EU's most important trade partner, with $2.7 billion of trade daily in goods and services. This impressive figure could be higher still if tariffs and non-tariff barriers to trade were reduced or removed.

Much of the media coverage on TTIP has so far focused on trade of manufactured goods. Rather less attention has been given to a sphere of commerce in which the UK economy excels globally – financial and professional services. I represent the City of London, a hub not only for banking but for a range of other related service businesses such as accountancy, insurance, consultancy, pension management and law. To give some perspective of those industries' importance to Britain, in 2012 the financial and associated professional services sector employed over 7 per cent of the UK workforce, produced nearly 13 per cent of total economic output, contributed £65 billion in taxes and generated a trade surplus of £55 billion.

The City is strongly supportive of the TTIP, but it has been consistent in its belief that no industry should be excluded from the partnership's scope, including financial and professional services. The benefits would come not only in terms of boosted trade but in reducing the potential for the kind of regulatory arbitrage that currently sees differences exploited in the implementation of financial standards, putting at risk financial stability. Some of these regulatory differences are unavoidable – the result of variations in

EU and US market structures. Others cannot be fully justified on prudential grounds.

As demonstrated so painfully in 2008, we tend only to get regulatory cooperation in times of severe crisis, with deals brokered at the eleventh hour to avoid market fracture. Should financial services be included within TTIP's scope, we could design a stable, long-term framework for the discussion and coordination of regulatory issues long before hitting the next crisis point. We might also create a larger, more efficient market place for EU and US financial institutions, solidifying their leading role in global financial regulation.

It is for these reasons that the European Union has been lobbying hard for such services to come within the bounds of TTIP negotiations. But there has been stiff opposition from the US Treasury, who suggest that TTIP is primarily a trade pact, not a forum for regulatory cooperation. The real fear seems to be that the US might lose sovereignty over regulation, but it should be made clear that this is not what the EU proposes. Nobody wishes to undermine existing regulations, even Dodd-Frank. But coordination is quite different to capitulation. We now need sustained, high-level political engagement to bring financial services within TTIP's scope.

I should finally like to make clear my concern that there is insufficient public awareness of TTIP – what is at stake and what are the challenges, problems and potential benefits over its implementation. Quite understandably, given the systematic undermining of the world's political and economic elite in recent years, there is a wave of distrust at the tenor of negotiations underway. There is a common perception that side deals are being brokered to benefit global corporations, with a risk to national sovereignty that might see our independent courts being made subservient to outside arbitration.

I believe it would be most helpful this afternoon if the Minister could clarify his position on these arguments and encourage the government to run a far more visible campaign on TTIP that would allow us all to have an open, honest discussion of its potential benefits and drawbacks. Those proposing TTIP need to show just what it can add to people's lives in terms of trading opportunities, jobs and better variety of consumer products. If there is a perception that this deal is being engineered in an opaque way, it is likely to fall apart, and we shall lose an enormous opportunity. Crucially, the United States must do the same. In that nation, protectionist sentiment and economic nationalism are now fast replacing the wave of enthusiasm on which TTIP initially rode. President Obama's leadership is crucial in this matter. He must set out a free trade vision backed by a personal commitment to seeing it through if European leaders are to spend their own political capital on getting a deal done.

Needless to say, progress in this field of influence will resonate strongly in the UK government's negotiations for reform within the European Union. It was the wily German statesman, Bismarck, who observed that 'politics is the art of the possible'. While I believe it sensible that the government does not raise excessive expectations as to what might be achieved in negotiations with our EU fellow members, it is worth observing that in the aftermath of last autumn's budget settlement, there appears to be a new mood towards some reform. One hopes that some of the UK's traditional allies, like Poland, Finland and the Czech Republic, will not feel encumbered by a resurgent Russia from making the case for institutional reform in the EU. Time will tell.

The debate over TTIP shows once again that the UK government's goal rightly will be to protect the Single Market while allowing the eurozone to develop a new range of its own institutions without prejudicing the UK's strength in financial and professional services.

‡

Ukraine – Russia's chance for an international renaissance, 2 March 2014

Trouble had been brewing in Ukraine since the refusal of President Viktor Yanukovych to sign an Association Agreement and free-trade deal with the European Union in November. Yanukovych, who had taken office in 2010, argued that his country could not afford to jeopardise trade with Russia in the face of opposition to the deal from the Kremlin, and suggested that, regardless, Ukraine would need at least €20 billion annually to bring its economy up to European standards rather than the €610 million on offer.

Protests to Yanukovych's decision quickly followed, with the streets of the capital Kiev filled daily with pro-Western Ukrainians keen to see their country move closer to Europe rather than Russia. A number of protestors and security personnel lost their lives as violence broke out and, in response, a compromise agreement was hammered out to make way for a power-sharing government and fresh elections in December 2014.

But events were to take a dramatic turn. The day after the compromise was reached, the Ukrainian Parliament abandoned the deal and instead stripped Yanukovych of his powers, issuing a warrant for his arrest for the death of the Kiev protestors. Yanukovych fled the capital as Russia waited to make its own move. On 26 February, President Putin ordered 38,000 Russian troops to the Ukrainian border in a show of strength, and the next day, unidentified military personnel surrounded airports and military bases on Ukraine's Crimean Peninsula. A week later, Crimea's regional Parliament announced a referendum to secede from the Ukraine and join the Russian Federation, while large pro-Russian protests broke out across eastern Ukraine.

In the midst of these events, I sought to understand President Putin's motives and mindset in fanning the flames of Ukraine's domestic conflict.

In the immediate aftermath of the Soviet Union's collapse, the symbolic evidence of communism's failure was inescapable. Along with the admission of ideological defeat – made all the more painful given the importance of 'face' and 'pride' to the Russian psyche – came financial meltdown and a sharp downgrading of Russia from global superpower to weak, also-ran failing state.

But there remained hope at the time that Russia in the Gorbachev era was a nation firmly on the path to multi-party democracy, rule by law and press freedom. These hopes persisted even in 2000 with the election of Russia's second President, Vladimir Putin.

Putin was keen visibly to demonstrate Russian willingness to become an important ally to the USA in areas of mutual interest. He accepted a second stage of NATO enlargement to the Baltic States, allowed the US to withdraw from the anti-ballistic missile treaty and stood shoulder to shoulder with George W. Bush in the 'war on terror' (a useful alibi, given his domestic problems in Chechnya).

With Russian troops on the streets of Sevastopol, the Russian Parliament backing Putin, and Russia's President reportedly telling Obama that he 'reserves the right' to defend Russian interests in east Ukraine, the cautious optimism of those years now seems hopelessly misplaced. As the past few weeks have shown, Russia is locked in an internal battle with itself, at once anxious to be taken seriously as a modern, open and successful nation, as exemplified by the success of the Sochi Winter Olympics, but equally determined to the point of paranoia at maintaining control over its historic sphere of influence.

The toppling of the inept Kremlin ally and former Ukrainian President, Viktor Yanukovych, has been an embarrassing and dangerous blow to Putin. Not only does it entail a loss of face in the world, but the speed with which peaceful protest morphed into overthrow has sent chills through Muscovite spines. Putin's government needs swiftly to limit domestic populist fervour and shore up Russia's interests on its southern borders while maintaining a veneer of international credibility. Round One may have been lost, but in Putin's mind there is all still to play for. As he knows, there is vanishingly little Western appetite for military intervention.

We have waited with bated breath over the past few days to see whether Moscow would seek to defuse tensions in Kiev or up the ante. Russia now appears to be moving quickly to stoke tensions among Ukraine's ethnic Russians, framing last weekend's events as an illegitimate coup by foreign-backed extremists whose ultimate hope is to marginalise and oppress. Russia has now made clear that it will 'strongly and uncompromisingly' defend the rights of its compatriots.

What we in the West fail to understand is that many Russians see the Gorbachev and Yeltsin era as a time of chaos, uncertainty and utter humiliation. Putin has been able to maintain domestic popularity by retelling the Russian story, filling the vast ideological vacuum left by the disintegration of the communist ideal with the notion of a Russian civilisation based upon patriotism, selflessness and deference to a powerful state. In doing so, he has tapped into a pool of resentment that goes beyond Russian borders to encapsulate many of those who dislike the US dominance of the past two decades.

Russia may not have the economic clout it once did, representing only 2 per cent of the global economy. But whether unashamedly supporting Assad in Syria, baulking progress to curtail Iran's nuclear programme or turning off the gas taps to Ukraine in the past, Putin has revelled in his nation's ability still to wreak havoc amidst Western foreign policy objectives. His unashamed international awkwardness has also allowed him to test our resolve. Time and again, he has found it wanting.

Russia knows that when it comes to Ukraine, there is little chance of broader-ranging conflict. The EU is firmly concentrated on fixing its economic woes and is still smarting from the almost immediate collapse of its brokered compromise to end the bloodshed. Britain is a diminished voice in global diplomacy since, in clumsily navigating the Syrian conflict, it relinquished decisions on military action to the whims of parliamentary approval. Meanwhile, President Obama's lack of interest in trans-Atlantic or Middle Eastern foreign policy is palpable.

If Putin decides to increase the stakes in Ukraine, our government will find itself with yet another colossal international headache. Putin's Russia will ruthlessly expose any even-handed indecision by the West and mercifully exploit it as a weakness. For all the internal economic turmoil of modern-day Russia, with its over-reliance on minerals and ugly future demographic profile, it shows every sign of diplomatically outgunning its Western rivals.

‡

Keep it simple – it's the deficit, stupid!, 12 March 2014

In advance of the 2014 Budget on 19 March, I set out some of the political criticisms that might be levelled at the Chancellor and recommended that he shrug them off, instead trudging steadily on with the coalition's central task of restoring order to the public finances. I also raised the idea of implementing our own brand of 'forward guidance', a strategy that new Bank of England Governor Mark Carney had devised seven months earlier at Threadneedle Street to indicate to markets that interest rates would rise once unemployment had fallen below 7 per cent. (The trouble with Mr Carney's gambit was that he had presumably not banked on the unemployment rate falling quite as rapidly as it did!)

Politics need not always be a complicated trade. Typically, the simplest messages are the ones that work best.

As the Budget provides a staging post on the road to May 2015, the desire to complicate comes at a potential political price to the Conservative wing of the coalition.

For much of the past three years or so, the British electorate have, perhaps begrudgingly, recognised that the coalition's avowed economic plan – the elimination of the structural deficit within the course of this parliament – has been the right path in response to the grisly economic circumstances.

Key to this plan was economic growth. Predicted compound growth of 2.7–2.9 per cent for the duration of the parliament accounted for over half of the deficit reduction programme. The international capital markets maintained their initial confidence in the coalition despite its first three years being characterised by stagnant growth. Fears that excessive borrowing on the scale that became necessary in 2010–13 would lead to higher interest rates proved unfounded.

The first glimpses of economic recovery and the healthy, consistent growth since spring 2013 have surprised many economic experts. They also put Ed Miliband and his team into a funk by summer 2013. The shadow Treasury analysis was like a broken record, and now that 'flat-lining' had had its day, how best to respond?

Over the next few months furious and furtive planning took place. I am reliably informed that only four people (one of whom was *not* Ed Balls) were in on the radical shift in strategy heralded by Ed Miliband's conference speech. The 'energy price freeze' promise was designed as the initial salvo in a Living Standards Offensive. As autumn meandered on, the theme was rolled out to include smash-and-grab raids on the Living Wage, utilities bills and latterly a return to the tried-and-tested offensive on the banks. For what it's worth, I predict that an all-out attack on the profits and opaque contractual arrangements of the global telecommunications operators will be next in line.

Labour Party command has been incredulous at the way in which they feel the coalition then proceeded to walk straight into the trap set. The initial reaction was to dismiss the Energy Price Freeze as a return to '70s-style socialism. Next up, it was written off as 'unworkable'. Finally, after a couple of weeks of media traction, the coalition hurriedly rolled out its own new proposals, trying to emulate and outwit the Labour version. All of which succeeded only in making living standards the economic issue at the expense of deficit recovery, growth and the ever-improving employment statistics.

Early New Year has allowed us to regain our footing and reset the Conservative message – we are following a 'long-term economic plan' that will benefit 'hard-working people'. If we can overlay this sober foundation with a sense of upbeat optimism and positivity about our nation in the coming months, we should have a solid base from which to bat away Miliband's attacks. It seems to have worked so far with a confident dismissal of Ed Balls's much-derided announcement in January that Labour would raise the top rate of income tax back to 50 per cent.

To complement consistent messaging on the deficit, we must also give the electorate a feeling of hope for the future under a Conservative government. Nevertheless, we should be wary too: if money can be found for tax cuts then our opponents will question the need for further reductions in the welfare budget – this at a time when even the Institute for Fiscal Studies calculates that only 40 per cent of the total planned spending cuts are in place.

So I wonder whether here we might cleverly borrow some tricks from the Bank of England. While the notion of 'forward guidance' has proved a mixed success so far for new Governor Mark Carney, it might be a useful tool for the Chancellor. I have always doubted the wisdom of promising instant, substantial tax cuts, as it puts in jeopardy our central mission to restore order to the public finances. However, reducing the tax burden should always be a part of the Conservative offering. As such, I would suggest that in his Budget speech on the 19th, the Chancellor offers his own brand of forward guidance, giving a clear signal that when progress on reducing the deficit breaks past a certain point, a series of tax cuts will kick in. That way, the electorate will know full well that while our priority is stability, our ultimate aim is a low tax, competitive economy.

Labour's messaging over the past six months has blended naïve populism with flagrant opportunism. Their appeal has rested not on their practicality but their exploitation of a deep sense of unease among many in the electorate that the current system does not deliver for them. Our response to this has too often been erratic and confusing, lending greater weight to policies which should rightly be dismissed as dangerous and unworkable. What voters need from us is consistency and simplicity.

Rather than getting blown off course, now is the time to cement our position as the calm, rational team that is slowly and patiently getting the UK economy back on track and the public finances under control. Substantial, radical reductions in taxes should only sensibly come when this mission has been accomplished.

‡

Has the government helped or hindered the economic recovery?, 17 March 2014

With his eye firmly on the general election, George Osborne declared his 2014 Budget one for the 'makers, doers and savers', made possible only because 'together with the British people, we held our nerve'. Growth

*forecasts received their biggest upwards revision for thirty years, to
2.7 per cent. Welfare spending was to be capped, while the personal
allowance would once again be increased, this time to £10,500. But
the rabbit out of the hat was gifted to older voters as the Chancellor
revealed he would be scrapping the requirement for pensioners to buy an
annuity, in a stroke transforming the UK's pension industry by allowing people to draw down as little or as much as they wanted from their
retirement pot.*

*I was asked by communications firm, Maitland, to write a piece for
their in-house magazine on whether I felt the government was helping
or hindering economic recovery. In the following article, I explained how
the Chancellor had transformed confidence in the public finances and, in
so doing, had ensured that the UK economy could now motor forward.*

In January, the government received the news it had so patiently
awaited. The Office for National Statistics was able to confirm that
in 2013, the UK economy had enjoyed its fastest rate of growth since
2007, expanding by 1.9 per cent. This unmistakable signal of recovery was further boosted by IMF and OBR predictions forecasting
growth of up to 2.4 per cent for the ensuing year.

It all seemed a far cry from the troublesome Budget of March
2012 and the unremittingly gloomy forecasts in the subsequent
Autumn Statement, when Chancellor George Osborne confessed
that the government was set by a distance to miss its debt reduction target. Taunts of economic flat-lining and persistent calls for a
shift to Plan B at that time were relentless. It would have been easy
to yield to this pressure. Yet the Chancellor has always recognised
one thing – confidence of the markets is key if Britain is to maintain the ultra-low interest rates that are, for now, so vital in keeping
the economic show on the road. Understanding what those markets wanted, the government has been granted permission to take
its time in fixing Britain's problems, and to stumble on the way
without more serious consequence.

In his Autumn Statement of 2010, the Chancellor had predicted
that by this financial year, the government would have reduced the

inherited £148 billion budget deficit to £60 billion. By contrast, it stands today closer to £111 billion. By the terms of its very raison d'être – namely to eliminate the structural deficit within a parliament – the coalition has not only failed but failed pretty miserably. However, Britain in 2014 enjoys ultra-low interest rates; unemployment is hurtling towards a rate of 7 per cent; migrants continue to flock here for the opportunities on offer; and business investment is up 8.5 per cent on last year. Meanwhile, in spite of doggedly and consistently higher borrowing than anticipated, the UK has been able to maintain top credit ratings in marked contrast to many of our competitors.

In short, the government has defied economy gravity and, for this, it must be congratulated. While the raw numbers suggest we still have a long, long way to go before eliminating the structural deficit, the coalition has always grasped what the markets have sought from it: a clear deficit reduction plan, a commitment to sticking to it and long-term reforms to address the competitiveness problem in the British economy. In all these areas, the coalition has made strides while maintaining social cohesion.

Key to achieving its goals has been sweeping change to the political mood music. At the 2010 general election, politicians of all stripes were content to focus debate very narrowly on how and when £6 billion of cuts should kick in. Once formed, the coalition moved very swiftly to revise Britain's narrative, making clear in its Emergency Budget that the nation needed to change course urgently. For much of the past three years or so, the British electorate has implicitly recognised that the coalition's avowed economic plan has been the right path in response to the grisly economic circumstances. The Labour Party has conceded this too by shifting debate onto the cost of living rather than deficit reduction.

The coalition has also directed a marked change in the national mood over welfare spending, education and the remit of the state. Rather than ducking tricky issues that previous administrations had shied from, the government has tackled head-on benefits entitlements, underperforming schools and pensions reform. Meanwhile, the Prime Minister's consistent theme that we are in a global race has invigorated pan-government efforts to attract foreign investment into key British infrastructure projects and boost British exports.

The Chancellor understands that markets require of him the self-assured skills of an illusionist rather than a mastery of detail. It is easy to find the flaws in the coalition's record, to point out where progress has been patchy, where policy implementation has been hashed. But the government's long-term economic plan and sense of direction have always been consistent. It is that dogged determination to reduce the deficit, coupled with a pragmatic approach to borrowing, that has provided government with the space to implement spending cuts and longer-term reforms without greater social upheaval. It is confidence in that plan that has allowed government to resist opposition pressure to hike taxes, and given businesses faith that we are on the path to stability.

Ultimately, it is only the hard work, enterprise and innovation of the private sector that can save Britain's economy. But growth can only take place if a government provides an environment in which commerce can flourish. The real achievement of this government is to shift resolutely public attitudes away from unsustainable excess. This has unquestionably helped Britain's nascent economic recovery.

‡

We need a rational debate on immigration
(*Sunday Times*), 23 March 2014

The Conservative Party went into the 2010 general election promising to reduce immigration to the 'tens of thousands' and had secured agreement with the Liberal Democrats at the coalition's outset to implement an annual cap on the number of non-EU economic migrants admitted to the UK.

I was unconvinced by the cap as I had seen its perverse outcomes – highly skilled, English-speaking professionals struggling to get visas for jobs in industries in need of their talent; innovative, entrepreneurial graduates declined the opportunity to stay on after leaving university; and high-spending tourists and students deterred from coming to the UK due to exhaustive visa procedures. Meanwhile, we were unable to do anything about the bulk of the migratory flow from the European Union.

In February, the Office for National Statistics revealed that the net flow of migrants to the UK had risen in the year to 2013 by 154,000 compared to the previous year, driven by a boom in EU citizens coming to work in Britain, particularly from Portugal, Italy, Spain and Poland. The public were fed-up and disillusioned, but Downing Street maintained that the coalition's immigration policy would remain firmly in place.

On 24 March, I launched a new group, Conservatives for Managed Migration, which called upon the Conservative leadership to drop the cap as a 2015 manifesto pledge and try to rebalance the national debate on immigration. In this preview piece I wrote for the Sunday Times, *I explained the group's aims in more detail.*

In spite of consistently ranking as a top voter priority, for years our nation's politicians ducked the touchy subject of immigration. Afraid of honest discussion, tough questions over the numbers of people coming here, and their integration into British society, were left almost totally unanswered by the political class.

Public resentment and anger fast filled the policy vacuum.

As that resentment has boiled over, so the political pendulum has swung erratically the other way. Former Labour Cabinet Ministers have since fallen over themselves to confess their mistakes in office, while the claim to have slashed immigration by a third has become a key campaigning mantra for the Conservative portion of the coalition. The rumbling threat of UKIP has only stiffened the resolve of mainstream parties to keep tough talk on immigration firmly on the front pages. The tone of debate suggests there is no middle ground between rabid, drawbridge-raising right-wingers and soft liberals bent on scrapping immigration controls.

In such a febrile atmosphere it has become almost impossible to have the rational debate we need. That is why I have decided to set up a new group, *Conservatives for Managed Migration*, to try to start that calm and reasoned discussion about immigration both within and beyond the Conservative Party.

It is a crucial discussion for two reasons. First, the current immigration crackdown has big implications for our nation and our economy. A cap on numbers is not only undeliverable but leads to an unhealthy focus on headline figures that is disconnected from reality. Since the government has precious few tools at its disposal to stem the tide of EU nationals, refugees and asylum seekers (protected by human rights legislation), government efforts to decrease numbers inevitably rest on keeping out many of the most desirable types of non-EU migrant – talented entrepreneurs, academics and business people. When the government fails to meet its own targets, voter distrust is only reinforced.

Second, the relentless focus on immigration by the Conservative Party seems to the outsider to border on near-obsession. The implicit message to the electorate is that my party is fundamentally hostile to those who were not born here, and deems the presence of settled migrant communities to be a mistake. This in spite of the fact that many immigrants in Britain demonstrate just the kind of vision, enterprise and family values that would make them natural Tory voters.

It would be wrong not to acknowledge the great strides the government has made in improving our dysfunctional immigration system. Abuses have been cracked down on – bogus colleges, sham marriages, fake students, health tourists and the like – and the Home Office is stopping the endless cycle of legal appeals for rejected applications. The government has also been striving to address some of the so-called 'pull' factors which have made Britain such an appealing destination for those exploiting generous Western health and benefits systems.

But the hostile tone of debate and the imposition of an arbitrary cap on numbers send out the wrong message about what my party stands for. It is also wreaking economic damage. Time and again, businesses and globally competitive universities tell me of the barriers they face in securing entry to Britain for the people we should be welcoming. By the same token, it seems impossible to deport that minority who do not play by the rules.

Britain's world-beating education sector draws fee-paying students from across the globe, many of whom go back to their home nations as tremendous ambassadors for the UK for decades to come. A 2011 report by the Home Affairs Select Committee suggested that twenty-seven contemporary foreign heads of state were educated in the UK. There is no cap on international student numbers, but the government's explicit objective has been to reduce student numbers as a means of bringing net migration to under 100,000 by the next election. The treatment of student and post-study work visas has now become a cause of regular complaint among top universities in my constituency, with prospective overseas academic staff now preferring to move to the US and Australia instead.

These complaints are echoed by senior business people. Barriers to entry include the complexity and cost of getting a visa, interminable queues at our borders, and long journeys to get approvals at far-flung overseas embassies. It is a cliché that a reputation takes years to build but can be lost in an instant. However, the UK runs a real risk of losing its hard-won standing as a country that welcomes trade, investment and talented students from around the world at a time when we most need international expertise and capital.

Our rhetoric at home needs to change too. Politically, the Conservative Party has always thrived most when it has adapted to or led change in Britain. We must avoid hysterical reactions to the problems of the last decade, when migration did indeed drift out of control. Nor should we be trying to recreate a Britain as it was in the 1950s. Those who have or will come here are not numbers – they are people. There are many minority and migrant communities who are bursting with the sort of entrepreneurial vision and family commitment that should make them natural Conservatives – but they are hardly going to embrace our party if we are rarely seen to embrace them.

The problem with the immigration debate is that it has long been stifled by a lack of candour. In truth, the movement of international business people, students and academics is not the nub of the issue. Although few support employers choosing an international worker over a similarly skilled Briton, or welcome with open arms each and every person wanting to make a new life here, equally most people accept that flexibility in a country's immigration system is now part and parcel of being a signed-up member of the global economy. Instead, worries about immigration broadly stem from a sense of rapid change to our communities alongside a feeling of impotence, a loss of control, over our ability to deport undesirables.

The aim of Conservatives for Managed Migration, launching this week, is to try to rebalance the national debate on immigration. We must and we shall make the positive case for welcoming those who can make our country greater, and for putting in place realistic and robust systems of control that can regain business and public trust. We believe that in doing so, we can make both our nation and our party stronger.

‡

HMRC's zeal over tax avoidance is harming investment in British film (*Daily Telegraph*), 28 March 2014

I had warned before of the potential for the Chancellor's tax avoidance clampdown to impose retrospective penalties on businesses and individuals who had engaged in tax arrangements that were, at the time of implementation, entirely legitimate. I was also worried about HMRC being given the power to appropriate disputed tax before it had properly determined what it was owed.

I was now being alerted to constituency cases where an increasingly muscular HMRC was taking action against investors who had previously engaged the Revenue in pre-clearance to utilise the government's own tax credits schemes. I highlighted these cases in an article I wrote for the Daily Telegraph.

As the New Year broke, Chancellor George Osborne beckoned the national press to Ealing Studios to showcase the thriving British film industry. His visit was timed to coincide with the welcome news that aggregate investment last year in UK-based film production had for the first time topped £1 billion. This has been aided by a tax break that has attracted huge sums of private cash into the industry. This week, in tribute to the creative sector's vital economic contribution, the Chancellor introduced a theatre tax break in his Budget to match those in place for high-end TV, film and televised animation.

I welcome this energy from government for the creative industries. My constituency is home to the globally competitive creative sector in Soho, and I campaigned for three years to get the animation tax credit that was successfully announced in the 2012 Budget. However, earlier this month, I listened to a tale of woe from a group of experienced private investors who have found themselves squeezed awkwardly between the coalition's ambitions for the creative industries and its other much-vaunted priority – a clampdown on tax avoidance. Their experience should be a warning sign to any investor who has sought to engage in an open and transparent relationship with HMRC. It should also give Treasury Ministers pause for thought as they aggressively pursue their anti-avoidance agenda in the months ahead.

Some years ago, the group approached HMRC with their model for private investment in the UK creative industries. After extensive discussion on its structure, the group was not only given the green light, but told that their vehicle was exactly the kind of thing the government envisaged. On the basis of this understanding, the group proceeded to invest more than £1 billion of risk capital into the British film industry, leading to the production of over sixty films including successful British titles like *Notes on a Scandal* and *Best Exotic Marigold Hotel*. To date, the partnerships have generated over £1.13 billion of income, with a further £1.08 billion projected over the remaining commercial life of the film slates. All of this income is taxable right here in the UK.

These investors were considered firmly as 'inside the tent' by

HMRC. Nevertheless, as a precautionary measure, they elected to place themselves on the Revenue's Disclosure of Tax Avoidance Schemes (DOTAS) register. As tax avoidance measures are now so widely drawn, it has been common practice to err on the side of caution and sign up to HMRC initiatives of this sort. With the tax authorities hiking the fine for non-disclosure in 2010 from £5,000 to up to £1 million, the incentive to DOTAS registry, which has hitherto had no downside, has only increased.

The investors thought nothing more of their DOTAS registration until a flurry of high-profile scandals came to light where film investment vehicles had been used by celebrities to slash their tax bills. Rather than sift egregious examples of so-called 'aggressive avoidance' from legitimate investment vehicles, HMRC threw a blanket of suspicion over any DOTAS-registered scheme. Keen to establish their vehicle's legitimacy as swiftly as possible, and exhausted by the consistent mismanagement of their case by HMRC, the investors elected to put their scheme before an independent tax tribunal.

Currently, if the UK tax authorities wish to challenge the legitimacy of a DOTAS-registered scheme in court, the taxpayer is permitted to hold onto the disputed tax while the case is being resolved. Since the government believes that this incentivises scheme promoters to sit back and delay resolution as long as possible, no matter how tenuous a vehicle's legitimacy, it has now accepted a modification proposed in its January consultation, *Tackling Marketed Tax Avoidance*. This involves extending the accelerated payments measure to *existing* DOTAS-registered schemes, such that disputed tax is paid upfront to HMRC and returned if a scheme is subsequently found to be legitimate.

The problem is, no exception is proposed in cases where taxpayers have demonstrably *not* 'sat back and delayed as long as possible'. Indeed, my investor constituents are desperate to get their dispute settled by an independent arbiter as a matter of urgency. In their case, it is HMRC baulking progress. Having secured a tribunal date, HMRC has requested an eight-month delay, conveniently pushing the case into the remit of any potential new legislation.

The reasonableness of the government's proposed policy is not in dispute. After all, legitimate investors understand the need to deal quickly with the tens of thousands of outstanding mass-marketed avoidance cases currently clogging up the courts. They simply propose an exception in the case of existing DOTAS-registered schemes whose promoters have taken all reasonable measures to enable a dispute to be brought before the statutory appeals tribunal.

The investors' arrangements are as far removed from a 'tenuous' tax avoidance scheme as it is possible to imagine. Indeed, had they been aggressive tax evaders or avoiders, it is highly unlikely that they would already have paid tax on £1 billion of taxable income to the Exchequer or sought to engage in such a transparent relationship with HMRC. They see it as a shocking breach of faith that the government is now attempting to impose a requirement on them to pay disputed tax upfront when it is HMRC actively delaying their tribunal. Worse still is the message being sent to other private investors who stand to be deterred from any future investment in the UK film industry.

DOTAS was designed to promote openness and transparency in investors' relationships with HMRC. It is now in effect introducing retrospective legislation with DOTAS declaration being used as a stick to beat legitimate investors who never planned on having the liquid assets to meet disputed liabilities. I fear this augurs ill for the government's broader, much-vaunted anti-avoidance plans, as well as its overarching aim to make Britain 'open for business'.

If the Chancellor wishes actively to encourage investment via additional tax credits, he must reassure legitimate investors that previously agreed, transparent vehicles are not at some point going to be subject to unplanned-for, upfront tax liabilities in the event of a sudden change to the rules by HMRC. Indeed, I have pressed consistently for government efforts on tax evasion to go hand-in-glove with the creation of a comprehensive pre-clearance regime. This would allow firms and their tax advisers to road-test proposed taxation schemes with HMRC officials. Ideally, if this were to work efficiently, no new scheme would be permitted to be marketed until approved.

Political alarm bells should now be ringing as Parliament presides over an unprecedented transfer of power to HMRC, itself too often a watchword for incompetence. This agency of the state is being empowered not only to apply the law, but to rewrite it.

The government's aims to encourage investment in British industry and clamp down on aggressive tax avoidance and evasion should not be incompatible. Shamefully, HMRC is making them so.

‡

Time to give our banks a break, 15 April 2014

One of the criticisms levelled at British banks ever since the financial crisis had been that they were failing to lend to small- and medium-sized businesses, the lifeblood of the economy and likely engine of any sustainable recovery. In this essay, I probed Liberal Democrat coalitionist Business Secretary Vince Cable's assertion that banks were starving business of credit, and assessed why the government's own policy prescriptions seemed not to be stimulating lending.

There is much to criticise in the ethics and conduct of British banks. Indeed, the catalogue of mis-selling and foreign exchange irregularities continues to this day.

But according to Business Secretary Vince Cable, British banks have also been hoarding cash and refusing to lend to credit-starved small- and medium-sized enterprises. 'If Britain is to emerge from this dreadful crisis,' he declared two years ago, 'business needs access to finance, just as plants need water – and the banks aren't supplying it.' Dr Cable's consistent stance that the banking system is suffocating enterprise is a view as widely shared as it has been accepted.

A reassuring story perhaps for those frustrated at the lack of investment even as the UK economy grows powerfully. But how much truth is there to this gloomy assertion? Are there really countless businesses to which our banks should have been lending, but have not?

Typically, on receipt of a request for borrowing, banks quantify the risk involved in lending to a specific business and forecast what they might lose if such a loan goes sour, an increasingly rigorous process subject to oversight by the Prudential Regulation Authority (PRA). Having quantified the risk, a decision is made on whether to lend, at what price and with what conditions. This assessment is naturally also affected by general economic conditions.

During the financial crisis, the level of expected loss from SME lending increased, particularly since there was a pronounced drop in commercial property prices. Banks tightened general lending policies accordingly. However, this tightening was at nowhere near the level or duration suggested by the Business Secretary, who has consistently implied that acceptance rates have been subject to rather more than a transient drop.

Smaller SMEs (fifty employees or fewer) saw the chances of their being accepted for lending fall from 78 per cent in January 2008 to 63 per cent a year later, before recovering to 76 per cent in January 2010. Acceptance rates for larger SMEs (no more than 250 employees) were 98 per cent in January 2008, but stood at 88 per cent in January 2010. The longer period of depressed approval rates for this group partly reflects the fact that it was this cohort most involved with the ailing commercial property sector.

Many businesses also characteristically reacted to the downturn by rapidly reducing their own risk – deferring investment, cutting back on borrowing and accumulating cash. By the beginning of 2010, applications for all borrowing from medium-sized business, and for loans to smaller SMEs, had fallen by 20 per cent from the level seen at the beginning of 2008. The truth is that this fall in demand has not yet been reversed. Indeed, it is possible that it would have been less pronounced without the misleading public perception, fuelled by politicians, that credit was barely available. Bank satisfaction surveys revealed that many customers *still* believe that credit is extremely elusive.

Nevertheless, if there has been a problem with lending, for almost four years it has been within the direct remit of the Business Secretary to address it. Arguably, the coalition's various policy prescriptions to increase bank lending have had little discernible impact.

The first of these, the Enterprise Finance Guarantee Scheme (EFGS), was established by the Labour government in 2009 and retained by the coalition as a key plank of its approach to increase lending to SMEs. The EFGS is designed to step in when a business has passed a bank's normal lending criteria but has insufficient collateral to offer as security. The government guarantees up to 75 per cent of the value of an individual loan and up to 9.5 per cent of the total lending provided by each bank within the scheme.

For the past two years for which data has been available, EFGS lending has contributed just 1.1 per cent of the lending by value provided to SMEs by major UK banks. Meanwhile, the quarterly contribution of EFGS under the coalition has declined to less than half that of the previous government. If our economy's great problem has been the senseless hoarding of capital, then the EFGS would appear not to be the answer.

That is not to say it has produced no economic benefit. Researchers at the Durham Business School found that, based on lending written in 2009, the EFGS created around one new job per business supported. Assuming the same level of benefit since the coalition entered office, EFGS has helped create 3,300 jobs per annum – praiseworthy, but essentially a drop in the ocean when compared to the 213,000 jobs created annually by bank lending without the benefit of government support. Interestingly, in the same analysis of job creation, it was found that over 90 per cent of new private sector jobs have no reliance on bank lending, suggesting that Dr Cable is exaggerating bank lending as the main barrier to economic growth.

The second policy prescription, Funding for Lending (FfL), hinges on the notion that a reduction in the cost of lending boosts demand. FfL allows banks to borrow from the Bank of England at rates lower than available in the wholesale market on the proviso that the benefit (typically a 1 per cent reduction in margin) is passed to customers. All of the UK's major SME banks, apart from HSBC, are now involved with FfL, but it is difficult to see what effect the programme has had since its launch in July 2012. The number of new lending approvals the year before launch, in July 2011, stood at 39,547. Twelve months after the launch, in July 2013, the equivalent figure for approvals stood at 27,019.

I suspect FfL's failure stems from the flawed reasoning behind it – that a 1 per cent discount in margin would stimulate significant extra demand. In reality, businesses usually borrow because they have a business need or see a business opportunity. The cost of borrowing is generally low relative to a business's revenue, and therefore a 1 per cent reduction in margin is not deemed significant enough to encourage unplanned borrowing. The Bank of England and HM Treasury have acknowledged that take-up of FfL has been poor, and have changed the terms from February 2014 to January 2015, refocusing the scheme towards SME lending and away from household lending.

The coalition's policies to stimulate lending have therefore been of only minimal economic benefit, perhaps because the charge that banks have been senselessly hoarding capital is simply incorrect. Indeed, if the government believes there really is a problem with access to credit and is serious about resolving it, it probably ought to have been focusing on the three variables crucial to increased lending: the number of businesses that request a loan, the average amount that is requested, and the percentage of requests that are approved (or the level of risk the banks will accept).

Throughout the recession, banks have sought to encourage customers to borrow via advertising campaigns, ring-fencing of SME funds and rewarding staff for lending. But many of their attempts have been drowned out by media and government suggestions that banks are failing to lend. Indeed, a source at the British Chambers of Commerce recently advised me that bank lenders he spoke to suggested that, in absolute terms, the money they have been trying to lend is as cheap as it has ever been. However, there is a strong perception issue at play since the differences between Base Rate and loan rates were much smaller before the crisis. If there has been any significant cost difference, it appears to be on arrangement fees rather than interest rates.

Targeting the third variable would involve banks approving more loans where there is a greater risk of loss by relaxing their lending criteria. If government were serious about increasing credit flow at all costs, it could support that relaxation by either underwriting the increased loss or encouraging banks with large taxpayer stakes (Lloyds and RBS) to engage in higher risk, higher margin lending. Unsurprisingly, to date, there is no evidence that the government has sought to do that. Indeed, the coalition has stipulated that EFGS support will only be available to businesses that meet normal lending criteria.

There is little to support the assertion that banks have 'senselessly hoarded' capital. At worst, they stand fairly accused of marginally tightening their lending criteria during the recession in response to the increased risk from lending to SMEs. But even this had been broadly reversed by the end of 2010. I suspect much of the decline in new lending is in fact related to a fall in demand. Vince Cable also overstates the importance of increasing SME lending to economic recovery. After all, only around one in ten of new private sector jobs created each year in the UK rely upon new bank lending to SMEs.

If the Department for Business, Innovation and Skills (BIS) really wishes to increase lending, it must first challenge the now-accepted wisdom about the availability of credit. Only then, if it insists on formal intervention, might the Department encourage lending to increasingly risky businesses. To date, it has shown no inclination to pursue either of these routes.

But then perhaps the banks – vulnerable because of their repeated failings – provide the Business Secretary with too convenient a scapegoat to relinquish.

‡

Let's not write the US off yet – China will rise, but will have pressing problems, 3 May 2014

With some forecasters predicting that 2014 would see China overtake the United States as the world's largest economy, I had travelled in March to Beijing, Tianjin and Shanghai and seen for myself the breathtaking pace of change since my previous trip in 2007. Reflecting on my observations, I thought it worth contemplating some of the challenges ahead for the Chinese economy.

The 2008 financial crash came laden with gloomy predictions for the imminent future of the West. One of the most dominant foresaw the passing of the Anglo-Saxon model of capitalism and with it the rapid demise of the United States, the nation which had surpassed all competitors in the twentieth century. In its place would storm China, the growth miracle of our time and the undisputed owner of the keys to the world's future. In contrast to the debt-loaded West, the foundations of the Sino-phenomenon were built on hard work, thrift and enterprise. We were all in thrall, swiftly swivelling our focus to the Masters of the Far East.

'The erstwhile expectation that by the middle of this century China and India will have attained the standard of living and international power on a par with the US now needs revising,' I wrote in October 2008. 'We may be there considerably sooner.'

'To put it simply,' I went on, 'money is power. Financial power and global political leadership go hand in hand. The bailout of US and European banks will essentially be underwritten by the flooding in the global capital markets of US and European government bonds, which will be mopped up by cash-rich sovereign wealth funds in China, the Gulf and Russia. Their money will buy them power. This power will be used to exert more influence – in the case of China and Russia, backed by military force around its borders. Our entire model of democracy and free markets will be put to the test.'

Nearly six years down the line, the confidence of the United States remains battered. President Obama's disengagement from foreign affairs is palpable, as President Putin and his supporters induce mayhem on Russia's western borders, and Syria's President Assad holds firm in an increasingly chaotic Middle East. Domestic battles on Capitol Hill suck Obama's energy. Gross national debt hurtles towards the $18 trillion mark. Engagement with China revolves around a 'Pacific pivot', with alternative Asian alliances nurtured in a bid to contain America's Far Eastern rival.

Meanwhile, in dollar terms, it is China that contributed more than any other country to the growth in global consumption between 2011 and 2013. As much of the US and European infrastructure deteriorates, China's high-speed rail network will have expanded by nearly two thirds by 2020, with almost every city with a population of over 500,000 connected into it. By 2030 China's cities will house nearly one billion people as urbanisation and modernisation continue apace. China can now boast the world's largest e-commerce market and some of the most sophisticated consumers on the planet. The Sino-superlatives could go on.

Many contend that China's vast foreign exchange reserves, increasingly educated and technologically savvy population and relative political stability will ensure that it will be able to overcome any future bumps in the road. Nevertheless, as the memory of the 2008 crash recedes, the scales are beginning to fall off our eyes as we examine China's remarkable ascent. Amidst the praise, uncomfortable, sometimes ugly, realities are creeping to the surface that suggest that, far from rapidly overtaking the United States, China may not match its magnitude in the twenty-first century.

Let's take a fresh look at the figures. In 2012, US GDP was approximately $15.7 trillion. China's was just under half that figure for a nation with four times the population. Core US defence spending remains larger than that of the next ten nations (China included) combined. While China is still posting annual growth rates of 7 per cent, it is quite possible that data on which GDP is calculated is deeply flawed. The Chinese statistics office itself has revealed that regional authorities have been overstating GDP by 10 per cent as provincial officials jostle for favour.

As the dangers of the West's debt bubble became evident six years ago, China set about inflating its own. This was primarily through construction works directed by local governments, aimed at counteracting the effects of the financial crisis on domestic employment and growth. Much of the cheap capital that flowed was invested sensibly on critical infrastructure, some of which I had the chance to admire on a whistle-stop trip to Beijing, Tianjin and Shanghai in March. But with pricing signals dampened, it became harder to ascertain which investments would eventually produce returns, and capital began to be misallocated on a major scale. Even sound projects like metropolitan subway systems now look likely to generate only enough cash to cover operating costs, not repay the original investment.

Since 2008, China's credit gap – the increase in private sector credit as a proportion of economic output – has risen by 71 percentage points, with a lot of new credit now being used to roll over existing loans rather than fuel growth. Total debt stands at 230 per cent of GDP, a figure that last year caused Fitch to downgrade China's sovereign credit rating for the first time since 1999. Meanwhile, reliance is mounting on the unpoliced and rapidly expanding shadow banking system, and China remains vulnerable to default by Western debtors.

It has been suggested that China's vast foreign exchange reserves, current account surplus and healthy domestic savings will ward off a credit crisis, and let us hope that is the case. Even so, the figures highlight China's central dilemma: how to shift the economy away from investment spending (which bestowed China with high growth and low unemployment and now accounts for nearly half the economy) to greater consumption, all the while avoiding economic pain and social disruption. China's new leadership understands the task it must undertake in restructuring the economy, and has asserted its willingness to let the rate of growth slide in order to achieve that goal. But it will need to be resolute if it is to take on the powerful vested interests benefiting from the status quo.

The squeeze on the labour market as a result of the demographic impact of its one-child policy (in contrast to a healthy US fertility rate) is also placing upward pressure on wages, reducing China's competitiveness and further undermining exports, which had already taken a hit from a taming of Western spending. In short, the two crucial elements of China's growth miracle – state-driven industrialisation and cheap exports – are now in jeopardy. Part of the answer, as China knows and I have already suggested, is to boost domestic demand. But for all the talk of a Chinese consumer boom, consumption actually trended downward as a percentage of GDP, from 46 per cent in 2000 to 34 per cent in 2010, so there is much work to be done.

Aside from these fundamental challenges, China faces well-documented problems over air pollution and land contamination that are cutting life expectancies and harming quality of life. Rapid urbanisation is exacerbating inequities between existing city dwellers and migrant workers, which have the potential to cause considerable social unrest. Endemic cronyism blights the political and economic sphere, and foreign multinationals are finding China an increasingly challenging country in which to do business, as sweeping new consumer protection laws, fickle consumers and high-profile corruption probes deter further engagement.

Just as it may have been rash to suggest a swift end to US supremacy, I would not wish to overstate China's problems. It remains a land of staggering potential with a leadership of enormous ambition, open about the challenges it faces as the Chinese economy matures. But the West should never have been dazzled into losing its confidence. For all its faults, the United States is similarly a place of huge opportunity, able better to innovate across myriad sectors, still the home for dramatic scientific advances and in the midst of a breathtaking energy and manufacturing boom.

As this century progresses, Chinese influence and power will undoubtedly grow. But in the foreseeable future the United States can surely rest easy. Looking over its shoulder, it will still find the challengers to its position as the pre-eminent economic superpower far behind.

‡

Where exactly does an EU exit lead us?, 20 May 2014

With the elections to the European Parliament scheduled for 22 May, speculation was rife that UKIP might make a major breakthrough. This only heightened tensions between David Cameron and his backbenchers over the EU, as fear spread among Conservative MPs that a decisive victory for UKIP in Europe might lead to parliamentary gains at the general election. Amidst this feverish atmosphere, I decided to make the case for our continued membership of the European Union, and cautioned that we needed to be more realistic about the likely success of any renegotiation of our terms.

As we all well know, the growing sense of unease over the past decade at developments in the European Union has made withdrawal tantalisingly tempting to many of our fellow Britons.

Indeed, those of us who believe our nation has a distinct, valuable economic and political contribution to make to Europe's future are facing an uphill battle to convince a sceptical public. Much persuasion will be required to convince voters that leaving the EU is contrary to the national interest. For a start, at a future referendum Conservatives would need to elevate analysis of the importance of our strategic relations with other EU nations beyond simply that of internal party management.

Closer to home, and sooner still, comes the Scottish independence plebiscite. Its conduct to date draws some important lessons for those who wish to see the UK (or whatever remains of it) leave the EU. Alex Salmond has failed until now to clarify what Scotland's post-UK relationship would look like – and this is probably harming his cause. The same risks apply to those who would have us withdraw from the EU. Once the emotional appeal of 'standing alone' wanes, a hard-nosed reality sets in – what next?

While opting out of future proposals for closer integration should pacify current sceptical UK opinion, it also makes further marginalisation of the UK within the EU more likely, and potentially prevents our overruling measures deemed to be against our interests. If the UK cannot retain influence from the margins, even EU enthusiasts will struggle to explain why it is in our interests to remain in the EU.

Geopolitically, it is difficult to argue that the UK outside the EU would retain its global influence, especially in a world increasingly dominated by continental-sized powers such as the United States of America, China and India. Harping back to a wistful place at the heart of the British Commonwealth is surely little more than that – an unrealistic, naïve reluctance to cast off post-imperialistic pretensions.

That is certainly how such a UK 'alternative to the EU' seems to Indian opinion formers. For Australians and New Zealanders meanwhile, the world has moved on. While the love-in with monarchy shows few signs of abating any time soon, these countries increasingly regard themselves as 21st-century Asian nations – and nor have they forgotten the sense of betrayal when we joined the EEC. As for Canada… well, their pride in the Royal Family owes more to the desire to differentiate historically from an internationally unpopular USA, but their economic and strategic interests lie firmly within their own continent.

Even for the dwindling number of arch-Atlanticists in our party, I fear that the prospect of swapping EU membership for NAFTA is painfully unrealistic, especially as the US political class increasingly turns its attention to relationships across the Pacific.

Moreover, the fantasy that the UK would be able in global affairs to compare itself with Norway and Switzerland in their relations with the EU (which, in any event, provide less flexibility than may initially appear) should have been put to bed by recent, terrifying PISA-OECD reports on UK educational standards. The plain truth is that we have more functionally illiterate and innumerate adults than either Norway or Switzerland has as an overall population. Our decades-long failure to educate a future indigenous workforce for the rigours of earning its way in the global race will be a massive drain on the UK welfare budget for generations. Let's face facts – we are simply neither nimble enough nor sufficiently well-endowed in commodity terms to reinvent ourselves as a Norway or Switzerland on the global economic stage any time soon.

Our reduced military capability and rapid geopolitical and diplomatic developments may soon contribute to the UK no longer enjoying the prestige of a permanent seat on such a narrowly drawn

UN Security Council. Similarly, the chances of the UK sitting at the 'top table' in international affairs and projecting 'British values' upon the rules of the international system of trade and diplomacy would surely be seriously undermined if we stood outside the EU.

Remembering Bismarck's maxim that 'politics is the art of the possible', we ought instead to build upon genuine progress at making the case for a new settlement within the European Union. In our project to remodel the EU, there is a growing band of potential allies, especially among Nordic and Baltic states. Even one of the original Six, the Netherlands, shows an open hostility to 'ever-closer union'. There has been a mood change within the EU since the budget settlement last year. Moreover, Angela Merkel in her visit to Parliament in March accepted explicitly the UK position that Europe needs to protect the Single Market and the UK's financial services interests while allowing the eurozone to develop its own institutions.

Nevertheless, if we are to stand any chance of success in extracting changes, we need to be much clearer about what we are trying to achieve, less belligerent in tone and more mindful of how we are perceived by fellow Member states. Many in France, for instance, are perplexed by British hostility to the EU. Their view of the European Union is one of a club vastly expanded eastwards at the UK's insistence, whose founding principles very much reflect British values of free trade, a huge Single Market and open competition. Moreover it is a club whose Members have gracefully granted the UK exemption from both the euro and Schengen area. In much the same way that many in Westminster believe that Alex Salmond will never be satisfied no matter the concessions or powers granted to Scotland, so the UK is beginning to be seen as an eternal complainer, whose appetite for European reform will never be sated.

Other member states accept that the institutions and rules of the EU are far from perfect. However, many believe that if the UK were truly serious about reshaping the EU, it would have been much more engaged with French, German, Dutch, Polish and Spanish efforts to make its everyday workings and institutions more effective. Rather than getting stuck in with the hard work of incremental reform, British politicians instead prefer domestic grandstanding that inevitably results in constantly refreshed shopping lists of powers that must be returned.

We also need to appreciate another continental reality: a resurgent Russia has and will focus the minds of many of the UK's instinctive allies for EU reform. Poland, the Czech Republic, Finland and the Baltic states will instinctively be reluctant to go out on a limb in opposition to mainstream EU and German interests. They want to stay firmly in the club. Poland and Lithuania also seek to hasten their path into the eurozone as the ultimate insurance policy.

UK politicians and electors alike need to appreciate that the long and winding road to EU reform will not be made easier by insistent – and unrealisable – demands for an exceptionalist set of UK opt-outs.

‡

Modi's India – finally open to business from the City?, 31 May 2014

On 26 May, Narendra Modi was sworn in as the new Prime Minister of India after the world's largest democracy gifted him a hefty personal mandate to enact sweeping change, as well as a gigantic victory for his Bharatiya Janata Party (BJP), which in time would become a formal sister party to the UK Conservatives.

The election had taken five weeks to administer as eight million electoral and security officials moved themselves and their electronic voting machines around the vast country. A record turnout saw 551 million votes cast, with electors delivering the ruling Congress Party its worst-ever result. Their campaign, led by Rahul Gandhi of India's infamous Gandhi-Nehru political dynasty, had failed to stop the remarkable ascent of former chai wallah Modi, who represented the hopes and aspirations of a new generation of young Indians impatient for change. After the failure of former Prime Minister Manmohan Singh's

Congress-led government to tame inflation and rein in corruption, opti-mism abounded that India was on the brink of something special. Modi promised a new era of reform, investment and economic liberalisation.

During his tenure as Chief Minister for Gujarat from 2001 to 2014, however, Modi had been severely criticised for his role in handling anti-Muslim violence in the state and his encouragement of Hindu nationalism, and had until 2012 been effectively boycotted by the UK. Nonetheless, David Cameron swiftly invited the new Prime Minister to visit Britain in a bid to reset our key trading relationship with India amidst hopes that Modi's leadership would prove the start of a boom for the Indian econ-omy. With India's Sensex stock exchange surging in the wake of the BJP's stunning victory, I wrote about my hopes that there might be fresh oppor-tunities for UK firms in the Indian market going forward.

Few would dispute that we have been here before. The opening up to UK investment of commercial opportunities in India has had many a false dawn over recent years.

However, the assent of Narendra Modi to the Indian Prime Ministership promises a new era for the City of London, whose professional services have frequently felt themselves thwarted by red tape and bureaucratic obstruction when doing business there.

It was commonplace until recently to speak of India and China in the same breath as the twin engines of global growth in the twenty-first century. It has understandably pained many Indians to see China storm ahead in the eyes of most global observers over the past decade. India's GDP annual growth rate has plummeted from 10.5 per cent in 2010 to 4.8 per cent last year. While Beijing and Shanghai now feature in the top twenty of the Global Cities Index that compares everything from human capital to cultural and business activity, this year shabby Delhi and chaotic Mumbai rank fifty-seven and forty-one respectively. As China's extensive high-speed rail network is on course to expand by nearly two thirds by 2020, progress towards India's avowed goal of adding 25,000km of new track to its own, rustier rail network is painfully slow – in the five years to 2011, only 1,750km was laid out.

India may have been battered by the storms afflicting global finance over the past five years, but it has many stubborn difficulties of its own making. Assuming continued annual growth of 8 per cent, the Congress-led coalition government of the past decade complacently failed to address India's serious structural problems, all the while undertaking major redistributive welfare programmes that risked higher fiscal and trade deficits.

Similarly, while the nation very successfully carved itself a niche as the world's preferred back office, supplying competitively priced, skilled labour in sectors such as the IT industry, it failed to harness its vast pool of unskilled workers to help build a broad manufacturing base of the kind that China so effectively engineered for itself. That would have required India's government to tackle the many barriers deterring investors. Instead, inflexible labour laws, crumbling infrastructure, hopelessly unreliable power grids, rigid policies on Foreign Direct Investment (FDI) and confusion over land rights remained unaddressed.

A package of sweeping measures announced in September 2012 had stoked optimism that India would finally start to tackle those problems head-on. But apathy and indecision soon took hold, and last summer, India's economy hit a crisis point that saw the rupee tumble and inflation run riot. Small wonder that the nation opted for change as it went to the polls. The mere prospect of a Modi government in the months preceding had already begun to enthuse the capital and equity markets, and attract talented Indians living abroad to consider returning home to join the Modi campaign.

As the Finance Minister who had overseen India's first, ambitious and highly effective programme of economic liberalisation in the early 1990s, there had been hope that Manmohan Singh would usher in a fresh round of deregulation when he took the reins as Prime Minister in 2004. That optimism got buried in red tape and central government indecision, so Indian leadership has form in dashing hopes. Nevertheless, Modi does have a recent, promising record for implementing economic change. Few doubt that Gujarat's infrastructure and economic activity improved markedly under his tenure

as that state's Chief Minister, where he achieved a far higher benchmark for growth than most Indian states, and built a reputation for
'fast-tracking' decision-making over key infrastructure projects. His
state, which accounts for just 5 per cent of the Indian population,
now produces a quarter of the nation's exports.

Modi's election manifesto focused heavily on the promotion of
job-creating, labour-intensive manufacturing. As Prime Minister, he
will implicitly understand that his greatest chance of re-election lies
in providing jobs to the low-skilled masses, particularly the young.
Meanwhile in China, wages rise, the workforce shrinks, and Beijing
is beginning to refocus from a state-led investment model to one of
higher domestic consumption. It is thought that up to 85 million
Chinese manufacturing jobs are now up for grabs, providing a unique
opportunity for India to step into the space China is vacating.

If that is to happen, however, Modi needs to use his mandate to
overhaul India's infrastructure, and use it quickly. Urgent action will
be required to build new or upgrade existing ports, power grids, rail
and road networks and more. The ending of electoral uncertainty
alone may be sufficient to bring many stalled projects back on course
– fortuitously, there are several in the pipeline that are well placed to
transition quickly from aspiration to reality. UK expertise is already
at hand when it comes to providing technical, construction, consulting, and legal services for precisely these types of projects, while
a number of participants have been able to tap into the immense
funding opportunities that the City of London provides through
public and private markets for both equity and debt.

Modi avoided specifics in his campaign but is reportedly keen to
privatise or give greater autonomy to a slew of state-owned enterprises (only four out of India's ten largest companies is currently
in private hands), possibly starting with the loss-making Air India.
Hopes are high that he will also give the green light to the liberalisation of a broader range of industries in the hope of attracting
fresh foreign capital and expertise in a market of 1.2 billion. The
BJP manifesto stated it would permit FDI in any sectors where it
would bring job and asset creation. While it specifically excluded

supermarkets, Modi began backtracking on that exception in the latter stages of his campaign, suggesting that his government need not stick to reversing the decision to allow FDI in multi-brand retail.

Might he also be the man finally to crack open the professional services sector? Top US and UK professional services firms have been successful at building a presence in leading Chinese cities via joint ventures. However, protectionist sentiment has hitherto crowded this route out in India, which has been a closed market for English law firms in spite of the similarities between our legal systems. It will require great political will from the centre to overcome stiff opposition to liberalisation from Indian corporate law firms, but the UK government must give vocal support to City professional services in working with Indian business.

In short, should the Modi premiership live up to its hype, there will be an array of sectors in which British expertise might be utilised.

This will all be music to the ears of David Cameron. At the outset of his coalition administration in 2010, he placed an expansion of trade with the East, in particular India, as a top priority. However, his high-profile trade missions, while entirely correctly intentioned, have failed to reap the rewards we all hoped they would. Nevertheless, the window of opportunity for British business in the subcontinent may prove narrow. In truth, Modi probably has only a couple of years to make his mark before vested interests begin to hammer at his door and the inherent inertia of Indian political culture sets in.

Furthermore, British firms will not be alone in wishing to take advantage of opportunities in the new-look India. In search of a home for some of its $3.8 trillion of reserves, the Chinese government earlier this year offered to finance 30 per cent of India's infrastructure in a targeted plan. It was an offer turned down by the Congress-led coalition, wary of relinquishing too much control to its regional rival. However, Mr Modi may well see a review of that offer as a key way to reset relations with his Chinese counterparts and a mark of his outward-looking intent. Meanwhile, both Japan and the US already have extensive involvement in the financing and engineering of Indian infrastructure, where they have been far more successful at taking advantage of the country's vast opportunities than the UK has, in spite of India's tough trading climate.

As this great Asian giant awakes to an exciting new era, there is a unique – but potentially only brief – opportunity for UK professionals and service providers to place themselves at the forefront of India's reform process. We must all now firmly hope that Modi's victory does not prove another false Indian dawn for British firms from a trading relationship that should hold such incredible promise.

‡

The eurozone crisis is not over – it could erupt at any time (*Daily Telegraph*), 13 June 2014

In the event, UKIP topped the national poll in the European elections on 22 May – the first time since 1906 that neither Conservatives nor Labour had won a popular national vote in the UK. Conservatives were pushed into third place, while the Liberal Democrats were virtually wiped out, left with only one MEP. The calls duly came for the Prime Minister to toughen up his negotiating stance with the EU before the proposed 2017 referendum.

In this article for the Daily Telegraph, *I assessed the health of the eurozone and looked also at the economic dangers facing the UK.*

The results from May's European elections are in, and a damning verdict of 'no confidence' in the European establishment issued. Taking their seats in the new-look European Parliament is now a bewilderingly diverse array of sceptics and single-issue campaigners from all quarters of the EU, while the number of MEPs from Eurosceptic parties has doubled.

In spite of this, there is a palpable sense of relief at European political conferences these days. No longer are continental leaders lurching from one eurozone crisis summit to the next. The more discussion centres upon the EU's political structure, the clearer the

overriding message that 'the euro crisis is over' – or at least the likelihood of any nation being forced out of the eurozone has now passed.
While the West seems unable to rid itself of its addiction to printing
money, the President of the European Central Bank, Mario Draghi,
has at least provided confidence and stability.

It is even possible to detect a faint whiff of smugness as emerging markets wobble in response to the Fed's cautious tapering of
its money-printing bonanza. Not for eurozone members, the easy
option of devaluation and inflation that the likes of India and Turkey
are now pursuing to motor their economies out of trouble. Instead,
they have gritted their teeth and endured tough austerity measures
and supply-side reform. A leaner, more competitive eurozone will
be the result, with the currency union remaining firmly intact.

That, at least, is the official political line.

It is interesting to note that this euphoric declaration of victory
is not even remotely shared by the German public, some 81 per cent
of whom in an April 2014 opinion poll reckoned the eurozone crisis
has further to run (only 7 per cent believe it is 'crisis over').

For now, however, the financial markets intend to make hay. Even
hapless Greece has proved able to get a bond issue away with investors helping themselves at Easter to €3 billion of five-year bonds
at 4.75 per cent. Much as we should all like to attribute this to the
innate strengths of the Greek economy, the truth gives less cause for
optimism. Nigh on six successive years of relentless recession and
a reduction of over one-quarter in GDP suggests that this revival
in fortunes owes more to confidence on the part of financial markets that fellow eurozone members will prop up Greece regardless.
Indeed if the economic fundamentals in Athens still look weak,
the more likely scenario for Grexit is if the increasingly unstable
Samaras coalition falls.

Now that a difficult set of European Parliament elections is
behind us, it should not be forgotten that the German constitutional court has still not categorically endorsed the European Central
Bank's assertion that it is empowered to buy up unlimited amounts
of government bonds issued by financially embarrassed eurozone

nations via the so-called Outright Monetary Transactions programme (otherwise known as Draghi's 'big bazooka').

The argument that the programme might infringe the powers
of the member states will become ever louder in German legal and
political circles if and when a eurozone default becomes imminent.
Until now, Mr Draghi's pronouncements have been a (rather successful) confidence trick – the reason the ECB has not bought up a
single euro-denominated government bond is that it cannot do so.

Having refused to approve formally of the ECB's new powers, the
German constitutional court (always aware of the nation's deep psy-
chological aversion to inflationary money-printing) has passed the
buck to the European Court of Justice. It is essentially playing for
time, all too aware that the outright monetisation of eurozone debt
would appal the German public, while understanding that the programme is the invisible glue holding the currency union together.
Without it, a new stage of the crisis is on the cards.

Smoke and mirrors have been similarly employed to cast a veil of
opacity over the eurozone's troubled banking sector. For five years,
the ECB has been quietly absorbing the toxic assets of members'
banks, doubling its own balance sheet in the process. We are told
this will mean that the results of their next stress test, due in the
autumn, will find them in rude health – a necessary conclusion for
any banking union. Yet no one truly knows which banks are solvent
or not, so deliberately obscure are their balance sheets.

In short, the eurozone remains in a state of limbo. No member
will countenance a return to sovereign independence, yet none has
fully endorsed the further relinquishment of power required for a
politically integrated currency union.

All this at a time when gradual monetary tightening seems, in the
US and China at least, to be the order of the day. In all likelihood,
we are only two or three years away from the end of this current
'upward' cycle of the global economy. Heaven help the eurozone if
this cyclical phase of the global economy comes to an end before austerity and macro-economic contraction in weaker European nations
has ceased.

Nevertheless, it is – as ever – wishful thinking to believe that economics, rather than politics, dictates the pace on matters concerning the eurozone.

Within days of the Russian annexation of Crimea, the Polish Foreign Minister, Radek Sikorski, announced that his country wished to fast-track its application to join the euro. No ifs or buts. It was made explicitly clear that this was a political decision designed to tie Poland more securely into the EU and German axis irrespective of its economic consequences. Indeed, the resurgence of Russia in the region has also persuaded Lithuania to follow suit, having previously taken a critical stance of their Baltic neighbours, Estonia and Latvia, for having rushed headlong into the single currency.

As ever, this does not augur well for the underlying economic stability of the eurozone, and the recent relative calm has allowed complacency to creep in. Events in Ukraine threaten to cast a long shadow over European affairs.

Needless to say, here in the UK we can scarcely be said to be sitting pretty as the next phase of the eurozone saga develops. We still undertake over two fifths of our trade with the eurozone. Indeed one of the main reasons we are apparently less exposed is that the UK economy, ironically enough given the domestic party political battles over immigration, has benefited from highly skilled migration from the weakest eurozone nations, which has helped accelerate our own economic growth.

Last autumn, the US Treasury expressed a fear that the eurozone is now adding a permanent deflationary bias to the global economy, and this too has the potential to blow our own recovery off the rails. The public has been lulled into a false sense of security with relentless talk of the deficit being driven down and a narrative that public services have been slashed. In reality, public debt has grown rapidly throughout the coalition's tenure, household debt remains uncomfortably high and the majority of public spending cuts will need to come after 2015. Deflation exported from the eurozone will make tackling that debt a far harder task. While the debt mountain will remain the same, the income to service it is likely to fall.

Similarly, British wages might have to be held down longer in order to compete with falling continental labour costs. This is before even taking into account the potential for an increasingly discontented eurozone citizenry to throw up new, market-jangling political challenges. It may be that our careful husbandry of the British economy becomes largely irrelevant when faced with further continental shockwaves.

The European currency union has lived to see another day. But there is no room for euphoria. The eurozone crisis is only dormant, with all too much scope for a fresh eruption.

‡

Temper your faith in the Lords of Finance, 1 July 2014

A year has now passed since the first foreign governor in the Bank of England's 319-year history sailed into Threadneedle Street on a wave of admiration. 'Mark Carney: The George Clooney of Finance', swooned the *New Statesman*, previewing the Canadian's arrival by praising his 'matinee idol good looks' and 'messianic' early beginnings. This seemed in stark contrast to the dry, inscrutable, academic manner of the departing governor, Sir Mervyn (now Lord) King, whose management of the prelude to and aftermath of 2008's financial crisis had come in for widespread criticism.

Meanwhile on the continent, European leaders worship at the altar of Mario Draghi, the suave Italian banker who replaced greying French bureaucrat Jean-Claude Trichet as President of the European Central Bank in 2012. Dubbed 'Super Mario', he has been hailed for staving off further crisis in the eurozone with the mere hint that he would use a 'big bazooka' of policy initiatives to keep the single currency going. As Draghi himself said with surprise, 'There was a time, not too long ago, when central banking was considered to be a rather boring and unexciting occupation.'

Yet the cult of the central banker is nothing new. Indeed, electorates and politicians have form in placing unbridled faith in unelected central bankers at times of extreme economic crisis and shattered trust in elected politicians. The problem is, such faith all too frequently proves to be distressingly misplaced.

The super-star central banker was initially an inter-war phenomenon, born from the unremitting faith the Big Four capitalist nations of the time (Britain, the US, Germany and France) placed in what Liaquat Ahamed in 2009 dubbed the *Lords of Finance* in his eponymous, magisterial book. In the 1920s, a quartet of elite bankers – the Bank of England's Montagu Norman, Benjamin Strong of the Federal Reserve, Emile Moreau of the Bank de France and Hjalmar Schacht, President of the Reichsbank – had dominated global finance. Labelled the 'Most Exclusive Club in the World', the press had been in awe of how the foursome steered Western economies through the aftermath of the Great War. But they failed to anticipate the deflationary effects of their protectionist policy prescriptions. By 1931 only Norman was still in place.

He, Strong and Schacht, entranced by the deadening orthodoxy of sound money, believed that returning the world to the gold standard would best tackle the impact of reparations and war debts. Here in the UK, even as strong-willed a politician as Winston Churchill, who became Chancellor of the Exchequer in 1924, was railroaded into supporting a return to fixed exchange rates in the face of establishment expertise and the accusation that any failure to act would be tantamount to admitting Britain's diminished global status. But the unassailable central bankers misaligned the rates of exchange and stoked up a credit bubble through artificially low US interest rates and colossal German borrowing. The road to ruin in 1929 and beyond was now set. For all the central bankers' immense prestige, the gold standard crippled their room for manoeuvre when the global financial system went into freefall.

Manifestly, the lessons of that era have been learned. Arguably, however, the extent and duration of active intervention by a new generation of central bankers after the 2008 crisis brings with it a different set of (to date unchallenged) problems that will, eventually, need fixing. We can only hope that events will allow us to do this at a time of our choosing.

As he celebrates his first anniversary at the helm as Governor of the Bank of England, Mark Carney has probably exceeded the high expectations that accompanied his arrival in mid-2013. To date, at least. Some of that has been down to luck and good timing: the delayed impact of unprecedented domestic QE stimulus and a lull in the eurozone saga provided that space of confidence that released pent-up demand in the UK economy.

Indeed, governor Carney's main strategic innovation – the promotion of 'forward guidance' – has proved an essentially cosmetic exercise. His inaugural announcement that ultra-low interest rates were here to stay, unchanged until such time as unemployment dipped below 7 per cent, was designed primarily to provide business with a sense of certainty and confidence in a bid to kick-start investment. It was also a political gambit by this most politically attuned of governors. The expectation was that, even with economic growth, unemployment would stay above the prescribed level until at least May 2015, the date of the next general election.

Purists might raise an eyebrow as to the notional independence of the Bank, especially as its inflation target had been surpassed each and every month for almost four years by the time the forward guidance was issued. If Mr Carney had enjoyed less goodwill, the fact that unemployment has fallen sharply and to a level below the 7 per cent threshold might have fatally undermined the governor's credibility. As it is, in spite of recent hints of a rate rise, the presumption remains that interest rates will remain at rock bottom levels until the general election is safely behind us, and there is little pretence that this is in large part a political calculation.

However, it would be a mistake to believe that the Bank of England's policy of ultra-low interest rates (now beached at an unprecedented 0.5 per cent for the past sixty-three months) comes without detriment to our future economic welfare. Near-zero rates have retarded the essential cleansing mechanism of capitalism. Countless so-called 'zombie companies' remain in existence as lending banks have no need to pull the plug on non-performers. This tying up of capital and labour in non-productive activity has engendered a false sense of security and boosted short-term employment levels. It also means that risk has been continually mispriced over recent years. All this suggests the creation of unsustainable bubbles in the economy and also augurs ill in the teeth of fierce global competition in the decade ahead.

Meanwhile, in spite of Mario Draghi throwing a blanket of promised bond-buying over the eurozone, the playing out of grinding austerity on the continent shows that one perennial economic truism has not been properly accounted for – every large debtor at some point realises that when owing huge amounts of money, threatening default can give one the upper hand. Greece, Portugal, Spain and Italy all now find themselves in this boat.

No matter the notional independence of these central bankers, politicians have been willingly complicit in their strategies. Since the 1990s, governments have been relinquishing control of monetary policy to independent central banks in the hope of freeing decisions from political intervention. While this should have helped governments and central banks in their principal task – the promotion of a stable monetary and legal framework that lubricates the economy with trust, the most crucial ingredient in any transaction – it has also had the effect of liberating politicians from the shackles of accountability and the urgent need to engage in tough economic reform.

Since 2008, the implicit message to central bankers has been to 'Keep things calm and keep the money flowing'. The US Fed, now under Janet Yellen, has accepted an employment target around which to frame its interest rate policy; the Bank of England aims to achieve a nominal GDP; the European Central Bank does whatever it takes to save the single currency. None of these goals has the maintenance of trust at their heart and all could eventually serve to undermine capitalism. Meanwhile, keeping monetary policy at arm's-length has allowed politicians, in the case of the eurozone, to preside over the transfer of unprecedented amounts of financial sovereignty with minimal popular alarm.

The contemporary cult of the central banker is, in part, a reflection of voters' despair with the political class across the Western world. Politicians, implicitly lacking faith in their *own* judgement, have been happy to relinquish responsibility to a new financial elite. Perversely, while bankers have never been held in lower public regard, elevation to central banker status has bestowed a new level of trust in Goldman Sachs alumni, Carney and Draghi. Central bankers have acted entirely rationally in insulating us from the most immediate, pernicious effects of the financial crisis. But they are essentially leading us into a world where risk is being improperly assessed. When the next downturn is in train, their actions may only exacerbate feelings of popular and political impotence. Just as with the financial superstars of the 1920s, we may well discover that their judgement is not so unassailable after all.

‡

Ukraine – a never-ending story, 17 July 2014

Since I had last written about the Ukrainian crisis in March, the conflict had both deepened and broadened. In Crimea, a referendum on 16 March proposing to join the Russian Federation had received the backing of 97 per cent of those in the province. While the West condemned it as a sham, Putin swiftly passed a resolution in the Russian Duma to absorb Crimea. Sanctions, travel bans and asset freezes against Russians followed as the EU and United States sought to increase international pressure on Putin.

The Russian President retaliated by fomenting rebellion in the Russian-speaking, eastern Ukrainian cities of Donetsk, Luhansk and Kharkiv, where protestors stormed government buildings. Secession referenda soon followed in Donetsk and Luhansk, with the Ukrainian government in turn launching military operations against Russian-backed rebels. By May, a fresh presidential election saw Petro Poroshenko take the reins, but with many eastern regions declining to hold the poll, from the outset he was unrecognised by considerable swathes of his own country.

Meanwhile, the mainstream media in the West was distracted by the emergence of a brutal new militia group ISIS which had declared on 30 June a caliphate in its newly won territory stretching from Aleppo in northern Syria to Diyala in eastern Iraq. Proclaiming its leader, Abu Bakr al-Baghdadi, the global caliph, ISIS purported to represent Muslims across the world and encouraged them to 'shake off the dust of humiliation and disgrace' by joining the new state.

Overshadowed by the barbarism of ISIS, the Ukrainian crisis receded to the back pages until events took a tragic turn on the day I published the following article. As it travelled over the Ukrainian village of Grabove, Malaysia Airlines flight MH17 was shot down, leading to the loss of 298 lives. Russian-backed rebels were blamed for the tragedy.

As the black flag of jihad has been hoisted over a large swathe of Iraq, it is perhaps unsurprising that the streets of Kiev have receded in the rear-view mirror of global crises. Ukraine's new President Poroshenko, elected in May, now appears to be robustly keeping separatists at bay in Sloviansk and Donetsk. President Putin seems content that his annexation of Crimea has kept intact Russia's defence interests in the Black Sea. Meanwhile, Western sanctions – or at least the threat of them – appear to be doing their job. Britain's Ukraine problem, while not over, is now under control.

Naturally, it is tempting to conclude that when an item falls off news bulletins, the moment of danger has passed.

Yet Putin still has no interest in the remainder of Ukraine becoming a united, more Western-facing nation. Indeed, his interest is in keeping battles in its eastern provinces raging. He will be relying on Europe and the United States to take their eyes off this ball – it must be made clear to him that this will not happen.

The Crimean crisis baffled many in the West, who failed to grasp why Vladimir Putin would engineer an old-fashioned, imperialistic land-grab that risked Western ire and Russian firms' balance sheets. Nor have they understood why reincorporation into Russia would seem such an enticing prospect for people only recently freed from the Soviet yolk.

But the Russian President is a master at fashioning strength from weakness. His handling of the Ukrainian crisis is a supreme case in point.

The toppling in February of inept Kremlin ally Viktor Yanukovych from the Ukrainian Presidency was a massively embarrassing blow to Russian prestige. In swiftly taking the initiative by first invading Crimea and then securing an (albeit dubious) democratic mandate for its return to Russia, Putin achieved several objectives.

From a position of fragile financial and geopolitical clout, Putin boosted his profile with a domestic and global audience as a champion for the interests of Russia and the Russian diaspora. His approval rating at home soared to 80 per cent after the Crimean invasion. The challenge and counterweight he presented to Western hegemony also won him quiet support among a broader community of states increasingly unwilling to dance to the USA's tune.

In practical terms, Putin has long feared encirclement by nations no longer within the Russian orbit. In taking a firm stance over Ukraine, which looked set to be absorbed into Europe's economic structure and NATO's ambit, he set down a marker that his nation would not tolerate further encroachment into its sphere of influence. Russia will not have forgotten the lessons from 1956, when a Hungarian uprising was brutally suppressed at a time when Western attention was focused firmly on the Suez crisis.

To his great enjoyment, Putin has also been able to expose to the full glare of global media attention the flimsiness of Western resolve. Bellicose rhetoric from NATO leaders was matched with inaction. Promises of protection remained unfulfilled. Just as in Syria, Russia was able to place itself at the centre of geopolitical negotiation and speculation without great cost. Putin now knows that in probing Europe's borders, he meets not a formidable armour but a soft underbelly. Meanwhile, he has further exposed US battle fatigue, already evident from American withdrawal from Iraq and Afghanistan, at the prospect of further global engagement. The lack of Western confidence in projecting its values and doing more than rattle sabres in support of those seeking its help will have undermined its alliances across the world.

On the face of it, Putin's objectives have been met by the actions he has already taken. He has ruled out further military encroachments, stilling Western nerves. But rest assured, the Ukrainian story is not over. Russia needs to keep this conflict live to ensure that there will be no further moves into its sphere of influence. The next phase of this Ukrainian battle of wills may see Putin navigating a far narrower course – stoking the flames of separatist passion through the provision of arms and the projection of power, while being able plausibly to deny Russian involvement. Without the money, desire or military reach to extend his nation more broadly, Putin now creates power through proxy wars and creative new mechanisms for mischief – the Russian state has become expert in the field of cyberwarfare, for example, with high-profile attacks on Estonia in 2007 and South Ossetia in 2008 wonderfully difficult to pin blame for.

So what should the West do? Make clear that it too has ways of getting its message across without needing to resort to hard military power. Foremost in its arsenal are sanctions, and we must realise that those already in place are working. The rouble is fast losing value, while capital is streaming out of Russia. Meanwhile, inward investment has plummeted and Russian companies are finding it far harder to access foreign credit. GDP growth this year will be close to zero. This is highly damaging to the Russian President.

Putin is surrounded by an elite keen to preserve their powerful business interests, dazzling wealth and access to the luxury goods, lifestyle, properties and schools offered by the West. The prospect of being placed on an international blacklist by Europe and the US, with assets frozen and visas cancelled, is a sobering one for Putin's cronies. Let us not forget either that many of this elite's companies have already had to make significant cash calls because of the double-digit collapse of the Moscow stock market.

If we are not to engage militarily in the Ukraine, we must at least continue to show the Russian President that we are serious when it comes to sanctions, even if this course of action harms our short-term financial interests (and I say that as the MP for a central London seat which has benefited enormously from Russian wealth in recent years). It may prove inconvenient, unpredictable and painful, but Russia needs to know that the benefit of the West's outward looking, free trade and liberal economic institutions will not be open to its companies and countrymen if it continues to test our resolve.

In the longer term, it is vital that Europe reduces its reliance on and exposure to Russian oil and gas. The United States should assist in this regard, removing all barriers to exporting its own energy resource to the region and encouraging Europe's energy independence by sharing new technologies, such as those around shale gas.

President Putin knew from the outset that Ukraine was a conflict that Western leaders wished would go away. In the world of power politics, he now needs to know that this is not a nation we are willing to allow to fall by the wayside. Should he remain determined to pour oil on this fire, we must have our own resolute strategy in response.

‡

Is protectionism part of the 'new economics'?, 5 August 2014

At the end of May, US drugs firm Pfizer admitted defeat in its attempt to launch a takeover of British pharmaceutical company Astra Zeneca. It had been a hugely controversial deal, as politicians feared for the future of seven thousand highly skilled British jobs and the creation of a monopolistic drugs giant. Similarly, US politicians raised their eyebrows at plans to shift Pfizer's tax residence to the UK in order to shelter its revenues from US taxation.

The deal reignited debate within the coalition about the desirability of foreign takeovers of British firms – a topic first discussed during the hotly contested purchase of Cadbury by US food giant Kraft in 2010. In his own contribution to the discussion, Business Secretary Vince Cable suggested that a raft of fines could be imposed on foreign firms if they failed to fulfil conditions to protect UK jobs and investment post-takeover. He also mooted the idea of widening the public interest test such that British firms could be better protected from hostile takeover. In this article, I examined the politics behind the Business Secretary's proposals.

'If Britain advertises itself as a tax-friendly country, it would be a strange position to adopt by saying to foreign firms, "you shouldn't come here"'. These were the wise words of Business Secretary Vince Cable, a little over a fortnight ago.

In the aftermath of the highly controversial, failed bid by US pharmaceutical firm Pfizer in May, for its smaller UK counterpart Astra Zeneca, Dr Cable had been rightly anxious to still market nerves. While the dust had started to settle, confused political signals had fed concern that rules on foreign takeovers would be tightened.

Yet, less than a week later, Dr Cable was upping the ante. Sketching out a new set of plans to govern the bids of international firms, the Business Secretary suggested ministers should be able to prevent foreign takeovers if they doubted the bidder's motives. This is designed to complement existing powers to intervene in deals threatening financial stability, national security or media plurality. Dr Cable's brave new world would also see hefty fines for foreign firms in breach of any conditions imposed during a takeover, such as guarantees on jobs and research.

It is, perhaps, an irresistible temptation. Politicians as a breed like to hand themselves additional powers to counter accusations of impotence whenever media storms take hold. But it is one which must resolutely be resisted if the UK is to maintain its reputation as an open, mercantile nation that embraces global investment.

Mr Cable's plans have already been criticised by BAE Systems chairman Sir Roger Carr, who has suggested the reforms could place governments in an invidious position, meddling in deals that should rightly be left to the market. This from a man who, when chairman of Cadbury in 2009, aggressively battled to defend the British confectioner against a hostile takeover bid by American food giant Kraft.

At that time, fears abounded among the public and shareholders alike that the beloved British firm would be gobbled by a low-growth, inflexible American behemoth, with jobs and factories shed in double-quick time. Indeed, shortly after the takeover, Kraft cut 200 jobs from its Cadbury division and announced the closure of its Somerdale factory. But this does not show the whole picture.

What nobody knew at the time was that Kraft was planning to split into two more dynamic entities. Cadbury was the final acquisition in this regard, giving the new snacks side of the business sufficient scale to compete in key markets like India. After the jobs were shed, £50 million of fresh investment flowed into the UK, £14 million of which was poured into the historic Bournville site to make it a cutting-edge research centre.

And here lies the point. Nobody knows what impact a foreign takeover will have on British jobs, innovation and competitiveness. Job losses often immediately follow mergers because the new entity is reducing overlap in the two firms' operations. Of course this feeds the very panic that preceded the deal, reinforcing the notion that foreign takeovers are 'bad for Britain'. But seldom is any analysis undertaken a few years down the line into the longer-term benefits of a merger. Our financial services and car manufacturing businesses, many of which are foreign-owned, thrive in the UK not because of jobs guarantees but because their operations in the UK are lean, well-managed and operate within a well-regulated and competitively taxed jurisdiction.

In adopting greater powers to impose conditions on any deal, ministers risk exposing themselves to lobbying from MPs naturally anxious to keep jobs and investment in their constituencies. Yet the preservation of a colleague's career by securing in their seat short-term jobs guarantees should not be the basis for assessing the worth of a commercial deal. That is a decision best dictated by shareholders. Furthermore, even if guarantees are written into any deal, how might they be enforced? Should economic or market conditions change, surely we would want the merged firm to be able to respond flexibly, shedding jobs in the short term if it allows for a company's longer-term survival, with all the benefits to jobs and growth.

Here in the UK, we have in place a takeover regime regulated by independent bodies (including the Competition and Markets Authority and Takeover Panel), as well as existing government powers, to frustrate truly disadvantageous bids. Should we succumb to short-termist meddling by ministers in addition to this regime, we open ourselves up to legal challenge and longer-term damage to our reputation as a liberal, open economy.

The Business Secretary's plans, revealed just under a year before the general election, must be called for what they are – protectionist, political posturings designed to booster the brand of a party which may soon have to consider a couple of merger bids of its own.

‡

A lesson from history and a pathway to the future, 12 August 2014

One year on from the failed vote on British intervention in Syria, the scales had fallen off our eyes when it came to the wisdom of arming groups opposed to President Assad. It was now clear that in addition to the Free Syrian Army, the nation had been infiltrated by all manner of militia, backed by a range of regional actors who sought to further their own interests at the expense of the hapless Syrian population. The most famous and feared of the militias was ISIS, but it was clear too that Assad was bringing in his own back-up from Russia and Iran.

In the absence of palatable choices, the West began to look at supporting Kurdish Peshmerga forces who had found themselves in the front line of the battle against ISIS, a group now lodged in the public's mind as the primary enemy and threat. I suggested in this article that this could represent the first steps in the eventual break-up of both Iraq and Syria.

Understandably, much current historic coverage has concentrated on the centenary of the outbreak of the Great War. But it was the Treaties of Versailles and Sevres, painstakingly negotiated at the end of hostilities, which have had a truly lasting impact – arguably to this day.

The spoils of the First World War involved victorious politicians and diplomats redrawing maps of the Old World from afar, taking little account of local sensitivities. In much of Europe, it was only after a second global conflict that national boundaries and ethnic populations were aligned. In 1945, some nine million civilians, mainly of German ethnic origin, were forcibly repatriated in a process that today would be described as ethnic cleansing. My late mother, then a five-year-old girl, was one of that huge number of displaced persons. Her birthplace, Breslau (now Polish Wroclaw), had been a Germanic town since 1242.

One small quarter of post-Versailles Europe, Yugoslavia, was spared that disruption. However, as we know, nationalistic fervour and old ethnic enmities resurfaced into a series of brutal Balkan civil wars during the 1990s. The massacre at Srebrenica of some 7,000 Bosnian Muslims under the noses of 400 Dutch soldiers in a so-called UN safe area was only the worst of many atrocities.

Peace in the Balkans has only been achieved by dismantling Yugoslavia into a collection of new 'nations' and inflicting the misery of displacement on millions.

The Treaty of Sevres divided up the Ottoman Empire of the defeated Turks. This vast and ancient empire had embraced much of the Middle East and Arabia. A new collection of countries was created: Lebanon on the Mediterranean coast was seen as a haven for Maronite and Orthodox Christians; Saudi Arabia brought together an array of small sheikhdoms. Iraq was the most contrived state – artificially created by French and British diplomats and populated by Muslims, Jews, Christians and tribes of various small minority sects that had somehow survived countless centuries in this cauldron of religious innovation.

I fear that what we now see being played out in Iraq with the terrifyingly swift emergence of the Sunni jihadists, ISIS, will lead to a similar outcome of a divided country with some of its longstanding population being permanently displaced.

I have written before about the plight of Christians in the Middle East and the Foreign Office's misplaced naïvety as the so-called Arab Spring developed. The West's collusion in regime change leading to the toppling of dictators we had previously supported in Egypt and

Libya, and our continued support of rebels against Assad in Syria, has destabilised the entire region.

These profound policy blunders, coupled with plentiful financial support from resource-rich Sunni backers in Saudi Arabia and Qatar, have allowed ISIS to thrive. The temptation on the part of war-weary electorates in the West to leave this part of the world to fight its own battles is entirely understandable. However, our political leaders need to spell out the consequences of allowing the humanitarian catastrophe to unfold and ISIS to gather increasing strength. Hundreds of UK citizens are already out in Syria and Iraq fighting for the fanatic Islamists; many seek to return to these shores and continue their terrorist activity.

In the Kurdish minority in Iraq, we have a faction we can and should urgently support. If UK involvement is to extend beyond intelligence cooperation and humanitarian help, our government will need to level with the British public now about the potential extent of our future involvement. UK airstrikes, drone attacks and the arming of and military support to the Peshmerga may follow within weeks. I suspect as part of a UN peacekeeping operation we shall (defence cuts permitting) at some point also need to put troops on the ground in Iraq and Syria. Alongside other Western nations, we will almost certainly need to offer asylum to substantial numbers of Christian and other minorities displaced in this conflict.

The public will need to be made aware that there is no guarantee of success. Our involvement here may lead to escalating atrocities and fearful terrorist attacks on British soil.

Last August's lost vote on potential action in Syria (ironically to support indirectly some of the very people who now form the nucleus of ISIS) has also set a clear precedent. No UK government can embark upon any such path without the consent and approval of Parliament. This is a fast-moving situation, but I would anticipate a recall of Parliament within the week.

‡

Forward guidance – a political gambit that has retarded true capitalism (*City AM*), 19 August 2014

In August 2013, Bank of England Governor Mark Carney had issued an explicit indication that interest rates would be lowered once unemployment had fallen below 7 per cent. One year on, I wrote the following review of his 'forward guidance' policy innovation for City AM, *questioning the extent to which economics can ever really be separated from politics.*

'It's a mistake to try and get too precise,' suggested Stanley Fischer last September, shortly before he was appointed as vice-chairman of the Federal Reserve. 'You can't expect the Fed to spell out what it's going to do. Why? Because it doesn't know.'

The Governor of the Bank of England, Mark Carney, may now be wishing he had shared Fischer's view on 'forward guidance' rather than make it the centrepiece of his first year at Threadneedle Street. The more mixed Carney's messages, the clearer it becomes that forward guidance (an indication of the Bank's intentions over interest rates) has been an essentially cosmetic exercise.

Governor Carney's inaugural announcement that ultra-low interest rates were here to stay, unchanged until such time as unemployment dipped below 7 per cent, was designed primarily to provide business with a sense of certainty in order that it kick-start investment. Back in August 2013, the safe presumption was that we would not see such a dip until early 2016.

Yet when joblessness fell faster than anyone predicted, Carney ditched its link to interest rates only six months after his announcement. Rate rises, he advised, would now be judged against a much broader range of economic indicators. So it was that at the launch of the Bank of England's most recent inflation report, the Governor highlighted stagnating wage growth as a major problem in the economy and another reason to believe there would be no rate hike before 2015. Yet, only days later, the Governor mooted the idea of increased rates *before* households begin to benefit from improved living standards.

A policy explicitly designed to give certainty seems now only to breed confusion. It is hard not to conclude that forward guidance has not just been an economic gambit, but a political one, with the Governor's primary goal to keep any rate increase at bay until next May's general election has safely passed. Either that, or the Governor implicitly believes that the recovery (as well as the finances of businesses and households) remains insufficiently robust to withstand the application even of a gradual increase in the cost of borrowing.

It is not surprising that questions are now being asked about the notional independence of the Bank of England, which had already been put in doubt after four years of flunked inflation targeting that were only brought to an end in December. I am not suggesting any formal collusion between the Treasury and the Bank of England, but Chancellor George Osborne has surely had an unspoken understanding with Governor Carney from the outset of their relationship.

The Chancellor was probably most attracted by the prospect of an incoming Governor prepared to maintain the rock-bottom rates that had been in place since 2009. Such rates have unquestionably staved off considerable personal misery for many and bought the government time to shore up a rapidly sinking ship. There is little doubt that resultant, inflated house prices have also injected the feel-good factor into the veins of an important quarter of the electorate. Meanwhile, with the date of destiny with the voters soon upon us, brave would be the Governor who risked his patron's scorn with a rate hike in advance of 2015's poll.

Nevertheless, the question that should be foremost in the minds of policymakers after five straight years of emergency monetary stimulus is: at what cost to the nation's long-term economic interests? Near-zero rates have retarded the essential cleansing mechanism of capitalism. This tying up of capital and labour in non-productive activity has engendered a false sense of security and boosted short-term employment levels. It also means that risk has been continually mispriced over recent years. All this suggests the creation of unsustainable bubbles in the economy and also augurs ill in the teeth of fierce global competition in the decade ahead.

Since, understandably, there is neither the commercial appetite nor political nerve to precipitate the bankruptcies and repossessions that would help wipe the economy's slate clean, expect ever more vacillation from the Governor to obscure the fact that in all probability, the Bank made its mind up on interest rates long ago...

‡

Politicians should listen to what voters are saying – and welcome international students into Britain, 25 August 2014

Continuing my Conservatives for Managed Migration campaign, I wrote the following foreword for a Universities UK report that published research on public attitudes to migration. While repeated opinion polls showed the breadth of public concern about immigration when it came to wages, jobs, cultural issues and the pace of change in towns and cities, Universities UK's detailed polling showed that the concern did not extend to international students. With international students from outside the EU bringing £7 billion annually to the UK economy, I argued that their number should be counted separately to broader statistics on migration since the clamour to reduce headline figures was damaging Britain's vital higher education industry.

Here in the United Kingdom we are rightly proud of our world-class universities.

Our global reputation for higher education excellence helps to explain why the UK is such an attractive place for people to study.

Almost 300,000 international students came to our universities in 2012–13. Only the United States matches the strength of this appeal to students from around the world.

A global brand such as this is also fantastic news for our economy. Top international students and academics keep our universities at the cutting edge of global knowledge, technology and innovation. The diversity they bring to campus life enriches the educational experience for British students and helps build strong links with other nations for decades into the future. They bring with them an estimated £7 billion in income, injecting substance into the UK's economic recovery. What better example of a true British success story in what the Prime Minister has called the 'global race'?

However there is a twist in this tale. The sheer strength of the UK's higher educational offering means that international students make up a significant proportion of those counted in the official immigration statistics. This often comes as a surprise to those who are not specialists in this subject. After all, few people have students in mind when they express concern about the impact and number of migrants coming to our shores.

This creates a dilemma when it comes politically to managing the tricky minefield of migration. Any uplift in the number of international students means greater scientific, economic and cultural benefit to Britain. Yet it also spells trouble for politicians trying desperately to cut headline immigration figures. A mark of our success therefore acts simultaneously – and perversely – as a badge of failure.

It need not be this way. This comprehensive report shows that students are among the most popular migrants with the public, in spite of their representing one of the largest inflows of people coming to the UK. Even the majority of those sympathetic to the overall aim of reducing migration believe that student migration is a good thing, both economically and culturally. So long as students are genuine, the public believes this issue should be kept apart from immigration policy.

At a time when Britain is seeking to promote industries that can take advantage of global growth driven beyond Europe, our higher education sector should be challenged and supported to *increase* our share of the rapidly expanding international student market. This is why it was always a mistake to include the student migrant flow within a target to reduce total immigration numbers.

Politicians are rightly expected to engage with public views and anxieties about immigration, and the government has admirably done so. It will, of course, be an important election issue for all political parties as we approach the 2015 general election. But it is time politicians made the case that there are different types of immigration.

This important survey shows that the public is quite capable of making those distinctions and in fact has a pragmatic and nuanced view about how to select the kinds of migration that best reflect our nation's interests and values.

There is a broad public consensus that international students are good for Britain: people welcome the income they bring to these shores; they are happy to see the skills they have gained here help UK firms rather than our international competitors; they are rightly anxious when they see other English-speaking nations aggressively target the lucrative international student market at the expense of British universities.

I very much hope that this report will reassure political parties in advance of next May that the public respects those politicians who put forward a mature and rational case for a managed migration policy.

Above all, this is great news for those of us who want our world-class universities to thrive and compete internationally. A welcoming approach to international students can clearly be seen to *reflect* British public opinion, rather than challenge it.

‡

Pension Schemes Bill, 2 September 2014

As the House returned after summer recess, attention turned to the Pension Schemes Bill, which set out a new legislative framework for private pensions following the Chancellor's dramatic announcement at the March Budget that the requirement to buy an annuity would be done away with. He had dubbed the reforms 'the most radical changes to pensions in almost a hundred years' and received wide praise for his boldness in bringing more consumer choice, flexibility and freedom to the pensions system. However, such reforms also brought consequences for pensions providers in the City of London, and I raised some of their concerns, as well as my own, about the finer details of the Chancellor's plans in my speech at Second Reading.

It is fair to say that, like holy matrimony, pensions reform is probably best entered into advisedly, soberly and discreetly. For good reason, the final year of a parliament is often *not* the best of times to embark upon radical reform in this area. It simply becomes all too easy for political adversaries wilfully to misrepresent your far-reaching proposals.

Yet there is no disguising that the notion of pensioners being able to unlock their life savings during an uncertain retirement is a revolutionary change.

As deficit reduction remains more straightforward to explain than achieve, these pension reforms also allow for fiscal loosening. For, once implemented, these proposals will release a vast dollop of cash for those over the age of fifty-five to pump into the economy rather than being forced to buy an annuity at woefully uncompetitive rates. Make no mistake – this is not somehow an unintended consequence. The red book to last spring's Budget made it clear – these reforms anticipate a boost to aggregate pensioners' spending to the tune of £320 million in 2015/16, rising to a whopping £1.2 billion in 2018/19.

I wholeheartedly support the Treasury's belief in the principle of freedom. Rightly, we Conservatives trust those who have worked hard and saved throughout their adult life to make their own decisions with their savings. Nevertheless, the generous tax relief that attaches to private pension savings has always been predicated on the basis that by providing for their old age, pension savers will not be a drain on the state. It will be more difficult to justify reliefs at such a generous level if the compulsion that goes with annuities or restrictions on access to savings is consigned to history.

I am also pleased that belatedly the coalition has consulted more widely on these plans. While one hopes that some technical issues are ironed out, I wanted at this stage to make some more general observations.

The government has been commendably vigorous in reforming the pensions system since 2010. Eligibility for a state pension will

only kick in at a later age; the earnings-related element of the pension
has been abolished; we now have a system of automatic enrolment
for employees. Many of these reforms have been undertaken for one
simple reason: we could not go on as we had in the past. Our understanding of retirement has changed beyond all comprehension since
the state pension was first introduced in 1909. Life expectancy then
was lower – so there was no point in continuing the pretence that the
state could adequately sustain decent incomes for generations that
will now live for twenty or thirty years *after* retirement.

If the emphasis is now firmly on self-reliance and the ever-greater
involvement of private providers, then the most crucial ingredient
going forward will be *trust*. If the law is essentially to compel citizens
via auto-enrolment to hand over an unspent surplus of hard-earned
cash to the unqualified or incompetent, there is little incentive for
anyone to save. Central to addressing this must be a pensions industry in which there is universal public confidence and which willingly
recognises a collective responsibility. We are a long way from this, as
we all know. The regulator, encouraged by government, now needs
urgently to engender a culture among the major institutions in this
field akin to that prevailing among the leading banks during the
early 1970s. Unfortunately, it is still clear that confidence in the pensions industry has not recovered after the debacle of Equitable Life,
with investment in a residential property seen as the more reliable
bet to all too many of those planning their retirement.

Meanwhile, if we are to reduce reliance on the state, we might
also reflect on the sobering fact that earlier this year, the Financial
Conduct Authority found the average pension pot to be a meagre
£17,700. For all the promotion of pensions, no amount of legislation will overcome the fact that many of our fellow countrymen are
too poor to save adequately for their retirement. I fear this will only
become truer for younger generations who find an ever-increasing
portion of salary dedicated to servicing high rents or mortgages
based on inflated house prices.

Next, I should like to touch upon coherence across government
pensions policy. On the one hand, the government is creating a new

regime which places much greater trust in the individual to manage their own retirement funds. On the other, its new system of automatic enrolment for employees suggests that it has little faith that people will take sufficient responsibility for saving in the years preceding retirement.

Similarly, while there is an implicit understanding that the state will no longer be able to provide citizens with adequate incomes in retirement, the government has made a costly commitment to a so-called 'triple lock' which guarantees that the state pension will increase in line with wages, prices or 2.5 per cent, whichever happens to be highest.

In short, the messages to the electorate on pensions remain mixed to the point of confusion – it would be helpful if the Minister could restate in this House what basic principles underpin government thinking in this vital area.

As I have alluded, as a Conservative I instinctively welcome the notion that people who have saved and planned their finances carefully should be free to spend their retirement funds as they see fit. It is exciting to see the Chancellor inject the principles of trust and self-responsibility right back into the heart of government policy. Nevertheless, it would also be wise for government to examine whether such policies alleviate or increase the burden on the state. In this regard, I should like to ask the Minister what examination he has conducted into the Australian system.

Some twenty years ago, the government there made similar decisions to those now being made here on annuities. However, I understand that the Australian government is now considering reversing that decision after the Murray Review, examining their financial system, found that roughly half of those retiring take money out as a lump sum with a quarter of that group exhausting their funds by the age of seventy. In addition, many had got themselves into debt in the years preceding retirement in anticipation of using the lump sum on retirement to pay off those accumulated debts. What safeguards do we have in place to avoid such an undesirable outcome?

Turning to guidance, I have received constituency representations from an industry specialist who is concerned that the new pensions 'guidance guarantee' has the potential to create widespread confusion among consumers and damage to regulated financial advisers. The Treasury has announced that under the new regime, everyone will be provided with free guidance from bodies such as the Pensions Advisory Service and Money Advice Service. The cost of this will apparently be borne by a levy on regulated firms.

Not only will the new levy add cost to the operations of independent financial advisers, but they will also essentially be funding a service that stands to undermine their own offering, since many customers will now take the view that it is not worth paying for advice. This in itself is not a problem for the consumer. However, financial advisers currently already operate in a very strict regulatory environment, whereas the guidance guarantee will set out generic options such as whether an individual should consider an annuity or income drawdown rather than specific recommendations. There is a danger, therefore, that many pensioners will see broad guidance as an inexpensive substitute to tailored, quality advice. My correspondent therefore recommends either that the government's delivery partners remove any suggestion that they will be providing *advice* rather than simply general guidance or else that policy is delivered through regulated, private sector firms, perhaps through a voucher system, which would offer consumers the kind of helpful, impartial and personalised advice that they need.

Finally, I should just like to say a word on unintended consequences. It has been clear for some time that the annuity system was not designed to fund the kind of long retirements we have seen as a result of improved life expectancies. However, there are implications for the health of the wider economy if we turn our backs on annuities in ever-greater numbers.

The vast majority of annuity money is invested in bonds, a crucial source of alternative finance for businesses beyond the traditional banking system. This helps spread risk in the system by ensuring that problems in the banking system, such as those we saw in 2008, do not completely turn off the tap of finance to the wider economy. Currently, those saving in defined contribution pension schemes buy approximately £11 billion of annuities per annum, with around £7 billion flowing to firms through corporate bond purchases as a result.

What consideration has government given to a collapse in such purchases should there be a sudden drop in the sale of annuities? While this may be offset by a fresh flow of money from those pensioners who decide to reinvest their lump sums, this cannot be guaranteed – as I have suggested, my fear is that without sufficient trust in the markets, property (and rental income received from it) will be the attractive destination for this cash.

Despite these concerns, I would like to finish my contribution by reiterating my admiration for the boldness of the coalition in trying to tackle a pensions system that clearly is not functioning well for the majority of our fellow Britons.

‡

Devo Max is a cheap last-gasp offer, but a federal UK may be the happy outcome (*City AM*), 11 September 2014

The shock landslide victory of the Scottish National Party in the 2011 Holyrood elections had given the momentum SNP leader Alex Salmond needed to push for a referendum on full independence for Scotland. By 2012, he and David Cameron had signed the Edinburgh Agreement, paving the way for a plebiscite by the end of 2014, with a simple Yes/ No question on whether Scotland should break away from the United Kingdom. The Prime Minister had promised to fight to 'keep our United Kingdom together with every single fibre I have', but a shock poll late in the campaign, showing Yes and No camps neck and neck, sent the three mainstream political parties into a state of panic. Frightened by the prospect of the Union breaking up after the 18 September poll, Cameron, Nick Clegg and Ed Miliband promised 'extensive new powers' for Scotland under a 'devo max' arrangement, should its people vote to remain in the UK. I was asked to write the following article for City AM *about the potential implications of such a deal for London.*

Whatever the outcome of next week's referendum on Scottish independence, of one thing we can be sure: the constitutional settlement that had helped make the Union such a success for three hundred years will be tainted.

This settlement had just about held together after devolution. However, many of us in the other Home Nations have been dismayed by the desperate promises of recent days to give the Scots ever more new powers in a last-gasp attempt to keep the United Kingdom together. Such rushed, short-termist thinking is no way to conduct constitutional change. In truth it will guarantee that the issue of Scottish independence will linger long after 18 September. The creeping resentment from England, Wales and Northern Ireland meanwhile – not to mention London and the regions – may well boil over if so-called devo max follows hot on the heels of a 'No' vote. Indeed London's claim for more powers is arguably much stronger than Scotland's, with near double the population alongside a far more successful economy with greater international reach.

The constitutional muddle left by devolution (a process which Labour naïvely hoped would kill dead Scottish nationalism) has left us with many now-familiar inequities. MPs from Edinburgh and Cardiff have been able to vote on health and education policies affecting Londoners and Mancunians, but not affecting their own constituents in this sphere. Under the Barnett formula, residents of Scotland have had much more spent on their healthcare and education than do my constituents. Scotland merits a Parliament. Wales and Northern Ireland only enjoy an Assembly while England is left unrepresented in the devolved UK.

The last Labour government was happy to leave those inequities unaddressed since it had most to gain from dangling a messy proposal for devolution, alongside House of Lords reform, before prospective voters in 1997. Conservatives, meanwhile, shied from promoting English votes for English laws lest this proudly unionist party be seen as cynical and negative on both sides of the border. It is unthinkable, however, that this uneasy bargain could continue were Scotland to be given yet more say over its governance.

It may then prove necessary to consider an option I have long advocated – four, full, national Parliaments in England, Scotland, Wales and Northern Ireland with all the existing powers of the House of Commons and over them a federal United Kingdom Parliament, which would debate defence and foreign affairs, make treaties and administer a cohesion fund for the poorer parts of the UK, funded by a per GDP levy on the national Parliaments. There would be no need for extra politicians, as the national Parliaments would simply send representatives to the UK Parliament and meet together for its debates, which could be held in the old House of Lords chamber.

This proposal also cuts the Gordian knot of House of Lords reform (we would become unicameral within the federal set-up) and provides an equitable structure that respects national differences. It would also strengthen the ties that unite us as a nation of equals. It might even prove just the medicine to reinvigorate British politics and restore the reputation and legitimacy of MPs.

This is, of course, a bold suggestion. But then the cheap, last-gasp offer of devo max might prove the catalyst for a constitutional overhaul perhaps even more radical than Scottish independence itself. Either that or the political class will once again complacently let resentments burn in an uneasy marriage of nations, the cost of which will surely be an increasingly alienated and disillusioned electorate.

‡

It's growth and recovery, all right. But how sustainable is it?, 14 September 2014

The Chancellor was given a nicely timed boost as he went into conference season, when the Office for National Statistics issued revised statistics on 3 September that showed the economy had grown more quickly than previously thought. Britain had enjoyed the third best economic growth in the G7, behind the US and Canada but beating continental rivals France and Germany. In this article, I probed the good news a little deeper and looked at the likely sustainability of the recovery.

George Osborne will hope to continue a welcome habit of confounding his critics. Steady progress at deficit reduction and austerity measures in parts of the public sector have not prevented a return to economic growth. Unsurprisingly, Labour have been forced to shift their line of attack to the continuing squeeze on living standards, as inflation continues to outpace wage rises. This is ironic, as by rights Labour should have little to crow about on this front – after all, real wages have been static for the average Briton since 2004.

Furthermore, the opposition's ill-disguised hostility to business and wealth-creation in reality leads them down an economic cul-de-sac: none of this is a sensible policy programme for a party aspiring to government within eight months.

So will this economic recovery prove sustainable? It is a familiar question that lies at the very heart of the election battle ahead.

For all the talk of 'our long-term economic plan' (the now famous OLTEP) the coalition in reality has two distinct economic strategies. Implicit in the OLTEP slogan is a recognition that the benefits of infrastructure investment, slashed in 2010 and restored last year, along with an aggressive programme of export-led growth in developing markets like China and India, will not come this side of May 2015.

These admirable, long-term investment projects certainly live up to Osborne's narrative, when in opposition, of promoting a new model of growth that does not rely upon consumer debt. The only snag with this revitalisation of the UK economy is that it will only begin to bear fruit well into the latter part of the decade.

Meanwhile, the coalition has a distinctly short-term plan to get the UK economy through the next election, which I reckon the Treasury feels cannot come too soon.

The surging growth of the past eighteen months owes much to the ongoing, massive monetary stimulus provided by five and a half years of near zero interest rates and £375 billion of quantitative easing. Funding for Lending provided the banks with an incentive to lend to the mortgage market, and consumers were similarly encouraged by assurances that credit would remain cheap for the foreseeable future. Indeed, in spite of a recent reorientation of the Funding for Lending programme away from real estate lending, barely one eighth of bank lending is used by companies for investment beyond property. Three quarters of *all* bank credit is still being gobbled by domestic house-holders to service mortgages and fund related consumption.

For so long as the Bank of England's attempts to calm the overheating London/south-east property market do not damage confidence, the economy should continue to expand at a steady pace until the election is behind us. It is possible that despite (or perhaps, given its notoriously inaccurate predictions, because of) the IMF's exuberance we may see some slowing-down in growth rates over these next three quarters. Manufacturing and construction data show clear signs of reduced activity although, perhaps thankfully, it is the UK's services sector that accounts for over three quarters of the national income.

So a fundamental rebalancing of the economy seems as far away as ever: paradoxically, the current strength of sterling continues to weaken our export performance and the UK's balance of trade. This also suggests that the elusive gap between growth rates in wages and inflation may widen again in the months ahead.

Nonetheless, the coalition's short-term economic plan is clearly on course and, unlike most other finance ministers in the G20, our Chancellor has the confidence of the markets.

It is in the medium-term where the economic fundamentals do not look so smart. I suspect the period 2016–18 may be difficult, whoever is in government. The budget deficit remains at a historic high of 6 per cent – double that of France and at a time when the German budget is almost balanced. Two thirds of the programme of public spending cuts have yet to kick in, and it may prove politically impossible to consider austerity at the level necessary to wipe out the deficit by 2018–19.

Interest rates will eventually need to rise. Indeed, this may even be forced upon the next administration by action in the global bond markets. In all likelihood, any prudent government will have to slam on the brakes by 2016, and bring to a halt this unprecedented era of cheap credit. The puzzle over the UK economy's declining productivity of recent times will require resolution. All this will test just how strong an economic recovery the UK is living through.

Only once interest rates begin to rise to 'normal' levels will the impact of our accumulated public and private debt take its full toll. Worryingly, this may all come at a time of further eurozone turmoil, with international strife leading to a slowdown in the global economy just as the current economic cycle turns down.

Yet there is one curious omission in the Labour party's critique of current economic policy. The fact is that, for all the talk of austerity, the coalition will have borrowed around £190 billion more during the course of this parliament than predicted at the time of the June 2010 Emergency Budget. Ironically, Labour's plans then to borrow a mere additional £50 billion over this period were derided by the coalition as irresponsible and potentially ruinous to the UK's economic health.

There are two reasons Ed Balls makes so little of this fact. First, this level of additional spending undermines the 'reckless austerity' charge levelled against the government. Second, he knows that it has only been the credibility engendered by Osborne with the international capital markets that has allowed such overspending not to have impacted on interest rates. A Labour administration over these past few years would simply not have been allowed to overshoot its budget without a strongly adverse impact on the cost of borrowing.

‡

High time to recognise the limitations of raising tax thresholds, 2 October 2014

'Let's not go back to square one;
let us finish what we have begun.'

As David Cameron took to the stage at Conservative Party conference on 1 October, he could breathe at least one sigh of relief. 'I am so proud to stand here today as Prime Minister of four nations in one United

Kingdom,' he began. '...The lead-up to the Scottish referendum was the most nerve-wracking week of my life.' Indeed, the shock poll that had shown Yes and No camps neck and neck had turned out to be an anomaly. Instead, those wishing to keep Scotland in the Union had won decisively, beating Yes campaigners 55.3 per cent to 44.7 per cent on an 84.6 per cent turnout.

But there were fresh troubles brewing in what was Cameron's last conference speech before the general election. At pains to emphasise that, by October 2015, he hoped to be delivering his speech as leader of a majority Conservative government – 'Coalition was not what I wanted to do. It's what I had to do' – few believed the Prime Minister's ambition was achievable. In the days before the Birmingham jamboree, stark polling by Lord Ashcroft warned that in the key marginal seats, Labour was pulling well ahead of the Conservatives, with Ed Miliband's party on course for a comfortable working majority.

Meanwhile, arrows were being fired from the right as UKIP sought to build on their European election breakthrough by causing chaos in the Tory ranks. On 28 August, Conservative MP Douglas Carswell had defected to Nigel Farage's party, and rumours spread like wildfire that more Tory MPs would soon be following his lead. Just a day before Conservative Party conference began, rebellious Tory backbencher Mark Reckless joined UKIP as well, claiming that his former party had not been serious enough about real change in Europe.

The Prime Minister responded by giving a full-blooded account of what a Conservative majority government would look like, appealing to our own ranks but also setting out a range of attractive policy ideas on full employment, competitive corporate taxes, sound management of the public finances, an increased minimum wage and a further hike in the personal allowance. In this article, I set out some of my reservations about the extent to which our tax-cutting policy could be pushed before we started to undermine our claim to be careful economic stewards.

Taking the lowest paid out of income tax entirely was a policy brought uniquely to the table by the Liberal Democrats in 2010... or so the junior coalitionists would have the British public believe.

The truth is a little more nuanced. My own constituency election address as far back as 2005 asserted an aspiration that no one earning less than £10,000 a year should be caught in the income tax net. After all, £200 a week is scarcely a King's ransom if you are working in central London. I know several other Tory candidates in the capital and beyond who made similar pledges.

I should confess that when I sought to repeat this pledge in my 2010 election address, I received a discreet call from Conservative Campaign Headquarters as we were about to go to press, asking me to rehash the wording. At that time, we hoped to expose the Liberal Democrats for having this as an uncosted promise in their manifesto. Four weeks later, the coalition had been formed and, hey presto, taking the low paid out of income tax was now firm coalition government policy!

No one denies that at a time of extended austerity this policy has proved popular. Putting the squabbling as to which coalition party deserves most credit for its implementation to one side, the real question now is the extent to which this policy should be extended into the future. The Prime Minister made his own views clear on Wednesday, as he brought Conservative Party conference to a triumphant close, declaring that a majority Conservative government would extend the personal allowance to £12,500.

It is sensible and exciting politics and I know many Conservative activists will be only too delighted to have clear daylight between our own approach and that of the Labour Party. Meanwhile, I was pleased to see that the increase in the personal allowance would be delivered *only* once the structural budget deficit has been eliminated. It is this kind of 'forward guidance' that I had advocated earlier this year when I suggested we make clear that once progress on reducing the deficit breaks past a certain point, a series of tax cuts kicks in. That way, the electorate would know full well that while our priority is stability, our ultimate aim is a low-tax, competitive economy.

But economically, how far can and *should* this policy be stretched?

What is crystal clear is that the raison d'être for creating the coalition, namely eliminating the deficit within the five-year fixed term of this parliament, has not even come close to being achieved. Indeed we are only two fifths of the way there and, as we know, substantial ongoing reductions in public spending will be necessary for several years to come if the UK's public finances are to be brought under control.

This bleak backdrop will also require some serious action to ensure the tax take is boosted. All the initiatives to clamp down on tax avoidance (aggressive or otherwise) can only achieve so much. Essentially, any future UK government will need to be mindful of the requirement to maintain as large a tax base as possible. Today, there are more Britons in work than ever before. That is a positive first step, but Conservatives should be determined to encourage as many in the workplace as possible to favour low *rates* of taxation. To put it bluntly, those earning below the threshold at which income tax kicks in have little incentive to support lower rates for those paying it. The larger that group the more difficult it will be for us as Conservatives to make a convincing, credible, widely appealing case for lower taxes.

We should also bear in mind precisely how this pledge has been funded so far. While all taxpayers have benefited as the personal allowance has steadily risen to £10,000 (soon to be £10,500), the level of earnings above the personal allowance at which the 40 per cent higher rate kicks in has decreased from £37,401 in 2010/11 to £31,866 in 2014/15. This has been creating a significant disincentive for lower to middle income earners to strive for higher salaries, and placing an ever-greater tax burden on a group of people that is far less likely than a low earner to qualify for any state support. I am glad to see the Prime Minister acknowledge this by complementing his announcement on the personal allowance with a pledge to raise the threshold at which the 40 per cent tax rate is paid to £50,000 by 2020. But it will be a tough deadline to meet, for all the reasons I have outlined.

As we shall see, 'soak the rich' is likely to be the catchphrase for *all* our political opponents at the forthcoming election. UKIP will seek to clobber non-UK nationals, while the Liberal Democrats are already lining up menacingly with Labour to push for a so-called Mansion Tax on homeowners as well as more punitive levies on banks and bankers.

Understandably, Conservatives wish to take a fair share of the credit for taking the poorest out of income tax and trying to address the poverty trap. However, by releasing ever more employees from the burdens of paying *any* income tax, we risk legitimising the politics of envy. We also shrink the tax base substantially, making our income tax take (which makes up over a quarter of government revenues) ever more dependent on smaller groups of taxpayers. Let us not forget that the top 1 per cent of UK earners *already* pay nearly a third of all income taxes.

A full throttled pursuit of class war rhetoric cannot ever be a vote winner for our party, especially at a time when we are widely (mis)-characterised as being solely on the side of the rich and powerful.

‡

Arbitrarily criminalising banking is a reckless way to reform British finance (*City AM*), 9 October 2014

On 7 October, two directors from banking giant HSBC quit their roles in protest at a new regime being brought in that allowed for bankers to be jailed for financial recklessness. The aim of the fresh rules was to stamp out the kind of banking misconduct that had helped precipitate the 2008 financial collapse and had so trashed the industry's reputation. Treasury Select Committee chairman Andrew Tyrie, who had called for the rule-changes, explained: 'The crisis showed that there must be much greater individual responsibility in banking. A buck that does not stop with an individual often stops nowhere'.

With concerns expressed by City folk that it would become increasingly difficult to fill executive boards, I outlined in this article for City AM *some of the potential unintended consequences of the new rules.*

'Just lock them up and throw away the key!'

The radical plan to prosecute bank bosses for reckless misconduct in the management of a bank is ringing alarm bells across the City, with a slew of top bankers now threatening to join the duo from HSBC in quitting the industry in protest.

The political allure of the proposal is clear. Since the financial crash and its consequent banking scandals (payment protection mis-selling and LIBOR rigging, to name but two), politicians have been under pressure to prove that the despised banking club is not simply 'getting away with it'. Scratch beneath the surface, however, and the plan to jail banking executives for collective behaviour falls apart.

For a start, how can recklessness be defined and then proven in an industry based upon risk-taking? One of banks' most crucial functions is to lend to business. Indeed, it is the very reason why they are deemed systemically important, and therefore too important to fail. Yet in 2012, 20 per cent of the 400,000 new business start-ups collapsed within a year, and it is anticipated that 50 per cent will not be operating by 2015. To lend to a new enterprise might on this basis be considered one of the riskiest things a bank could do. Similarly, it is pretty risky to lend to people purchasing a home with a high loan to value ratio, yet that is precisely what the government has been encouraging banks to do via its flagship Help to Buy policy.

So when does commercial risk become recklessness? I would contend that the latter can only be defined in hindsight, when a particular lending decision spectacularly fails. What about those banks who in the run-up to the financial crash sought to rely upon what was widely regarded as independent advice from credit rating agencies? Banks can try to avoid such a scenario by cutting off credit to 'risky' ventures but that path would surely only lead to stagnation in the wider economy. The very purpose of banks would, at a stroke, be undermined.

In an unwise perversion of the British justice system, these proposals would also reverse the burden of proof. It seems that executives accused of recklessness will now have to demonstrate their innocence rather than have the Crown prove their guilt. If those running businesses are haunted by the clink of prison keys as they manage their organisations, they will be tempted to lead by committee, surround themselves with armies of lawyers and hide behind bureaucratic procedures in a bid to disperse responsibility. In a globally competitive market, that is no way to run a company.

Supporters of 'holding individuals to account' counter that sanctions of this type will only come into play where a bank has been bailed out by the government. The Bank of England and the Financial Conduct Authority also concede that the likelihood of successful prosecution is very slim since, as they implicitly appreciate, any laws on this would be littered with loopholes. How long, for instance, does executive responsibility last? Would it be current or past management teams who end up in the dock? Instead, it is argued, this proposal is designed to act as the ultimate guard against reckless behaviour. In the meantime, the fear of prison should get those wild bankers to behave more sensibly. Maybe. Or it could simply make banks mindful not to locate key staff in London for fear of arbitrary sanction. That fear alone will not undermine London's future as an important financial centre, but demonstrates that the government is vulnerable to populist pressure and creates a sense of dangerous uncertainty.

The great flaw with banks, the one at the heart of the anger these proposals seek to quell, is that in taking enormous risks with other people's money, they have been able to pocket any gains while transferring losses to the hapless taxpayer. Threatening bankers with imprisonment is not going to resolve that asymmetry. The only thing that can is the pain of commercial failure. That will involve, insofar as possible, removing that implicit taxpayer-backed guarantee, something governments have sought to do since the financial crisis via a wide range of other, more effective, reforms.

Better that bankers should be subject to the same commercial and legal incentives and punishments as everyone else. If they commit fraud, if they lie and cheat the system and break the law, they should be pursued and penalised. But let us not risk criminalising an entire industry and warping British justice by pretending these ideas will have any positive impact beyond the enticing headline.

‡

The crackdown on 'no win, no fee' risks handing a victory to dodgy directors (*City AM*), 16 October 2014

In representing the City, I would frequently speak to the banking community about government policy and its likely effects. But the Square Mile has always been about much more than finance, with just as lively a community of insurers, lawyers, entrepreneurs and other professionals working within its bounds. In this article for City AM, *I explained some of the concerns of insolvency practitioners over changes to 'no win, no fee' legal cases.*

One of the hazards of policymaking is that many of the best laid plans can have curiously unintended consequences. Meanwhile, in implementing policy, government can often find its left hand undermined by its right. So it has been with the Ministry of Justice's laudable bid to halt spurious and costly civil litigation, an initiative which now risks compromising a crackdown on rogue directors by the Department for Business, Innovation and Skills (BIS).

The Legal Aid, Sentencing and Punishment of Offenders (LASPO) Act was introduced in 2012 by the coalition to protect the taxpayer and public interest by severely curtailing the use of 'no win, no fee'. These are the types of legal cases made infamous by the personal injury advertisements that have plagued a generation of daytime television viewers. It was a popular move, designed to free up court time and cut costs for companies, individuals and public institutions targeted by vexatious and unworthy litigation.

The changes were implemented for all types of litigation. However, insolvency litigation was given a specific carve-out on the basis of it being in the public interest – when such litigation is successful, HMRC receives returns from the insolvent estate, while creditors like small businesses get some of their money back. Meanwhile, claims brought in such instances are neither frivolous nor disproportionate in cost, and since alternative funding tends to have a high acceptance threshold and high cost, far fewer cases would be pursued without 'no win, no fee'.

From 1 April next year, however, the government intends to end the insolvency exemption. At a stroke, this risks putting the Ministry of Justice in direct conflict with the efforts of BIS, in its *Transparency and Trust* project, to clamp down on rogue company directors who take money or assets out of a business that subsequently goes into liquidation.

The vast majority of corporate insolvencies do *not* involve directors who have acted unlawfully. But in those cases that do, the 'no win, no fee' system has worked well in helping insolvency practitioners fund investigations into corporate wrongdoing. Since, for obvious reasons, there tends to be very little or often no money left in an insolvent company, often there are no practical alternatives to 'no win, no fee' when it comes to funding this type of litigation. This was confirmed in a recent study by the University of Wolverhampton, which also revealed that £160 million a year is being recovered from dodgy directors under the existing system, and returned to those to whom it is rightfully owed, such as businesses and sole-traders awaiting payment for goods and services provided. The current system also incentivises rogue directors to settle before a matter is taken to court, keeps insolvency costs down, ensures that creditors do not have to stump up for legal fees, and acts as a deterrent to other directors.

Should the LASPO regime be extended next April to insolvency litigation, it is likely to prove unaffordable for creditors to pursue directors and third parties holding onto their money, particularly for sums less than £50,000. This might sound like small change to large organisations, but for any small business it can be the difference between survival and going under. Claims are also more likely to be dragged out, increasing costs to creditors. Why should directors who have wilfully engaged in wrongdoing get away scot-free? The Ministry of Justice should be under no illusion – it is those dodgy executives who will be the only winners if these proposals are implemented.

The maintenance of the current set-up ought to be a no-brainer, but the MoJ insists that LASPO must be applied consistently and it will be pursuing the changes on this basis. The UK's insolvency profession has proved itself incredibly effective at mopping up after business failure, but this plan looks set to make its job much harder. It is the smallest of businesses and the taxpayer who will end up bearing the brunt. It seems a high price to pay for 'consistency'. The Ministry has eight months to think again. BIS, small firms and insolvency practitioners will be fervently hoping it does so.

‡

A global brand being recklessly neglected, 16 November 2014

In October, the Vice Chancellor of Oxford University, Professor Andrew Hamilton, had intervened in the debate over student migration to warn that the government's tightening of the visa system was damaging the UK's ability to attract the most economically valuable international students. He used his Annual Oration to push political parties to drop student migrant targets from their manifestos as the general election approached. However, with the Clacton by-election on 9 October giving UKIP its first-ever Member of Parliament in Douglas Carswell, and Mark Reckless in with a good chance of keeping his Rochester & Strood seat under UKIP colours at the 20 November by-election, the Conservative Party had little appetite to give ground on the controversial subject of immigration.

'Whenever I travel in the world, particularly in China and India, one question persists,' reflected Professor Andrew Hamilton last month, '"why has the UK adopted a visa system so hostile to student entry?" Frankly, it baffles me too!'

As Vice Chancellor of Oxford University, Professor Hamilton understands both the colossal economic opportunity that international students represent to the UK, as well as the aggressive competition to attract their business from rivals like Australia, Canada and the United States.

Rocketing growth in Asian economies has ensured tens of millions of Chinese, Korean, Malaysian and Indian citizens are added to the ranks of the global middle class every year. This affluent new cohort has a hunger for higher education that Asian universities have not yet the capacity to cater for. This has created an exciting opportunity for developed nations over the past decade, similarly hungry to find new areas of growth for their ageing, undynamic economies at a time when state subsidies to universities are necessarily being cut.

It has been a match made in heaven, with the considerable added bonus that a sustained flow of international cash and top postgraduates and academics into universities helps grow associated high-value sectors such as science, technology and engineering. In the UK, this has created a virtuous circle, allowing the talented to cross-pollinate and combine with money and commercial opportunity. But that delicate ecosystem is now under threat. Asian nations understandably want to retain the talent on their own soil and are resolutely building up their higher education institutions. Competitor states like Australia and Canada, meanwhile, want to increase their slice of the action.

Depressingly, the British response to this has not been to up the ante. Instead, we have allowed a debate about the number of immigrants in our country to morph inadvertently into a crackdown on the flow of international talent into our universities, impeding one of the most important growth industries we have. The fact that Prof. Hamilton's lament was echoed by the Nobel prize-winning scientist, John O'Keefe, who warned that the system was now creating a 'very, very large obstacle' to recruiting top global scientists, should make sirens go off in the corridors of power.

Officially, the Home Office places no limit on the number of students who can come to our shores to study, with visa allocations in place for academics. Reality suggests, however, that the cumulative effect of the government's immigration policies, coupled with the hostile tone of public debate on immigration, are acting to deter the best postgraduate students and academics from signing up even to our elite institutions.

Over the course of its term, the coalition has implemented a stricter, more complex and more costly visa regime for non-EU students. Restrictions on the routes into employment have been imposed that make it difficult to find meaningful job opportunities for those keen to develop their early careers once their courses end. The government has recently legislated via the Immigration Act for students and academics to pay fees upon entry for the NHS (not an insignificant annual sum for a PhD student staying for a few years with his or her spouse and children). And the tone of debate on immigration has toughened as Ministers have danced increasingly to UKIP's tune. When prospective students calculate the cost of visas, upfront health and rent payments and high academic fees, then contemplate the bureaucratic complexity and sense of general public hostility, they will ask a simple question: 'Do other nations hold out a more attractive offering?'

This is perhaps why in 2012–13 we saw the number of international students coming to the UK to study at higher education institutions decline for the first time ever. Worryingly, that decline is most profound among the postgraduate population, with a drop in numbers of 2.8 per cent between 2010–11 and 2012–13, and a frightening 52 per cent decline in the number of Indian postgraduates coming to the UK. This has broad repercussions, since non-EU students tend to focus on subject areas like engineering, computer science and maths, where they will often outnumber UK and EU students, making this contingent particularly critical to course viability in some of the areas where the UK wishes to maintain a cutting edge. The Russell Group has regularly pointed out that the combined teaching income for so-called STEM subjects does not cover the average annual cost of teaching that resource-intensive subjects require, such that UK and EU students are taught at a loss. This makes the continued supply of international students essential to the basic economic viability of undergraduate STEM teaching in even the most prestigious universities.

These concerns are raised time and again by the elite universities in my own constituency. At Imperial College, recently placed joint second in the world university rankings, 40 per cent of doctoral research postgraduates come from outside the EU, and in 2012/13 they received over double the sum of Home and EU students' fees in academic fees from overseas students (£103.8 million versus £48.2 million). Indeed, this top university calculated that for every lost international student, two and a half home students are required to make up the fall in income. These elite institutions wish to see the flow of students removed from net migration figures, with students and academics excluded from payments for the NHS and post-study routes into work reinstated. They also seek policies that think holistically about how to enhance the UK's attractiveness in terms of scientific and technological innovation.

When high-flying education consumers turn their backs on the British offering, the damage goes way beyond the loss of income from the individual student. There is the cost of lost opportunity, whether from the new generation of global ambassadors that we failed to foster or the research scientist that did not get the chance to find the next big breakthrough in the UK. There is harm to the domestic offering to British and EU students, whose courses are often subsidised by the academic fees of their international counterparts, particularly in specialised postgraduate courses. And, of course, there is the economic damage from losing the fees, investment and daily expenditure of the international student body. Precious wonder that our competitors in this lucrative market are licking their lips at the prospect of the UK becoming a more unappealing financial and social proposition.

Britons relish our reputation as a world-leader in the high-end technological and scientific innovation that often begins with a breakthrough in the university lab. Britons are proud of our consistently high rankings in the university league tables. But in today's world, those things can only be sustained if we accept that the brightest minds must be given easy passage here. Public unease on immigration does not extend to students and academics, beyond the abuse of visas in the further education sector that we saw under the last government and which has rightly been stamped out. So let us not only recognise that but challenge and support our higher education sector to *increase* the UK's share of this exciting, lucrative and rapidly expanding market.

‡

Some strategic thoughts for the Autumn Statement and beyond, 30 November 2014

> *'Red warning lights are once again flashing*
> *on the dashboard of the global economy'*

On 13 November, David Cameron flew to Australia to join other world leaders at the G20 summit in Brisbane. He and President Obama both used the occasion to dress down President Vladimir Putin about his ongoing violations of international law in Ukraine, promising to isolate Russia further from the global community if he continued to arm separatists. But Cameron was also to use the conference as an opportunity to warn people back home that the job of fixing the economy was far from complete. With the Japanese economy unexpectedly returning to recession, the eurozone still in crisis and demand from emerging markets slumping, the Prime Minister cautioned that 'red warning lights are once again flashing on the dashboard of the global economy'.

His downbeat message was derided by Ed Miliband – 'I think that is what is known as getting your excuses in early.' But it helped to establish the danger of veering from the coalition's economic plan, casting the Labour Party as a risk that the UK could ill afford to take. This set the scene for George Osborne's Autumn Statement on 3 December, which I previewed in this article by warning that if the coalition really thought Labour presented a risk, we ought to stop stealing policy items from Miliband's populist agenda.

One of the great paradoxes of this strangest of political times is that sustained growth and clear signs of domestic recovery have made the economy a less salient issue to voters. It is almost as if these upward trends are now being taken for granted by voters unaware of the hardship and challenges that continue to lie ahead.

Perversely, in the circumstances, perhaps only renewed economic turmoil will persuade the voters that the prospect of Labour's return to office is a risk too great to bear. As David Cameron wisely warned a fortnight ago at the Brisbane G20, global instability and uncertainty make it clear that we cannot detach ourselves from the gathering international economic storms.

Indeed, George Osborne's single biggest achievement of these past four and a half years has been to continue to convince the markets that we have a workable plan. Market confidence would in all likelihood collapse if a Labour-led government emerges in May: a run on sterling and markedly higher borrowing costs would follow.

However, our delivery of this message has been impeded in part by the fact that the coalition may inadvertently have prepared the ground for some of the damaging policies that the Labour Party might in government wish to implement. This makes the tone of this Autumn Statement even more important than usual.

There are inevitably times when short-term political expediency trumps principle. A politician would have to be in denial to suggest otherwise. But sometimes the coalition has sacrificed principle either to stave off immediate criticism or to rob Labour of the initiative by adopting its interventionist rhetoric.

Let us take this year's Finance Act as an example. At a time when the government was vocally celebrating the imminent 800 year anniversary of the Magna Carta, it oversaw the passage of legislation that permits Her Majesty's Revenue & Customs (HMRC) to confiscate a citizen's property *before* the courts have established who is legitimately entitled to it, via the innocuously named *Accelerated Payments Regime*. This essentially provides a mechanism for retrospective taxation of the sort we were so up in arms about recently when the UK was presented with an unprecedented £1.7 billion EU budget adjustment.

It also built on foundations laid by the previous year's legislation, under which a General Anti-Abuse Rule (GAAR) was introduced without the provision of a firm definition as to what constitutes tax abuse. This move effectively led to an unprecedented transfer of power from Parliament to HMRC, with this agency of the state now authorised not only to apply the law, but to rewrite it. If such changes had been introduced by a Labour Treasury team, Tory shadow Ministers would have (rightly) been making a principled stand opposing such new powers.

The political thinking behind all of these moves has been clear. With Labour ratcheting up the rhetoric over tax avoidance by the super-rich and global corporations, Conservatives have needed to be on the front foot, neutralising criticism that ours is the party that looks after its rich friends. But on what intellectually consistent basis could a future Conservative opposition criticise a left-of-centre government that sought to take ever more draconian retrospective action against the corporations and wealthy individuals that it relishes taxing to the hilt?

We are in a similar bind over bankers' bonuses. I appreciate that the Chancellor could not have been more robust in defending Britain's banks from a European Union bonus cap and Financial Transactions Tax which threaten to undermine London's global competitiveness as a financial centre. We properly make the case that the cap would only place upward pressure on base salaries, giving banks less flexibility to manage costs and making it tougher to claw back rewards in the event of failure. Yet, only this spring, the Treasury was impervious to the concerns of RBS executives as it moved to block plans to give key staff bonuses, at a stroke undermining a commercial operation in which the taxpayer has a hefty stake. What is our line of attack should a putative Chancellor Balls wish to micromanage commercial decisions of this nature?

Let us look again at the Bank Levy, a tax introduced in 2011 on banks' balance sheets to compensate taxpayers should their backing be required for any future bailout. Sensibly designed to reduce risk by encouraging banks to minimise public exposure to large balance sheets, the levy has failed to raise the targeted £2.5 billion per annum since it came into force. In truth, this is a good news story

– as banks have duly downsized and protected themselves against the need for a future bailout, there have been fewer assets to tax. The trouble is, the government has realised it now needs to raise the cash for both financial *and* political reasons. As a result, it has hiked the rate of the levy no fewer than eight times in order to hit the £2.5 billion target, creating an unstable, uncertain tax regime in this sector. It has also ensured that the levy is now considered part of the budgetary furniture to the extent that Labour plans to use it to fund future spending commitments.

When it comes to foreign investment in the UK, inconsistencies in the coalition's avowed rhetoric give succour to interventionist voices within the Labour Party too. Take Pfizer's takeover bid for Astra Zeneca. Labour took delight in criticising the government's wise decision not to interfere in the abortive takeover. However, rather than defend itself through careful explanation of the dangers of protectionism, the coalition instead attacked the previous Labour administration for hypocrisy, before flirting with the idea of extending the national interest test in foreign takeovers. I appreciate how politically sensitive the Pfizer deal was in some constituencies, but the government's expedient response fundamentally undermined Conservative principles and will surely make it harder to articulate the case against an interventionist approach by a future Labour administration.

On property taxes, we have correctly launched an uncompromising attack on Labour's plans to levy a charge on so-called 'mansions' priced beyond £2 million. Incidentally, it seems to me that most central London Labour MPs *also* think the mansion tax as proposed is sheer madness! Yet, by the end of its tenure, the coalition will itself have ramped up taxes on that end of the market at least seven times, whether through a hike to 7 per cent stamp duty at the £2 million plus level, the imposition of capital gains tax on overseas owners, or the 15 per cent levy on empty homes owned by companies. The Treasury now raises more in stamp duty from one London borough (Kensington & Chelsea) than from Scotland, Wales and Northern Ireland combined. There is similar inconsistency when the coalition proudly contrasts its emphasis on personal responsibility to the nanny-statism of the Blair–Brown era. In spite of robust encouragement of an enterprise-led, job-creating economy, the coalition has arguably helped build on Labour's legacy by pursuing punitive regulatory policies on legitimate businesses, whether through plain packaging for cigarettes or exploring the prospect of sugar, fat and salt taxes and further advertising restrictions on junk food.

Conservatives are right to point out the very real economic threat posed by the mere prospect of a Labour administration. This must be both our primary message in the months to come, and the underlying theme to this week's Autumn Statement. However, in truth, the job of turning the UK economy around has only just begun. It is likely that by May 2015, of the seven largest annual deficits in UK history, five will have been recorded in each of the years of the current administration, whose watchword has been austerity.

We are surely mistaken to believe that the real and impending economic threat posed by a Miliband government might be politically neutralised by stealing choice items from Labour's wardrobe. Not only will the electorate begin to question whether there is truly anything to fear from a change of administration, but if we find our opponents back in charge, we might find that some of their worst policies have our fingerprints on their foundations.

‡

Stamp duty overhauled in the Autumn Statement, 4 December 2014

> *'Britain faces a choice.*
> *Do we squander the gains... or do we finish the job?'*

As a vital pre-election scene-setter, George Osborne's task in putting together the Autumn Statement had not been an easy one. With UKIP gaining ground, and Labour apparently getting cut-through with its message on the cost of living – Ed Miliband consistently lamented the 'joyless, payless recovery' – he needed to tell voters that he was a successful

Chancellor while simultaneously convincing them that there was much more work to be done to put the UK on a sustainable footing. His job was made even harder by unhelpful figures from the OBR suggesting that the deficit was far larger than the coalition had forecast it would be by this stage in the parliament, with the government having to borrow much more than intended over the next five years, as oil revenues collapsed alongside weak receipts from income tax and stamp duty.

With limited room for manoeuvre, Osborne announced a new 25 per cent 'Google tax' to be imposed on technology firms who tried to shift UK profits to foreign tax havens; a small increase in the personal allowance; a freeze in fuel duty; and the abolition of air passenger duty for children. Ever mindful of the 'optics', however, he reserved a surprise reform of stamp duty as a final flourish. A tax cut for the majority of homeowners would be funded by a huge hike in stamp duty for the most expensive homes. I questioned the wisdom of placing an ever-larger tax burden on an ever-smaller group.

Yesterday, Chancellor George Osborne stayed true to Autumn Statement tradition by pulling a rabbit out of his Red Box. A much -needed overhaul of the antiquated stamp duty system has been implemented in double-quick time, banishing in a sweep the duty's perverse slab element that saw properties taxed at set rates on their *entire* value once they crossed various thresholds.

For 98 per cent of home buyers, it is anticipated this will translate into a reduced stamp duty bill. The welcome overhaul is also designed to end the strange distortions that the tax introduced into the property market, with properties clustered at prices just below the thresholds. The cost to the Exchequer of these changes will in part be offset by a hike in stamp duty rates for properties worth over £937,500.

Those buying a £2 million home will now have to find £153,750 in cold hard cash to hand over to the Treasury, up from £100,000. Meanwhile, those purchasing a property valued at £5 million will have to pay £513,750 in duty, coincidentally precisely the same amount as the cost of the *average* London property. These amounts need to be paid upfront to the Exchequer, direct from income that has already been taxed. These are *colossal* sums. I do not anticipate many tears being shed across the country for this group of house purchasers. But anyone with experience of the central London property market will tell you that £2 million does not a mansion purchase. In my constituency, it is likelier to get you a two-bedroom flat.

I am sympathetic to the *politics* of the move, particularly this close to an election. The Chancellor has well and truly shot Labour's fox and I would have hoped as a result that this change might put a few additional nails in the coffin of the opposition's poorly thought-out 'mansion tax' plans. Depressingly, spokesmen for the Labour and Liberal Democrat parties insist that this policy remains in play even after the stamp duty hike. Nevertheless, since my constituency contains the second largest number of properties valued at over £937,500, I am predictably less than delirious about this element of the stamp duty changes and the rhetoric that has been used to justify it. It is unfortunate that a Conservative government has hailed these changes on the basis that 98 per cent of homebuyers nationally (91 per cent in the capital) should be better off, while soaking the remaining 'rich' 2 per cent.

Indeed this Autumn Statement has helped entrench the notion that it is legitimate to single out for 'public enemy' status groups in UK society who can be subject to arbitrary super-tax treatment. This torrid list includes banks and bankers, the nebulously defined 'rich', multi-national corporations, non-domiciled individuals, sin companies such as tobacco firms and, increasingly, those who deign to live in London. By focusing our fire on these minorities once again, we risk unintentionally legitimising Labour's unrealistic assertion that all its spending commitments can be funded by ever-more draconian taxes on a small number.

It is revealing that the Office of Budget Responsibility crunched the numbers on stamp duty and concluded that the Autumn Statement's changes will likely cost the Treasury £800 million annually in foregone receipts. In other words, even the vast additional tax levied on relatively expensive properties will be nothing like enough to offset changes to the other end of the scale. Put simply, this is because there are not enough 'rich people' property transactions to tax – and it is worth remembering that the likely result of this policy will be the suppression of the number of transactions.

This merely reiterates the point I have made time and again – Labour is highly unlikely to find sufficient numbers of 'the rich' to fund its ever-growing spending promises. If anything, yesterday's deficit figures should have drummed home that what we really need is a much broader tax base. Instead, the movement of travel is to place an ever-larger burden on an ever-smaller group. Opinion polls may tell politicians that the public hates bankers, aspirational and wealthy Brits, non-doms and big global corporates. But the Treasury will not half miss them when they leave these shores.

‡

Unpredictable perhaps, but unprecedented?, 4 December 2014

All eyes in Westminster were now firmly trained on the 2015 general election, and speculation on its likely outcome was a constant in parliamentary conversation. Would UKIP make a substantial breakthrough and, if so, might any surge affect Labour as much as the Conservatives? Would the Liberal Democrat vote hold up? And what likely shape would any post-election coalition take?

I looked to elections past to see whether they might give us any clues as to how May's events would play out.

Whisper it softly, but for three quarters of the electorate, next May's election will be anything but unpredictable. As the Westminster village gets itself into a frenzy of excitement about the outcome, the stark truth is that at least 500 of the UK's 650 constituencies will absolutely, assuredly elect an MP of the same party allegiance as they did in 2010. In all likelihood, a fair few of the remaining 150 battleground seats will do likewise.

So why all the fuss?

Well, unless the opinion polls over recent years have been consistently wrong or they change markedly over the next five months, we appear to be heading for a second consecutive indeterminate overall result. Not bad as a repudiation of the first-past-the-post electoral system, designed to produce 'strong government'! It will also be the first time this has happened for over a century, and arguably since the Third Reform Act of the 1880s.

Genuinely competitive politics beyond the two main parties has only been with us since 1992. As a consequence, tactical voting has become institutionalised. What promises to be new this time is the rise of UKIP as a parliamentary force, and the strong potential in Scotland that the SNP will make a Westminster breakthrough well beyond even its October 1974 performance.

All this suggests that scores of quirky, unanticipated results may be the order of the day on 7 May. Indeed, the disillusionment with conventional party politics stands to be compounded if vote shares and seats won become hopelessly unaligned. Current polling evidence suggests that Labour may end up as the largest single party even in the event of securing some 3 or 4 per cent less of the popular vote – i.e. perhaps more than a million fewer votes – than the Conservatives.

Similarly, incumbency and careful targeting is likely to provide the Liberal Democrats with a substantially larger number of seats than UKIP can realistically expect to win, even if the new insurgent force of British politics secures (as now seems highly likely) third place in the popular vote. None of this will help restore public trust or confidence in a political system or electoral process that worryingly many now feel is broken.

So what of the historical parallels… and can any lessons be drawn?

Ninety-one years ago this month, in December 1923, there was arguably the only instance of a genuine three-way party outcome in modern British politics. As Lewis Baston observed last year, it was this election coupled with the contest thirteen months previously that marked the point at which the Labour Party overtook the Liberal Party (itself riven by Lloyd George- and Asquith-supporting factions) as principal contender for office to the Conservatives.

What 1923 has in common potentially with next spring's election is that the number of extraordinary and unanticipated constituency results may prove far higher than normal. That general election was the second of three contests that took place within just two years. The Conservatives remained the largest party (having surprisingly won a comfortable majority in 1922 following the dissolution of the coalition) with 258 seats. Labour won 191 seats and the Liberals 158 – up to a peak from 117 the previous year, only to fall back calamitously to just forty seats in 1924. The volatility in the third party's performance was the cause of the sheer unpredictability of so many 1923 constituency battles. It remains the only UK general election in which three parties secured over 30 per cent of the vote.

Remarkably, the Liberals won a handful of seats (such as Aylesbury, Basingstoke and Blackpool) which had even eluded them seventeen years previously in their famous 1906 landslide victory. As well as making hay in the West Country, Manchester and on the Tyne and Tees, a huge swathe of market town English seats fell to the Liberals. Places like Harborough, Salisbury, Gainsborough, Chichester, Sudbury, Devizes and Sevenoaks turned Liberal for just one short parliamentary term, returning in 1924 to trusty Conservative hands, where they have remained ever since. Some of the poorest London districts, such as Hackney Central, Camberwell and Islington East, were won from the Tories, but by the end of that decade favoured the radical edge of the Labour Party, which has been able to rely upon such seats for the past seven decades.

Perhaps May 2015 will prove a similar election. Some of the seats that unexpectedly change hands may indeed quickly return to type. Others, by contrast, may take on a fresh allegiance for decades to come. Who can tell? For all of the three mainstream traditional parties the current mood is one of fatalism and some defeatism. All sorts of assumptions have now been washed away. Until recently (with due respect to our own 40/40 candidates) it seemed pretty difficult to see how Labour might lose seats to the Conservatives. One of the reasons Ed Miliband has faced such a barrage of off-the-record briefing in recent weeks has been the realisation from alarmed Labour MPs that perhaps their dismal 2010 performance of 29 per cent of the vote under Gordon Brown might not, after all, prove to be a low point from which a political bounce back is guaranteed. Suddenly, twenty or so Labour MPs in Scotland alone cannot take for granted their continued parliamentary career. Meanwhile, the rise of UKIP directly threatens a handful of English Labour MPs, while others rightly worry that, in their particular seat, the Conservatives might just come through the middle to win if UKIP disproportionately threatens Labour's core vote.

These may prove to be very uncharted electoral waters. We have always assumed that in a first-past-the-post system, voters will gravitate towards one of two parties. Traditionally, unless a new party makes a substantial breakthrough within two or three electoral cycles, it risks being squeezed… or so we all thought.

Perhaps the wise money should now be on a headlong rush towards a renewed push for electoral reform. This is especially so if UKIP proves not to be a flash in the pan, both in May and, more critically, still at by-elections during the next parliament. Anyone out there in the Conservative Party willing to make the case for AV?

‡

A European good news story (*Daily Telegraph*), 19 December 2014

On 1 November, former Prime Minister of Luxembourg Jean-Claude Juncker formally began his five-year term as the European Commission's new President, taking over from Jose Manuel Barroso. He had not been David Cameron's choice. Indeed, the Prime Minister had launched a high-profile campaign to stop the Luxembourger, whom he had condemned as the ultimate Brussels insider, unable to lead the kind of reform that the EU desperately needed to retain legitimacy. In the end, Cameron was able to secure only the support of Hungary's Viktor Orban, with Juncker's candidacy receiving the twenty-six votes of the remaining country leaders. The inability of the Prime Minister to influence the choice of Commission President augured ill for the imminent renegotiation of Britain's relationship with the EU, and gave succour to Tory Eurosceptics campaigning for Brexit.

There was some consolation to be found in the release of Juncker's first work programme, however, which I previewed in the following article for the Daily Telegraph.

The dramatic plunge in the Russian rouble and the knife-edge presidential votes precipitating elections in Greece provided more than enough copy for financial journalists this week. So it was perhaps no surprise that Tuesday's launch of the European Commission's 2015 work programme raised barely a flicker of interest. While the European Union has tended only to make UK headlines when a bust-up is brewing, it was nonetheless a shame, given that (whisper it softly) the European Commission is beginning to say things that should be palatable even to sceptical British ears.

David Cameron has made it his mission to wake continental counterparts up to the pressing case for EU reform, summed up so powerfully in his 2013 Bloomberg speech. With European leaders' primary focus on keeping the euro afloat, too often this has appeared to be whistling into the wind. The anointment of Jean-Claude Juncker as the new President of the European Commission – a candidate whom the Prime Minister vociferously opposed – seemed only to underscore the lack of enthusiasm for UK government's agenda.

Yet this newly launched work programme, outlining the EU's legislative schedule for the coming year, contains just the kind of language and proposals that he has been seeking. Entitled 'A New Start', the Commission has committed itself to doing things differently with 'less EU interference on the issues where Member States are better equipped to give the right response'. As an opening salvo, 403 laws face being thrown on the scrapheap, and the legislative agenda has been slimmed down dramatically to only twenty-three new initiatives. This underlines the Commission's commitment to focusing on the 'big things', ensuring that needless regulation does not distract from the central mission to tackle high unemployment, slow growth and, most encouragingly, the EU's lack of competitiveness in the global marketplace. So far, so good.

But it is the focus on expanding and sharpening the operation of the Single Market that should provide the Prime Minister and UK Conservatives with most cheer. The Single Market provides one of the finest examples in global economic history of international cooperation to the benefit of hundreds of millions of Europeans. This vast economic zone, boasting a combined GDP greater than the US and Japan, provides a level playing field in which UK businesses can trade. It is the primary reason why Britain signed up to the EU and why many Conservative MPs wish that relationship to continue.

The Commission wishes to move towards an Energy Union and open up the opportunities of the digital Single Market, allowing consumers to enjoy cross-border access to digital services and creating a level playing field for companies in a vibrant digital economy. It is also putting forward a new agenda on migration to address directly the concerns expressed by Cameron and others that the Single Market should mean free movement of workers, not people. This should help the government in its mission to crack down on benefits tourism of the type that so incenses the British public. Completing the trade deal with the United States remains high on the agenda, as are efforts to prevent corporate tax evasion. This neatly ties into the Chancellor's efforts to get better cross-border cooperation on global tax issues, particularly in establishing a system which ensures the country of taxation is the country in which profits are generated.

As ever with all matters European, we should apply caution! The EU clearly has a tumultuous year ahead and it is quite possible that the Commission's agenda will be blown wildly off course by events in the eurozone. With little detail on the proposals, there is also plenty of room for the Commission to slip in new rules later that are firmly not in the UK's national interest. But Mr Juncker has promised that this will not be a business-as-usual Commission. For now, as a matter of faith, I believe it absolutely vital that British MPs and MEPs take his approach at face value. As a mark of our own commitment to restyling the relationship with the EU in a way that will best restore Britons' confidence, we must now properly engage rather than carp from the sidelines.

The Commission's work programme, far from opening the way for further clashes between London and Brussels, underlines just what can be achieved when the UK tries to lead and properly involve itself in the European debate. More focused, better regulation. Movement on migration rules. Real progress on completing the Single Market. A focus on competitiveness. These are all things firmly in the UK's national interest – much more so than the narrow, isolationist and backwards-looking agenda that all too many Eurosceptics wish us to pursue.

2015

General election year began with the United Kingdom intact, but divided. *The Scottish National Party may have been decisively defeated in their bid for an independent Scotland, but their domestic support base had been invigorated. Nigel Farage's UKIP could now boast two Members of Parliament and its strongest-ever contingent in the European Parliament, increasing tensions between David Cameron and his Eurosceptic back-benchers, who demanded ever-tougher talk from him in Brussels.*

Nick Clegg and his Liberal Democrat party struggled for relevance, kicking off the New Year with the promise to 'provide heart to the Conservatives and spine to Labour' in any post-May coalition. Ed Miliband's Labour were up five points in Ipsos MORI's first poll of the year, but this placed them only neck-and-neck with Conservatives instead of providing the commanding lead they probably required to form a government.

Twelve months of unexpected turmoil in global affairs in 2014 had seen Russia's President Putin fashion strength from a position of weakness as he extended his influence in Ukraine and Syria, showing up the West's absence of resolve either to defend Europe's eastern borders or to take decisive action in the Middle East. It seemed as though the post-Cold War consensus in the West that Russia might eventually develop into an economically integrated, modern democracy had been based on a flawed interpretation of events.

After thirteen years of military operations, by year end the UK had withdrawn all but a handful of troops from Afghanistan. ISIS, on the other hand, could claim to control Mosul, Iraq's second city, as well as a swathe of territory from Syria to northern Iraq. The United States seemed more concerned with controlling violence within its own cities as riots in Ferguson, Missouri, shone a spotlight on the depth of the USA's race relations problem.

The European Union was similarly caught up in a web of its own difficulties. With eleven of its twenty-eight members boasting double-digit percentage unemployment tallies by the end of 2014, the EU could look forward in 2015 to projected growth of only 1.5 per cent (1.1 per cent in the eurozone). The European Central Bank was now turning its mind to money-printing as the spectre of deflation loomed – by November 2014, the inflation rate stood at a worrying 0.3 per cent.

In the global economy, Chinese growth was slowing too, weakening demand yet further. Oil prices had begun a steady slide, dipping below $60 a barrel. Big banks continued their reign in the headlines as Citibank, HSBC, JP Morgan, RBS and UBS all received hefty fines for rigging foreign exchange markets. Meanwhile, the investigation continued into the bizarre mystery of Malaysian Airlines flight MH370, which had disappeared on its journey from Kuala Lumpur to Beijing. The 2013 outbreak of the Ebola virus in west Africa had by now become a full-blown international health emergency.

2015 looked like it might be the year of unpredictability, economically and politically, in the UK and across the globe.

Some numbers to reflect on, 8 January 2015

Welcome to 2015! With election year finally upon us, regular readers of political articles can be confident of an endless stream of wordy (and perhaps even worthy) speculation about the outcome of what is universally agreed to be the most unpredictable general election in a generation. So I thought it might make a change if, in this short piece, I focused instead upon a few *numbers* worth bearing in mind over the coming months.

7.3

This was the extent (in percentage terms) of the Conservative lead over Labour in the national vote in 2010. So remember – a Tory lead anything smaller than this in May implies a net *loss* of seats to the main opposition party.

There is a tendency to lull ourselves into a false sense of security when looking at opinion polls, as if being level pegging with Labour is somehow a competitive performance. In fact, even a 3.5 per cent Conservative lead (not something we have achieved in a single opinion poll since before the Budget of 2012) would imply a swing to Labour of almost 2 per cent, which, repeated on a uniform basis across the UK, would make them (just) the largest party in Parliament.

25–35

All things being equal (of which more in a moment) this is the range in numbers of seats Labour needs to gain from us in order to become the single biggest party in Parliament. Put another way – to achieve this key goal, Labour needs to regain roughly three in every ten of the seats it lost to us in 2010. While we had a mountain to climb last time, in 2015, Labour has to conquer only a hillock.

My '25' assumption is that the gains made from the Liberal Democrats and losses to the SNP or UKIP even themselves out between the two main parties. Clearly a Labour collapse in Scotland cannot be discounted at this stage, so it is prudent to work on the basis of the SNP gaining twenty seats from Labour (hence the '35' upper threshold figure). Watch for the variation on our own theme, namely 'Vote SNP, get Cameron', which Labour hopes will get traction. Labour surely starts as hot favourite to win back most of the net thirteen seats it has lost to Liberal Democrats in 2005 and 2010 (Bristol West, Leeds NE, Cardiff Central and Cambridge represent the only realistic exceptions), so it is only if the Liberal Democrats slip well below thirty seats nationally (they won fifty-seven in 2010) that the Conservatives are likely to be the net beneficiaries.

For their part, UKIP will probably secure as much parliamentary representation in previously safe Tory areas as in marginal Tory-held constituencies, in effect depriving Labour of anticipated gains.

We shall hear much before 7 May about the 'swing back' from opposition to the governing party that typically occurs in the months before an election. We all remember the dizzy double-digit leads that Labour had in mid-term during the 1980s on the road to consecutive defeats. As late as August 2009, the Conservative poll lead was 16 per cent: surely Ed Miliband's Labour should have been much further ahead if his party is to have any chance of winning? Instinctively, this seems right, but it is worth reflecting on the relative stability of opinion polling (at least that involving the two largest parties) over the past two years. One reason why there may at most be a very modest 'swing back' in the months ahead is that, since 2010, there has been no appreciable shift of voting intention from Conservative *to* Labour. In short, there is nothing much to swing back.

The two important shifts in voting intention in the past five years have been the upsurge in UKIP support (disproportionately, but by no means exclusively at Conservative expense) and the immediate transfer of roughly one in four Liberal Democrats to Labour on the formation of the coalition. All the polling evidence suggests that this radical left-wing element of Liberal Democrat support in 2010 is resolutely determined to vote Labour next time. So no swing back from this quarter, at least. Indeed, this demographic alone has provided Labour with something like a 6 per cent uplift in its polling figures and, whisper it softly, is the least likely to be persuaded by an aggressive anti-Ed Miliband campaigning line.

Naturally, merely becoming the largest party in Parliament does not *necessarily* make for a sustainable government. Indeed, if Labour achieves a narrow lead over the Conservatives in seats this year, it is likely to have won fewer, perhaps significantly fewer, votes than us. Imagine if this constitutional quirk (which occurred in 1951 and February 1974) is compounded by UKIP gaining (as now seems likely) a higher vote share than the Liberal Democrats, while winning a fraction of the number of seats – a quite plausible scenario. While in truth this owes more to Labour's efficient garnering of votes on lower differential turnouts in its safer seats rather than any intrinsic bias in the electoral system, the public perception of the election being somehow stolen would be strong. This would compound the sense from millions of Britons that our voting system and democratic framework as a whole is not fit for purpose.

1992

Ah, such happy memories for us Conservatives!

Since it became clear that the coalition's raison d'être of eliminating the structural deficit within this parliament was not going to be achieved, Conservative strategists have had a keen eye towards framing the May 2015 election as a rerun of that 1992 contest.

Unfinished business on the economy; a profound lack of trust in Labour's economic credentials; a weak, disrespected opposition leader with derisorily poor public opinion poll ratings; a widespread sense of disbelief that the current opposition leader has what it takes to become Premier. All the ingredients are there, and while, as it stands, much of the British public reckon there is little difference between members of the UK's elite political class, in truth there is probably more to choose economically in the offer between the main parties than at any time in the past thirty years.

Naturally, there are some differences too. In 1992, John Major was able to cast himself as both the continuity and change candidate. Memories of the Winter of Discontent and Union power meant that Labour was still regarded as extremist by much of middle England; the relentless press campaign against Neil Kinnock may well be repeated this time out, but newspaper readership has slumped over the past couple of decades – how many voters now pay much attention to what *The Sun* or *Daily Mail* have to say?

It is also sobering to recall, however, that despite Kinnock's famous failure to win the hearts and minds of the British public in April 1992, his Labour Party actually made a net gain of thirty-nine seats from us at that election. Superior organisation on the ground then meant that Labour performed disproportionately well in the key battleground marginal seats. Worryingly, Lord Ashcroft's polling and local election results suggest a similar thing may well be happening at grassroots level today. On a uniform swing, Labour in 1992 would have gained only nineteen seats, and John Major's triumph would have yielded a parliamentary majority of sixty-one, rather than twenty-one. History might then have turned out very differently...

9

This is the number of first-term Conservative MPs who have announced that they will not seek re-election in May. A variety of personal reasons, the ever-lower public esteem for politicians and a distaste for parliamentary life all have some part to play in this unprecedented rush for the exit, but it also has electoral implications. The psephological phenomenon known as the double-incumbency effect provides evidence of a 2 to 3 per cent boost in the average performance of MPs seeking re-election for the first time.

In 1987 and 2001, the elections immediately after landslides which brought exceptionally large new intakes to Parliament, the number of seats lost by the governing party was considerably lower than the average national swing would have supposed.

By rights, we Conservatives should anticipate a similar boost in 2015, especially in view of our inability to implement boundary changes (probably the only silver lining to this failure). All nine of the 2010 retirees who have announced to date are in seats held by Labour between 1997 and 2010, but won back last time. In four of these seats, we defend a majority less than 2,000. In the type of very close-run election that many predict this May, a markedly more difficult battle to retain even a handful of seats might make all the difference between being in government and losing office.

While each retiring MP has his or her own reasons for stepping down, this also suggests that they have each made a hard-nosed assessment of the likelihood of their re-election. It is perhaps instructive that none of the fifty or so from our 2010 intake who inherited Conservative held seats has (yet) decided to call it a day.

Nonetheless, in this most unpredictable of electoral showdowns one thing is absolutely clear – there is still everything to play for!

‡

Some home truths on the NHS, 22 January 2015

*On 19 January, the MP for Bristol North West, Charlotte Leslie, did
something unthinkable for someone in a marginal seat in election year
by suggesting that the NHS in its current form was not designed to deal
with the challenges of modern-day England. This at a time when Labour
had started the political year with a sharp attack on the coalition's running of the health system, certain that on the NHS it had a firm electoral
advantage over we Conservatives. In this article for ConservativeHome, I
lamented the lack of honest debate over the future of the NHS, supporting Charlotte in her attempt to bring some sanity to the issue.*

It is a brave politician who speaks openly and honestly about the
NHS. That my colleague Charlotte Leslie has done just that this
week – mere months away from a general election – makes her contribution to the health debate both refreshing and courageous.

As a member of the Health Select Committee, Charlotte has
observed at close quarters the acute problems the NHS faces in coping with rapidly increasing demand for its services. Placed 'at the
heart of our sacred taboos', she has described political support for
the institution of the NHS as a 'religion' that 'prevents anyone from
sensibly discussing solutions'.

In contrast to this candid assessment, we have shadow Health
Secretary Andy Burnham, whose disingenuous posturing on the
NHS is almost sickening in its hypocrisy. Having held the health
brief in the last government, Mr Burnham is surely more aware than
virtually anyone of the enormous challenges facing the NHS and of
the institution's staggering complexity.

As he well knows, the primary problem is not one of 'privatisation by the backdoor', 'profits before people' or 'Tory cuts'. It is, in
truth, one of near-insatiable demand and the difficulties an inflexible system has in coping with it. This demand issue was going to
kick in no matter who was holding the reins. We have a population

living ever-longer, a booming birth rate, an array of complex co-morbidities and the welcome creation of innovative, life-prolonging medical advances once disease has taken hold. In 1948, if you were lucky enough to reach retirement age, life expectancy was three to four years. A heart attack or cancer was essentially a death sentence. Today, retirement often lasts decades with a significant proportion of that time spent being in ill-health, recovering from life-changing medical conditions.

Add to that a host of issues that have been a decade and more in the making, which will take equally long to fix. We are still reaping the dubious rewards, for instance, of the 2004 GP contract that disincentivised out-of-hours provision, a PFI-funded infrastructure investment programme that has left many hospitals with cripplingly huge annual debt repayments (some for decades to come) and a progressive recruitment crisis at A&E and GP level.

Since the very same Mr Burnham as Health Secretary paved the way for private providers in the NHS, and the current government has presided over a real terms *increase* in the health budget since 2010, we shall put to one side Labour's primary, opportunistic criticisms. Arguably, they are on more fertile ground when it comes to the concerns raised over the reduction in social care budgets at local authority level, as well as the robustness of mental health provision – two items which both have a significant impact on so-called 'bed blocking' in hospital units. Insofar as the coalition is culpable for adding to the list of NHS woes, however, its main mistake was to expend huge amounts of political capital on a reorganisation that very few people properly understood or were able to communicate effectively.

The Prime Minister's initial instinct to let his erstwhile Health Secretary, Andrew Lansley, get on with the job and implement his plan to give GPs more control was admirable. As shadow Health Secretary for six years, Lansley was fully immersed in his brief – a master of detail, confident that his policy wonkery in opposition could be successfully translated into practical reform. But, once in office, opposition to his supply-side plans was fierce, and as MPs got deluged by email campaign after email campaign, the government seemed unable to answer in the simplest of terms what the reforms were all about.

As a result, they became pockmarked with messy compromise, drastically reducing their potency and effectiveness. But worse still, this episode has meant that any opportunity for sensible and open discussion about the future of the NHS has been taken firmly off the table for a decade. Politically, it is now simply too hot to handle. It is a great shame, for I have in my constituency two outstanding teaching hospitals in Barts and St Mary's Paddington, and after the initial confusion following the removal of Primary Care Trusts, we now see much better cooperation between GPs, hospitals and other care providers, and improved surgery opening hours. Meanwhile, the NHS as a whole recently topped the rankings for quality and efficiency when compared by the Commonwealth Fund to eleven other Western healthcare systems. Indeed, what the NHS achieves in my constituency and beyond, week in, week out, is literally incredible. When the Health Secretary praises the hard-working doctors and nurses in the NHS, he knows they are performing miracles – nationwide, over a million more people have been treated in this parliament than the last.

The dismal Lansley experience also revealed the powerful forces against change within the NHS, and the opposition that reformers face from those who spray around the word 'privatisation' to deter any discussion on efficiency. On this note, it is worth pointing out that if the Mid Staffs scandal had happened on the watch of a private provider, these same voices would have been calling for emergency legislation to hound out firms from the NHS for ever more. As it was, they took a vow of silence until Hinchingbrooke Hospital hit the headlines, allowing them to crow with delight that even mutual providers cannot be trusted with the NHS. It is worth noting too that in spite of the hyperbole about the loss of 'our NHS' to the profit-chasers, the state still provides 94 per cent of its services.

The public forgets that bodies like the British Medical Association are powerful trade unions, not the independent, dispassionate and professional observers they would have us believe. But such bodies know that they hold a trump card – any change in policy that they do not like can be warded off by browbeating the public that it will bring closures, a reduction in service or pressures on staff that put lives at risk. It is a tactic Labour deploys to great effect itself. It is difficult for reformers to explain succinctly the many reasons behind all that is being done to change and improve the health service. In contrast, the opposition knows it can always condense any negative headline on the NHS down to three simple words: 'Stop Tory Cuts'. Indeed, such campaigns on the NHS are meat and drink to Labour campaigners. These are messages with which they not only feel entirely comfortable but provide them a reason to get out of bed on a Saturday morning and knock on doors!

In the face of all these challenges, debate on the NHS has essentially been shrunk to one about funding alone. But we are all colluding in a fundamental falsehood. As any Member of Parliament will tell you, there are two types of conversation about the health service – the public one, where talk of hard-working nurses is accompanied by hasty promises of further cash, and the private one where NHS staff candidly admit that the current service is unsustainable and that we must urgently discuss future priorities, changes to the system, and our willingness either to provide more funding at the expense of other public services or tell the public that there is a limit to what the NHS can offer.

I hold out little hope that such a frank conversation will be brought out into the open in the next few months. As a result, it is understandable that we wish to make the economy the central issue of this forthcoming election.

Regrettably, I remain unconvinced that many of the NHS's self-proclaimed champions care as much about patients as they do about preserving the integrity of 'the system'. Insofar as we Conservatives wish to make the health service a campaign issue, it should be to contrast ourselves as a party of solutions, not of ideology; a party that focuses on caring for patients, not protecting the institution. In this vein, Jeremy Hunt's placing of patient care at the centre of his vision for a 21st-century National Health Service is something about which we must rightly be proud, whether in getting GP surgeries to open at times more convenient to working people or efforts to increase hospital transparency and accountability. The truth is, the NHS – like any institution – must innovate and adapt, or it really will be in peril. Conservatives should place themselves ahead of that curve, not confine themselves to a game of one-upmanship over the cash.

‡

Could a review of council tax be the antidote to Labour's mansion tax?, 14 February 2015

The referendum in September 2014 was meant to have settled the question of Scottish independence. Instead, it had left a nation bitterly divided. In spite of being on the losing team, the referendum campaign had been the making of SNP leader Nicola Sturgeon, and her party's surge in popularity was sending Scottish Labour into panic. Lord Ashcroft polls conducted in January of sixteen Scottish seats suggested that even Labour political heavyweights like Douglas Alexander could lose their seats in May.

Jim Murphy, who had been elected in December as Scottish Labour leader, needed to fight back, and did so by proposing a tax raid on London and the south-east to fund Scottish health spending. In this article, I hit back at Scottish Labour's politics of envy, but acknowledged too that Conservatives needed our own solutions to inequities in the taxing of property.

As the New Year dawned, Jim Murphy triumphantly announced that Labour would 'tax houses in London and the south-east to pay for 1,000 new nurses in the Scottish NHS'. The coupling of Labour's mansion tax policy with its battle-to-the-death north of the border with the SNP was doubtless deliberate. The Scottish Labour leader knows only too well that his focus on two targets of Scottish resentment – London and the well-off – would play wonderfully with his audience.

Alas, these messages resonate south of the border too. The notion of Londoners as a cash cow able to fund all manner of policy promises has gained widespread traction in recent years. The capital city sparkles with success and is brimful with confidence at a time when other parts of our Kingdom struggle. Increasingly, people speak of London's alienation from the rest of the UK as the metropolis gobbles talent and makes its compelling case for ever-increased infrastructure budgets.

Meanwhile, the issue of housing in London itself has become toxic. Boosted by the weakness of sterling and the perception of the UK as a safe haven, foreign money has flooded the capital's prime housing market. As the international enclave expands in the central boroughs, so too have prices been driven up in outer suburbs. It is getting tough now even for well paid professionals to buy homes, as population growth exacerbates supply issues, high rents gobble funds for deposits and prices get a boost from artificially low interest rates. As a result, passionate debate about the imposition of a 'mansion tax' now rages as a means of addressing the resentment felt both from the rest of the country towards its capital, and from those Londoners excluded from the property bonanza.

I have written before about why I vigorously oppose such this levy, which has been advocated by both Labour and the Liberal Democrats. Undeniably, however, we Conservatives risk being left behind in public debate on these issues if we fail adequately to address the resentments behind the mansion tax's popularity. I think our voice on these issues can be found if we grasp the nettle on council tax.

The council tax was introduced as the primary source of collecting income from residents by local authorities in April 1993, hot on the heels of the ill-fated and short-lived poll tax. As we know, the levy for councils in England is calculated by allocating a dwelling to one of eight bands, A to H. This allocation is made on the basis of a property's assumed capital value. But that assumption has been based on prices as they stood on 1 April 1991. The tax is not even particularly proportionate to property values, with the same amount levied on all homes valued at over £320,000 in 1991 prices. This means that around half of all houses in the capital are now placed in the same council tax band even if their size, location and value are vastly different. A Knightsbridge oligarch, for instance, is paying £1353.48 annual council tax for a £60 million home – exactly the same as properties worth one thirtieth that sum.

If the outdated system of valuation seems ludicrous, it can be explained by a concern among politicians that the process of revaluation would be contentious, difficult and potentially costly to voters. But there is a solution that is neither overly complex nor anything like as painful as a mansion tax. More important still, it could come with a big upside when it comes to the provision of affordable housing.

Currently, all banding ratios are set down in statute, but the government could allow local authorities to set their own bands for H and above, with Bands A to G remaining at their existing statutory ratios. A ceiling could be set so that council tax would always be limited to, say, Band J being three times the existing Band H charge to ensure that this does not become a mansion tax by the back door.

Let us take Westminster as our example here. In this central London borough, a Band H property would now probably be worth over £2 million, and there are now just under 15,000 of such homes. But there is a vast difference between a £2 million flat in Pimlico and a home valued at £60 million at One Hyde Park. So the local authority might be empowered to impose two additional bands – there could be, for instance, Band H for prime properties worth between £2 and £5 million; Band I for so-called 'intermediate prime' properties in the £5 to £15 million bracket; and finally Band J for super prime properties worth over £15 million. Incremental targeting of the highest value properties could be accompanied by a new, localised council tax support scheme that would allow specific instances of individual hardship to be addressed.

Crucially, however, the government ought to ensure that all additional council tax or prime property tax income over and above the existing band structure could be retained by the local authority on the specific proviso that it be earmarked exclusively for affordable housing in the area. This positive, localised proposal could be a far more eye-catching and exciting way of countering the envy-driven mansion tax and tackling perceived housing inequality.

It would also chime perfectly with the spirit of the age. There are strong currents pushing towards further devolution of central powers. London in particular would surely be able to make a compelling case for localised revenue-raising if Scotland is to become ever more autonomous. Meanwhile, the enormous and growing pressure on London's housing supply will see an ever-stronger case being made for money raised in the capital from its prime housing stock to be retained in-city for the provision of affordable housing. Politically, there is a strong case to make too. Residents in prime central houses are paying around a third of what they were in rates compared to the 1980s, while the burden for those further down the scale has increased proportionally. Reformers should take this opportunity up with relish.

This proposal avoids the complexity of revaluation, though it should regardless be noted that such complexity is fast reducing with the rise of online property sites able to provide accurate historic and current market assessments. Would it really be difficult for a system of self-assessment to be established, such as that set up in France for the 'wealth tax', whereby the worth of the equity in a property is submitted on an annual basis and can be challenged by the Town Hall if it is thought not to be an accurate assessment of market value?

While we Conservatives must never give in to the politics of envy, the wider support for a mansion tax among many fair-minded people is in part a reflection of a collective failure to review property taxes comprehensively. It is time we finally tackled the outdated system of council tax in a way that allows for genuine local discretion and gives local authorities a new route for boosting affordable housing at a time when London in particular desperately needs it.

‡

Tax avoidance – a practical glossary, 23 February 2015

> *'Any civilised country built on the idea of the common good must*
> *have common rules, shared and respected by all its citizens.*
> *But in Britain today, we risk having one rule for the rich*
> *and powerful and another for everybody else.'*

Tax evasion was the story that kept on giving for Ed Miliband's Labour Party as fresh scandal erupted in February, this time related to banking giant HSBC, whose Geneva branch was alleged to have encouraged its customers to dodge tax payments. The story descended into a political row when it emerged that Conservative minister Lord Green had headed up the bank at the time the practice was undertaken. The Prime Minister was grilled on why he had not carried out proper checks on the peer before he was appointed to government, and got in further hot water when it was revealed that nine Conservative Party donors were listed in files relating to the clients of HSBC's Swiss subsidiary.

Ed Miliband knew that large corporates or rich individuals not paying their fair share was the cause of deep anger and resentment among ordinary voters, and chose to place an 'aggressive' review of HMRC at the heart of his speech to Labour's Welsh conference. I took the opportunity to set out what constituted tax avoidance and what was classed as evasion – two terms that had become woefully interchangeable in political discourse.

These past few weeks have been characterised, in domestic political discourse at least, by rows over 'tax avoidance'. Now that dust is beginning to settle over this toxic partisan issue, it might be helpful to cast a little more light on the matter.

In essence there are *four* distinct categories of conduct where the term 'tax avoidance' commonly applies as an often confusing catch-all.

First, **tax efficiency/mitigation**. This is the category embracing investment in personal pensions, ISAs and even Ed Miliband's now notorious 'deed of variation'. In summary, these are forms of legitimate tax planning, openly recognised and approved by the Treasury.

Second, **genuine tax avoidance**. A term covering schemes carried out at the behest of professional advisers, which enable taxpayers to reduce their liabilities but in a manner which was *not* envisaged by Parliament when drafting the relevant legislation or tax statute. This category involves the exploitation of loopholes, which are invariably later closed down by the Treasury once their use becomes widespread.

Thirdly is **tax abuse**. More controversially, this subset is typically tackled by the imposition of retrospective legislation or retroactive Treasury decree. The GAAR (General Anti-Abuse Rule), for example, is designed to sweep up tax minimisation schemes that even a reasonable person would not regard as fair, just or equitable, even though they fall within the law.

Naturally, the insidious impact here is that clamping down on tax abuse involves a reversal of the usual legal burden of proof. As a result, the State (via HMRC) is regarded as the legitimate owner of monies and taxpayer citizens are required to prove that their financial affairs are ethically and morally justifiable as well as legally robust.

Finally there is **tax evasion**. This is simply illegal activity (such as squirrelling away funds in a Swiss bank account without disclosing their existence), which is normally subject to criminal sanction. Unfortunately, the terms 'tax avoidance' and 'tax evasion' have increasingly been used interchangeably by politicians, which has assisted in muddying already murky waters in this sphere.

In all fairness, the avowed aim of the coalition government during its terms of office has been to promote even more transparency in this policy area. However, given the importance to the UK of financial services, it is neither prudent nor realistic, whatever the communiques at G8 and G20 summits may say, for the UK to go out on a limb over tax policy without global cooperation and internationally binding agreements. As such, the controversy surrounding 'tax avoidance' is unlikely to disappear any time soon.

Closer to home, there is one important weapon in our armoury. UK tax remains fiendishly complicated; indeed, in 2012 our tax code overtook India's to become the largest in the world. Complexity is the godparent to avoidance. In tax matters, as in political life as a whole, it is always best to **keep it simple**. Easier said than done! To show that the government's heart is in the right place, it set up within three months of taking office in 2010 the Office of Tax Simplification (OTS). The good news is that virtually every one of the tax reliefs it has recommended ending in its reviews over recent years has been scrapped. Unfortunately, in Budgets since 2010, three times as many *new* reliefs have been created as the OTS has in its work been able to mark out for abolition.

‡

The fracturing of the austerity consensus, 14 March 2015

'Deficit down, growth up, jobs up, living standards on the rise, Britain on the rise; a budget for Britain – the comeback country'

In hindsight, the Chancellor was thought to have overplayed his hand at the Autumn Statement. His prediction of surpluses in 2018–19 and 2019–20 had led many commentators, as well as the opposition, to question the scale of spending cuts that were likely to be required in the next parliament. The Tories, so the line went, were seeking to shrink public spending as a proportion of GDP to levels 'not seen since the 1930s'.

Having promised that the deficit would be cleared by the end of the coalition's term, the expectation had been that most of the painful reductions in departmental spending would have been over. It was not clear, in this election year, that the public was willing to accept a further round of restraint, and fresh debate had begun as to the effectiveness and desirability of government austerity – a theme I explored in the following preview of the Chancellor's final Budget on 18 March.

In the event, the Chancellor implicitly acknowledged he may have gone too far by using the Budget to pare back his austerity plans, pushing the idea of a small surplus emerging only in the final year of the next parliament. With an eye on the votes of Middle England, he announced measures to help savers, with changes to ISAs and the removal of the punitive tax charge levied on pensioners accessing their annuity, alongside another hike in the personal allowance up to £12,500, a further fuel duty freeze and a penny off a pint of beer.

He was also able to announce record employment levels, with the jobless rate down to 5.3 per cent, alongside more optimistic growth projections from the OBR in spite of their downwards revision of growth in 2014. Taken as a share of national income, the deficit had halved since the coalition took the reins in 2010, requiring £30 billion of additional savings in the next parliament to get the books balanced. Labour snapped that the Chancellor was attempting to hide an extreme plan on spending that could see NHS funding slashed, with Ed Miliband suggesting that nobody could believe 'the trust fund chancellor' and his 'Bullingdon Prime Minister'.

The Liberal Democrats, meanwhile, continued their strategy of differentiation, distancing themselves from the coalition's least popular policies and portraying themselves as a moderating force against a Tory Party gagging to slash spending. This strategy extended itself to presenting their own 'Yellow Budget' – rather a flop when Chief Secretary to the Treasury, Danny Alexander, delivered his address to an almost deserted Chamber.

The Greek debt crisis of spring 2010, and the austerity agenda it heralded, brought tear gas and smoke bombs to the streets of Athens. But it also ignited an otherwise colourless general election campaign being fought two thousand miles away in the UK. Seemingly overnight, the storm in Athens provided the context for a toughening of the economic message that had been long overdue here. If we failed to elect a government sufficiently determined to tackle the UK's gaping budget deficit (or so the story went), financial calamity of the Greek variety would soon be visiting our shores.

Five years on and the perennial Greek financial woes once again provide the backdrop to a domestic general election campaign. This time, however, its dictation of the mood is subtler – and potentially more dangerous.

After half a decade of grinding reform, acute debt servicing and squeezed public expenditure, the Greek electorate has rebelled against the austerity consensus by electing a radical Syriza-led government. Cast as the plucky leftist challenger to Germanic fiscal rigidity, the new Greek leadership has since won a four-month bailout extension. As ever in the eurozone saga, more time has been bought as politics continues to outweigh economic realities. Expect to see the anti-austerity agenda debated more widely over the coming months, and the sustainability of the eurozone without Greece. Incidentally, the strongest critics of Athens at the moment hail not from Berlin, but Ireland, Spain and Italy, who feel that they have swallowed their ECB austerity medicine and finally see light at the end of the tunnel.

The Greek situation matters to the mood of the UK electorate. For a start, voters may well reflect on how little has changed since they last went to the polls. In spite of it all, the eurozone has muddled through courtesy of ultra-low interest rates, sheer political will and the markets' incorporation of Grexit risk into their assumptions. For all the talk of imminent collapse and economic meltdown, the reality has in many ways been far more benign. As a result, talk of looming disaster no longer carries the weight it once did.

Second, challengers to the consensus are on the march as the schism grows between northerly eurozone members and those with a more Mediterranean outlook. Extreme leftist movements are swiftly going mainstream in places like Spain, where the fledgling Podemos party commands 30 per cent in polls in spite of being in existence for only eighteen months. This is largely a reflection of voters' desperation, but it also indicates a growing appetite for a radically alternative way of thinking that has been embraced, albeit in different form, on these shores.

Finally, global quantitative easing programmes have not (yet) proved inflationary. In fact, the imminent threat in the West is now one of *de*flation, which is why the European Central Bank has belatedly and cautiously turned to the printing presses itself. Add to this the fact that interest rates remain at rock bottom and continental governments continue to be able to borrow from the markets at suicidally cheap rates. In short, we have now had over half a decade of sustained borrowing and money-printing, and the roof has not fallen in.

Looking across at Greece in spring 2015, therefore, the British voter might mistakenly conclude that the risks of choosing a path other than austerity are not quite what they were five years before. Would it really be that economically reckless for the British government now to borrow a little more in order to give the NHS, social services and perhaps even our armed forces what they need, particularly now that the economy seems to be growing so robustly?

The coalition has spent much of its time in office carefully building a consensus on the necessity for sustained spending constraint. That narrative was bought into by the electorate perhaps more readily than we might have imagined. But the reaction to Chancellor George Osborne's most recent Autumn Statement showed its potential limits. When he forecast a budgetary surplus by the end of the decade, he was roundly attacked for the scale of spending cuts that would be required over the next parliament to reach such a target. This has given Labour a window of opportunity, allowing them to put forward an 'austerity lite' agenda, a theme they are likely to build on over the coming weeks.

Opinion polls have long suggested an indeterminate outcome following May's ballot, with the Scottish Nationalists substantially boosting their representation north of the border. New SNP leader Nicola Sturgeon has already called on Ed Miliband to champion an alternative approach to austerity that could see an additional £180 billion spent on public services by 2020, and would be a condition of any pact between their parties. Labour has shown itself receptive to such a prospective deal by choosing to use last week's opposition day debate to reject the government's 'failing austerity plan'. We Conservatives comfort ourselves by thinking it a great danger for Ed Miliband to be cast as Britain's own Tsipras or

Hollande, devoid of any support from big business. But the nagging doubt is that such a characterisation would be in tune with the mood of the times, which is increasingly distrustful of the establishment and large corporations.

This all adds up to a political problem, certainly. But it is also an economic one. The coalition has hitherto done an excellent job of convincing the public that it has presided over a period of sober restraint. Yet, while Greece has borrowed £185 billion under its bailout plan since 2010, the coalition itself looks set to have borrowed £572 billion by the end of its term. One of the Chancellor's most impressive achievements has been to maintain the confidence of the markets in spite of this. But the truth is that while we have talked the talk of austerity, a fair bit of the heavy lifting is yet to come. Assuming we continue to ring-fence health, schools and international aid, the OBR forecasts that spending on non-protected departments will need to halve from £147 billion in 2014–15 to £86 billion in 2019–20. The job of fixing the public finances is not even halfway through and will need to be completed at a time of increasing, not diminishing, risk globally.

We are entering uncharted waters within the international economy. Far from paying down debt since the financial crisis seven years ago, the 16th Geneva Report revealed in September that the total burden of world debt has increased from 180 per cent of global output in 2008 to 212 per cent in 2013. Much of this increase was driven by China, which vastly expanded credit in the aftermath of the financial crisis to keep the global economy going, and has woven a large amount of risk into its economy as a result, primarily through the inflation of a rampant real estate bubble.

Meanwhile, central banks have hit the printing presses with gusto. The United States may now be winding down its programme of quantitative easing, but Japan, the world's third biggest economy, has been cranking up its own version in an audacious attempt to tackle deflation. Net global QE by the European Central Bank and Bank of Japan is due to hit $400 billion a quarter, with the latter's programme so colossal that it is essentially buying up Japan's entire bond market. These are unprecedented policy interventions that ought to be highly stimulative. Yet all the evidence suggests that the effectiveness of quantitative easing in reviving economies is ever more in doubt. It begs the question, how will this all end?

I have written many times about my concern that excessively loose monetary policy, alongside the racking up of ever more debt, will eventually spark another financial crisis on a potentially more devastating scale. When all the normal market signals have disappeared under a mountain of cheap money, it remains nigh-on impossible to make a rational investment decision, ensuring that risk is always and everywhere mispriced and creating enormous danger at the point at which you try to return the economy to some kind of normality.

The situation in Greece may indicate a fracturing in our own consensus on austerity, but we cannot allow Ed Miliband and his fellow travellers to develop that theme unchecked as we approach May's general election. The UK remains hugely overleveraged at a time when there are considerable risks in the global economy that could well lead to fresh financial crisis. The greatest signal the Chancellor can now send to the electorate and markets that he is serious about fixing our public finances is the delivery of a deeply unexciting Budget. No glittering giveaways. No electoral sweeteners. Just the sober message that no matter the rumblings on the continent, Britain understands that the need to live within our means is every bit as pressing as it was five years ago.

‡

So what's so unsustainable about minority government?, 30 March 2015

As fevered speculation continued about the likely outcome of May's election, behind closed doors few parliamentarians believed Conservatives could secure a working majority. The best we could hope for, most of us mused, was to be the largest party, at which point we would have to decide whether to try to form a coalition once more or to push on as a minority administration. It seemed impossible that after five years of austerity, the electorate would reward us with more seats than in 2010.

Over a century has passed since two consecutive general elections produced indeterminate outcomes. Hung parliaments – at least while a first-past-the-post voting system persists – may be the new norm. But should coalition government invariably follow?

Certainly opinion polls and betting over the past year suggest we may well once again be in this territory come May. With the two main parties typically hovering at just above 30 per cent in the polls, at no time in the past four and a half years has it looked less likely that there will end up being a majority Conservative or Labour government. Yet Nick Clegg and Ed Davey are adamant that the Liberal Democrats will not prop up a minority government with 'supply and confidence'.

Even those of us who supported a second 2010 election (and believe even without hindsight that this would have best served the national interest) recognise that the mood of the nation at the time dictated, following Cleggmania, that the Liberal Democrats had earned their place(s) at the cabinet table. I suspect this will categor- ically *not* be the case in the wake of May 2015's poll.

My working assumption until early 2014 was that the erstwhile third party of British politics would recover from its dismal single- digit poll ratings and end up with at least forty seats. However, it now seems more likely that the junior coalition partners will end up with no more than one tenth of the popular vote. While this may well still provide the Liberal Democrats with a multiple of the number of seats that UKIP win (even on a markedly smaller vote share), I suspect it will be difficult for them to have the credibility to *insist* upon a coalition. In truth, the sort of indeterminate outcome to the next election which most commentators now expect will only have one certainty – that the Liberal Democrats will be seen as the big losers. How can they surf the national mood to stay in office?

We may also be heading towards an election outcome where the largest party does not win the most votes (this happened in both

1951 and February 1974). That might well be compounded by the party coming third in the national vote, securing far fewer seats than the fourth party and the SNP (which contests only fifty-nine of the 650 constituencies). Do not discount that the combination of the first and third parties' seats will still not comprise a majority. This all augurs ill when it comes to maintaining public support for the current electoral system. Indeed, 2015 could be the election outcome that brings the first-past-the-post system to breaking point, although our electoral system has hitherto had an uncanny knack of reflecting the national mood. Despite all the fevered speculations, it may still do so in May.

The potential triumph of the SNP also raises the intriguing prospect that minority rule will become more palatable. Alex Salmond has already indicated that no deal will be offered that keeps Conservatives in office (a pre-emptive strike to the Labour charge that 'Vote SNP, get the Tories'). Nevertheless, if the SNP were able to secure thirty-five or more seats, reducing Labour to a fraction of their present strength and all but wiping out the Lib Dems north of the border, the strong argument made in 2010 that the Conservatives could not form a plausible government with a solitary seat in Scotland would not necessarily play out. One of the unsung benefits of coalition was that the government was able to claim twelve MPs with Scottish seats. But a massive SNP advance might, in Westminster political terms, simply turn Scotland into 'another Northern Ireland' – a place where political party allegiance as we know it in the rest of the UK is simply 'different'.

In May 2010, there was an almost unseemly headlong rush to 'do a coalition deal'. By late spring this year, however, the alibi of imminent economic crisis is unlikely to be there. It is also the case that the financial markets are unlikely to take fright at the prospect of weeks of political horse-trading. In truth, by 7 May political uncertainty of some sort will already have been factored in by the markets. Nor will a hung parliament be such a novelty, so the UK political class would, I suspect, be rather more relaxed about coalition negotiations taking weeks rather than days. The next Queen's Speech may not be delivered until June. In the meantime, special party conferences may be the order of the day before any deal is endorsed by potential coalition parties; such delay will also result in plenty of 'noises off' from MPs and party activists, making it far less likely that even the most determined leaderships will be able to railroad a coalition deal to fruition as happened in 2010. Even if the numbers were to allow for a Labour–Lib Dem coalition, I suspect that tribal loyalties will probably hold firm, not least as Labour have over the past five years reaped the benefit of the 'left-wing vote' not being as divided as it has been since the formation of the SDP in 1981.

It strikes me that, despite all its apparent inherent unsustainability for a fixed five-year term, minority government becomes potentially a more palatable, practicable and popular option.

What is the problem with a minority administration anyway? The arguments *against* such an arrangement are well rehearsed. Progress on getting the government's legislative programme through Parliament could grind to a halt, with each detail subject to painstaking negotiation. This could serve to heighten public scepticism about politicians' ability to deliver solutions to the nation's problems. Some would also point to financial market uncertainty but, as I have suggested, this may already have been priced in by Election Day.

It is also worth remembering that we have already had a minority administration in one house of Parliament over the past sixteen years without insuperable difficulty. Naturally, this has constrained governments to a certain degree, but in the House of Lords they have had to negotiate with other parties to get business done. From time to time (in fact rather frequently) votes have been lost in the Upper House, but arguably better legislation has emerged. What is so objectionable about extending this practice to the elected House of Commons? Perhaps minority government will truly allow Parliament, and MPs, to rise to the occasion.

We Conservatives should instinctively support the passing of fewer Acts of Parliament and better, more extensive scrutiny of legislation. Minority government will make necessary thorough pre-legislative scrutiny of government Bills, and the whips will need to be pragmatic at the prospect of losing clauses in their legisla-tion where they cannot persuade a Commons' majority. Life will assuredly go on, but (say it in hushed terms) the influence of party managers will go into decline!

In fact, a minority administration might well last the full course of a five-year fixed-term parliament, but only if party managers realise at the outset that a fundamental change of mindset is required, along-side a reversal of the trend since the Blair years for power to flow towards the executive and away from the legislature. This means a fresh style of operation and attitude from Whips' Offices quite unlike that which they have been accustomed to when coalition government commanded a clear majority. Flexibility will be their watchword, with coalitions of support built as and when they are needed.

There is an assumption that a minority government would – even *could only* – operate through confidence and supply agreements. But the avenues open to party managers, especially in a six-party set-up, might be broader than that. Let us not forget that the opposition parties themselves may not collectively form a majority, and have their own electoral anxieties and vulnerabilities that leave them open to deals. This makes ad hoc pacts, such as an agreement not to vote down a Budget or support for key items or parts of legislation, a distinct possibility. This would especially apply if the government were able to appeal to the public over the heads of its opponents by putting forward sensible, considered policy proposals. The desire among opposition parties to avoid a return to the polls (on costs grounds, if nothing else), and the difficulty in dislodging a govern-ment once it holds power in such circumstances, should also never be underestimated.

As the two main parties are becalmed in the polls, and support for smaller parties waxes and wanes with greater volatility, a minor-ity administration that puts forward a measured and thoughtful legislative programme, calling for public and parliamentary sup-port on each of its agenda items, might well prove just the tonic for an electorate disillusioned by the inability of majority govern-ment to reflect its views. For a nation that continues to face some

relentlessly tough economic choices after May's poll, sharper legislation and more open public debate over its difficult decision-making
would also be no bad thing.

‡

The London Powerhouse: universities are at the heart of the capital's success (*City AM*), 30 March 2015

*As part of the 'rebalancing' agenda that sought to make the UK economy
less reliant on London and its financial services industry, the Chancellor
had developed a 'Northern Powerhouse' strategy to improve infrastructure and incentivise economic growth in and around the northern cities
of Manchester, Leeds, Liverpool, Newcastle and Sheffield. In response,
City AM began a series of articles about the 'London Powerhouse',
exploring what makes the capital thrive. In my piece for the newspaper,
I focused on London's flourishing higher education sector and suggested
how northern cities might try to replicate some of its successes as part of
the Chancellor's exciting new strategy.*

Dreaming spires and cloistered courtyards. The image of Oxbridge
has for centuries defined the idea of excellence in Britain's global
higher education offering. But in the twenty-first century, it is London's elite universities that are tearing up the script.

Last September, Imperial College shared second place with
Cambridge in the QS World University Rankings, hot on the heels
of Harvard. UCL, meanwhile, tied with Oxford for fifth place. A separate 2014 study rated UCL higher than Oxbridge for research strength.
It is a brand being aggressively built upon as it draws up expansion
plans for a new campus, UCL East, on the former Olympic Park.

The relentless rise of London's institutions in the university league
tables coincides with our city's seemingly unstoppable growth as a
premier destination for global talent, capital and ideas. Oxford and
Cambridge Universities dominate their respective cities, whereas
London's universities are threads in a complex metropolitan tapestry.

While London's students may not get the authentic 'university town' experience, they are more than compensated by a vast pool of opportunities.

Just as the metropolis has married financiers with start-ups to create a booming tech sector, our universities have become adept at collaborating with the city's business, philanthropic, government and research communities to widen their offering. My constituency is home to three of the capital's top universities – Imperial, KCL and LSE. Their expansion plans have fascinated over the past decade. In 2007, Imperial integrated its medical faculty with St Mary's and Hammersmith hospitals. Today, Imperial College Healthcare is a globally respected centre for medical research, with patients benefiting from cutting-edge care and academics able to trial new treatments on London's uniquely diverse population. Imperial is similarly collaborating with Aviva Investors on a new White City campus, Imperial West, to support science start-ups and ensure that the UK benefits commercially from breakthroughs made in its university labs. The plan is to ensure that the university will soon be virtually independent of public funding.

Amidst healthy rivalry between London's top institutions, there is also partnership. Imperial, King's and UCL, for example, have joined forces with government and others to build the ground-breaking Francis Crick Institute for biomedical research in King's Cross. Once open, this will complement the arrival of Central St Martins in nearby Granary Square, whose student population has already injected life into the urban revival of this once seedy quarter of central London. In fact, the investment of universities in formerly forgotten corners of the city is proving central to the sustainability of some of London's biggest housing and commercial regeneration projects.

So compelling is the proposed mix of good transport links, housing, flexible commercial space and cultural facilities at Stratford's Olympicopolis, for example, that Loughborough University wants a piece of the action – it has snapped up the former broadcasting centre to help expand its postgraduate offering in engineering, digital technology, sports and the creative industries. This is only one of a number of non-London universities acknowledging the importance of having a presence in the capital as part of their international offering. Naturally, London's institutions thrive because of their academic excellence, but it is the fact that so many high-fee-paying overseas students want to study in our city that is the real key to their storming success. The financial clout of this international contingent has also given London universities the confidence to expand.

In the aftermath of 2008's financial crash, there was much talk of the pressing need to rebalance the economy away from banking and finance. That task has been completed very successfully in London with the creative, tech, research and education sectors all thriving. But this has only served to entrench the capital's dominance in the wider UK economy, rather than address the other rebalancing act of boosting the regions.

How the rest of the UK's universities compete with the southern academic powerhouse is the real challenge now. Some experts warn of a 'relentless decline' of the other leading universities in England. A fifth of government research funding is now claimed by the top three universities – the so-called 'golden triangle' of Oxford, Cambridge and London – and it is the capital city that has over 100,000 square metres of new research facilities in the pipeline.

If the Chancellor's Northern Powerhouse and broader devolution agenda is to work, he should examine how London's universities have not just integrated academic excellence into the heart of this global city, but provided a compelling educational offering to the world through relentlessly building links with the worlds of industry, commerce, government and finance.

‡

Osborne should prioritise taxpayer value over rapid RBS privatisation (*City AM*), 10 June 2015

Well, a lot had happened since my last article, not long after which I had vacated my parliamentary office to begin a fourth bid to represent the Cities of London & Westminster. Following a campaign where polls made headlines over policies, I had gone along with the gloomy view that there would be a virtual dead heat between Conservatives and Labour.

The Guardian's final ICM poll, published for 7 May's front page mere hours before the polling booths opened, had been as follows:

	Seats	Vote share (%)
Con	273	35
Lab	273	35
LD	27	9
UKIP	2	11
SNP	52	5

It seems it had been a little wide of the mark. The outcome turned out to be nothing short of earth-shattering, as the SNP triumphed in all but three seats in Scotland, the Lib Dems collapsed and even Labour won twenty-six fewer seats than in 2010:

	Seats	Vote share (%)
Con	331 (+24)	36.9
Lab	232 (-26)	30.4
LD	8 (-49)	7.9
UKIP	1 (+1)	12.6
SNP	56 (+50)	4.7

The Conservatives' ability to secure a working majority had left most of us dumbfounded, and pre-election speculation on the likely form of a post-May coalition swiftly turned to excitable chatter on how we had pulled off such a victory.

There was little doubt that considerable credit could be attributed to our consistent lead against Labour on the two key questions of leadership and economic stewardship. I had always maintained that Ed Miliband had more to offer than the cartoon portrayal of him in the mainstream media. Nonetheless, Miliband's failure to earn either the nation's respect or a place in its heart gave his party an enormous difficulty to overcome from the outset. Meanwhile, with Ed Balls leading on economic strategy, there was no sense of a clean break from the Gordon Brown era of boom and bust.

However, we Conservatives were also lucky in three distinct ways:

First, who would have guessed after the conclusive Scottish Independence referendum result of September 2014 that the Scottish Nationalist Party would have virtually swept the board north of the border, humiliating Scottish Labour, but also alarming middle England with talk midcampaign of constructing an anti-Conservative coalition? The thought of a party not even contesting 591 of the 650 UK seats holding the English to ransom did untold damage to Labour in key English marginals.

Then there was the fate of the Liberal Democrats. Their disastrous strategic error was not to campaign in defence of their record in coalition with the Tories, but to seek differentiation at all times. Thus, they forfeited credit for the economic and political stability of 2010–15 but also cast themselves as part of the potential chaos of a future grand centre-left coalition. With hindsight, we were all blindsided by the apparent strength of Liberal Democrat incumbency. Yet, as the party nationally was consistently beached at 7–8 per cent in the polls, losing two thirds of its voters, it really should not have come as a surprise that even its most popular incumbents would be unable to resist the tide. The truth is that very few sitting Liberal Democrats would be able to withstand the loss of even one third of their vote. And so it proved.

Finally, the continual reporting on tight opinion polls may well have helped distort the outcome in the Conservative Party's favour. Imagine if throughout the final month of the campaign we had been consistently 5 to 6 percentage points ahead of Labour. The focus of the campaign would then surely have been on the party's proposed spending cuts. Instead, the virtually universal view that we were heading for a dead-heat and the post-electoral coalition deal surely played firmly into our hands by galvanising those who may otherwise have stayed at home.

The emergence post-election of new grassroots populist leaders Jeremy Corbyn and Tim Farron of the Labour and Liberal Democrat

parties respectively, both with unproven general vote-winning quali-
ties, suggested that domestic politics would be characterised by a sense
of shambolic chaos in the months and years ahead.

As the new parliament dawned I also realised that, in starting my
fourth term, I was no longer the Young(ish) Turk of self-regard but, in Con-
servative terms at least, almost an Old Stager. Of my 329 party colleagues,
fully 257 had entered the House of Commons after me, yet only thirty-seven
of us had ever experienced a Conservative-majority government.

After five years on the Intelligence and Security Committee, I was
given a fresh challenge as vice-chairman of the Conservative Party, head-
ing up our International and Outreach Office. Before the final result
was even declared on 8 May, political pundits had turned their minds to
the now-certainty of a referendum on our membership of the European
Union, and the Prime Minister's promise first to try to renegotiate our
EU relationship. In my fascinating new role, I was now to have the
opportunity to speak with European allies from our sister parties on the
continent, as this key moment in history played itself out.

Meanwhile in London, the City fraternity waited to hear what
Chancellor George Osborne was likely to do with his renewed Treasury
mandate at June's Mansion House dinner. In the days leading up to
the event, it became clear that he intended to signal the government's
readiness to begin selling-off taxpayers' shares in RBS. He had chosen the
same theatre two years before to announce his intention to put the pub-
lic stake in Lloyds Banking Group up for sale, and had carefully been
selling the shares on the stock market ever since, taking our ownership
of Lloyds down from 43 per cent to just below 18 per cent by June 2015.
But was the time now ripe to give RBS the same treatment? In this piece
I wrote for City AM, I sounded a note of caution.

Almost seven years on from the £46 billion taxpayer bailout of RBS,
it may seem perverse to ask, 'Why the rush?' when it comes to selling our remaining 79 per cent stake in the still-ailing bank. But
this is precisely the question that must be posed if, as anticipated,
Chancellor George Osborne sets out at the Mansion House tonight
a timetable for the Treasury's exit from the banking business.

The then Labour government received plaudits for its October 2008 rescue package of RBS and the Lloyds Banking Group (the product of Lloyds TSB taking on the insolvent HBOS), which saw vast swathes of the British banking sector brought under public ownership. In swiftly shoring up these ailing British institutions, broader economic calamity had been avoided and the cash machines would continue to churn out their notes.

But beyond that short-term goal, the erstwhile government never set out an accompanying long-term strategy over the public's eventual exit from the banking business. This absence of a clear plan continued under the coalition government from 2010. Everyone seems to agree on the desirability of as rapid a withdrawal as possible from RBS and Lloyds. What has too often been less pressing is the need to extract maximum value for our collective share. Alongside these considerations has been a broader imperative to get some semblance of normality back to the finance sector, allowing two of our Big Four banks to operate freely as commercial entities. Yet at times, there has also been a sense that politicians have sought to use taxpayers' shares in the banks as a mechanism by which to deliver political messages on tricky subjects like executive pay or SME lending. Never has it been entirely apparent which of these jostling objectives is given greatest priority by the Treasury.

In signalling last month that he would like to deliver £23 billion of privatisations over the next financial year, the Chancellor has indicated that a Conservative-majority government regards a quick-fire public withdrawal from the banking sector as its most urgent priority. Instinctively, I have plenty of sympathy with that view. Nobody expected back in 2008/09 that taxpayers would still own nearly four fifths of RBS in 2015. I also appreciate the Treasury's enthusiasm to stimulate wider participation in the market by potentially offering a share discount to smaller investors in Lloyds, as well as assisting in the deficit reduction plan. There is probably a lot of truth too in the notion that RBS's shares will only continue to be depressed by the state's majority ownership, creating a vicious cycle which may mean that taxpayers will always face a loss when selling up their stake.

Nevertheless, RBS and Lloyds are very different beasts. The former is simply not strong enough for the Treasury to replicate the successful drip-feeding of Lloyds shares into the marketplace that has seen our collective stake in LBG drop to just under 18 per cent in recent months – and bring in a £3.5 billion paper profit to the Treasury. Whereas Lloyds has done well in offloading its riskiest investments and getting back in the black, RBS remains in a dismal state in spite of the herculean efforts of chief executives Stephen Hester and Ross McEwan. By the end of the last financial year, it was still holding £349 billion of risk-weighted assets, and some analysts concluded RBS to be the worst year-to-date performer in the European banking sector after the Greek banks. Remember that this is before taking into account significant forthcoming penalties from a variety of regulatory investigations that will see the balance sheet take a further short-term hit. In short, RBS is unlikely to be turning in a sustainable profit before this decade is through – in selling its stake any time soon, the taxpayer would be looking at a loss of £13.4 billion.

In respect of Lloyds, I am still to be convinced that a specific discounted retail offering, such as that which received such unexpected enthusiasm over Royal Mail, is strictly necessary, as the Treasury looks to sell its remaining stake. The fact that Royal Mail was seven times oversubscribed has no doubt encouraged the cash-strapped Treasury, but public ownership in the part-nationalised banks is of a different magnitude to the original £1.7 billion Royal Mail deal. In short, any discount might well represent a significant loss to the taxpayer. In all honesty, the existing, careful, drip-feed approach being coordinated so successfully by Morgan Stanley should continue.

The Chancellor's zeal to see the swift return of the banking sector to private ownership is to be commended. But our overriding priority must be to exact the greatest return for taxpayers' stake in a global finance sector whose recovery remains fragile and uncertain. If that means that even as late as 2020 the majority of RBS remains under some form of public guarantee and ownership, it is a price we should pay.

‡

Europe and debt: twin challenges for
the new government, 18 June 2015

I was asked to speak at a City conference to an audience of financiers and international business folk anxious to understand where our party was coming from on the European issue and keen to hear about some of the economic challenges likely to face the new Conservative government. I took the opportunity to set out some of my own thoughts on the emotional case for our remaining in the European Union, alongside its economic advantages, and to highlight my continued worry about the ever-expanding sea of global debt.

Just two months ago, many of us had assumed that the UK was heading into a period of potentially damaging political uncertainty. I know there is much relief from the City that minority government or the prospect of a Labour/SNP alliance *instinctively* hostile to business has been avoided. Nonetheless, there remains some foreboding. The stark truth is that the spirit of the age remains more hostile to enterprise, profit and wealth than any of us whose careers began only in the last quarter of a century have experienced.

Thankfully, the Chancellor of the Exchequer has already made some moves towards addressing some of the areas that had most strained the coalition's relationship with the City. The era of new regulation upon new regulation is over; the bank levy will be tailored to a genuine rescue fund rather than a bottomless pot of cash to assist in deficit reduction; the public finances will, if all goes to plan, be converted via sustained growth and public spending cuts. Tax-rises will only be on the agenda if Plan A fails to have the desired impact on deficit reduction.

Now I wouldn't be a real-life Conservative MP if I were not to turn my attention, especially with this pan-continental audience, to matters European.

If the UK is serious about maintaining a workable relationship within the European Union, one of our nation's most important alliances, we need urgently to stand up to the fantasy that the EU is a constant conspiracy by foreigners to undermine British interests.

One lesson of last September's Scottish referendum is to make a case that owes as much to emotional as economic or rational impulse. The United Kingdom of tabloid myth is a nation that has always stood proudly apart from the continent, with our unique culture of entrepreneurship, intellectual endeavour and empire developed in isolation from Europe. In truth, the story of the UK – from ancient invasions of our shores to British military adventures on the continent; the trading of goods to the sharing of intellectual ideas; familial exchanges among continental historic monarchies to the nurturing of relationships between ordinary citizens – is one of centuries-old cross-pollination with our European neighbours. Philosophical battles and religious frictions across this continent have shaped the collection of secular nation states that, while infused with Christian values, are (thankfully) ruled by law, not religious ideology.

Naturally, Europeans might happily operate as an unbound collection of individual nation states. But the question is whether we can continue to achieve more in close alliance. Last autumn, many English, Welsh and Northern Irish folk reacted with dismay as our Scottish counterparts willingly contemplated throwing away a framework of values and institutions within a UK in which national differences could flourish.

The challenge for Europe has always been to balance creative friction and competition between nation states without sparking war. It was a balance which European leaders struggled to resolve until the formation and gradual expansion of the EEC. For all the Union's faults – and they are legion – perhaps too often we take for granted the fact that three generations of Europeans have been able to take for granted peace on our continent. This is a remarkable historic achievement that must be celebrated more whole-heartedly. Indeed, with the UK's own near obsession of commemorating both twentieth-century World Wars, not to mention Waterloo, this should not be a difficult case to make. Nor is it one which is forgotten by our eastern European parties, who cling even closer to the Union in the shadows of a resurgent Russia.

I am proud of all that the UK has brought to the European Union. We act as an essential bridge between the EU and the

English-speaking world. We provide a crucial counterweight to the established Franco-German axis and we bring real economic clout. We should now defend the Brussels institutions that we have helped create as providing a decisive means for international cooperation in insecure, testing times. In my view, the Council and Commission are a bulwark of collective continental security rather than reflecting an irretrievable loss of British national sovereignty.

The Single Market, meanwhile, provides one of the finest examples in global economic history of international cooperation to the benefit of hundreds of millions of Europeans. This vast economic zone, larger than the combined GDPs of the US and Japan, provides a level playing field in which UK businesses can trade. This has allowed the City of London to supply legal, financial and professional services with ease to our European neighbours. Our fledgling IT firms, to name but one industry where we enjoy a competitive advantage, have been able to access markets swiftly without complying with twenty-seven different sets of regulations. British car manufacturers have been able to enjoy a resurgence with the investment that has flowed from foreign firms seeking a base from which to access the continent.

The founding principles of European cooperation include free labour movement. In the fierce domestic debate about immigration, it is worth making the case forcefully that the UK economy, not least here in the City of London, has and remains a huge beneficiary of skilled migration before seeking (rightly in my view) to promote tougher sanctions for those EU migrants neither willing nor able to contribute economically to another country. Our system of welfare benefits will need to be contributory, like much of Europe, rather than paid out automatically to migrants – and the indigenous population – on the basis of need.

Nevertheless, if we are to stand any chance of success in extracting significant concessions, we need to be less belligerent in tone and mindful of how we are perceived by fellow Member states. Many in France, for example, are perplexed by British hostility to the deal we enjoy in the EU. According to their view, the EU is a club that has vastly expanded eastwards in the past decade at the UK's insistence. The founding principles reflect British values of free trade, a massive Single Market and open competition for goods and financial/professional services. Moreover, it is a club whose other Members have granted the UK permanent exemption from both the single currency and Schengen area.

Margaret Thatcher famously handbagged her way to a rebate in 1984, but thereafter it was the *implied* threat that helped her negotiate favourable deals. To many in Brussels, the UK is nevertheless seen as the eternal complainer, whose appetite for EU reform will never be sated. Ironically, it is exactly the same sentiment that the remainder of the UK has towards the seemingly endless devolutionary demands of Scottish nationalists.

I accept that for those without the continental blood I am proud to have in my veins, it is difficult to attach a romantic ideal to Europe. However, one monumental moment that still brings a tear to my eye when I watch it again is the sight, thirty years ago at Verdun, of French President Francois Mitterand grasping German Chancellor Helmut Kohl's hand as they stood together in commemoration of those who died in the fiercest battles of the Great War.

Deep down I believe there *is* an emotional case to make for Europe. Not perhaps its bland institutions and faceless bureaucrats, nor the reconciliation of competing national interests that means its rules reflect the impurity of compromise. Nevertheless, the European Union remains a powerful symbol of togetherness in a world crumbling into ever-smaller blocs of ethnic, religious and nationalist narrowness.

Please forgive me now if I turn to a more general economic theme.

I believe on matters economic the new government would be wise to raise its horizons beyond European adventures to addressing the sustainability of the UK's recovery in an ever-expanding sea of global debt. It is important that we recognise precisely the message from the markets in the pricing of that debt – and how that bleak assessment contrasts with the healthy projections of real economic growth in the years ahead.

In June 2010 as the last parliament began, the Chancellor assumed the then £1.32 trillion of accumulated national debt would cost £66.5 billion annually to service. Yet now, half a decade on, after a passage of 'austerity' that in fact has produced successively five of the seven largest annual deficits in UK economic history, the debt pile has risen to £1.63 trillion. But here's the rub – this expanded borrowing and enlarged debt will, apparently, require a mere £51 billion a year in debt interest. So much for the penalties to be paid by any government daring to borrow and spend recklessly!

So why are the herd of investors in the capital markets pricing government debt with such deceptive, perhaps ever-dangerous, calm? Incidentally, it is worth noting these record low interest rates apply to government bonds issued by all but the most basket-case economies in the eurozone. In large part, there is a fear that deflation may be here to stay and a prolonged period of stagnant, very low growth may be in the offing. In such uncertain circumstances taking on government debt may indeed seem the safest bet. Add the impact of quantitative easing and the regulatory driven excess demand for bonds, which has helped reduce the cost of borrowing by governments.

However, at the self-same time, our own OBR, along with the IMF, projects healthy *growth* for the UK economy in the years to come. Not a Japanese-style deflationary stagnation implied by the pricing of government debt, but solid growth year-on-year at a rate of 2.5 to 3 per cent. The trouble that lies ahead for the UK economy is that, once the markets catch up to this reality, it is surely a racing certainty that the costs of servicing that ever-growing pile of debt will rise – and fast. In short and paradoxically, it is a sustained economic recovery that risks blowing a huge black hole into future years' budgets as the UK continues to grapple with the vastly expanded debt accumulated over the past decade. This is why drastic and determined government action on deficit reduction remains so critical for the medium-term health of the UK economy.

At the beginning of the year, analysis by the McKinsey Global Institute revealed that global debt – the accumulated borrowing of

governments, companies and households – had risen by 17 per cent
since the final quarter of 2007, when the collapse of Bear Stearns
and Lehman Brothers was in the offing. Even here in the UK, all
too often the efforts by households to pay down debt have been out-
weighed by further government borrowing. It is difficult to envisage
how this will all end – other than very painfully.

None of this is new – for it was as long ago as June 2006
that the central banks' club, the Bank of International Settlements,
struck a firm note of caution about the dangerous levels of
accumulated debt that had been built up in the global economy.
Government debt, personal debt and over-leverage. This was two
years before the crash, remember. When the crisis came in autumn
2008, the classic Keynesian solution to the crisis was QE.

Nevertheless, the racking up of debt on this scale represents the
biggest experiment ever conducted in the global economy. Seven
years on from the eye of the financial crisis storm, and a considerable way presumably into the next upcycle of economic activity, all
that has happened is that an even greater debt pile has accumulated
without any collective plan to pay it off having been conceived, let
alone put into practice. Short of the unleashing of a burst of unprecedentedly high levels of output and sector-wide productivity growth,
or else a programme of fiscal contraction hard to imagine in an era
of welfare entitlement and dependency, not to mention universal
suffrage, it is impossible to see how the developed world will ever
be able to repay these levels of debt.

Even history may not provide much of a comforting guide, as we
may really for once have entered an era that is 'different this time'.

Historically, governments have dealt with large debt overhangs
by allowing a little inflation to develop. As we know, this is *always*
perilous, as a small dose of rising prices often leads to higher levels
still (in fairness, the huge post-crash stimulus has not, despite natural fears, triggered such an orthodox outcome). The alternative is
to induce what economists call 'financial repression'.

The double whammy of the 1930s depression and the cost of
fighting the Second World War in the following decade left Western

economies with equivalent debt levels relative to national income. Between the 1950s and 1970s, yields from government bonds were set at just below inflation. As a consequence of the alchemy of compound interest, our collective borrowings, albeit in an era of persistent and strong economic growth, were in time paid down to manageable levels.

While this might be a comforting parallel, there are also some key differences. Most importantly, we live in an age of free cross-border capital flows and much of our borrowing comes from international sources. The model of squeezing creditors by negative real interest rates and rising prices does not work when credit is denominated in a foreign currency or in a deflationary era. We need only to look at the travails of the eurozone to see the limits of imposing financial repression when nation states are locked into a monetary straitjacket.

Not that we should be too complacent closer to home. Such a high share of UK government debt is now controlled by foreign creditors that any significant weakening of sterling would render our own public finances extremely vulnerable.

We hear much of the fact that one third of UK government bonds have been mopped up by the Bank of England. This has helped keep interest rates artificially low (seventy-six months now at the emergency 0.5 per cent level). However, potentially more distorting still is the fact that over 40 per cent of our gilts are owned by foreigners. In an uncertain world, these overseas creditors may take on the chin the repressing impact of artificially low returns on their bonds yielding less than the underlying rate of inflation. However, they may be far less sanguine at the impact of currency risk. If the currently benign market sentiment about sterling, despite record current account deficits, were to turn and the pound to fall, sterling denominated gilts in the hands of foreign investors would lose value. The prospect then of such overseas creditors losing confidence in the UK economy and selling off their bonds would have a potentially disastrous impact on the cost of servicing our debt. This is precisely what I suspect would have happened in the event of an indeterminate general election result, particularly if the outcome had been a minority Labour administration. While that eventuality has thankfully been avoided, we should remember that the economic fundamentals remain delicate.

For this reason, it is all the more important that government here and across the developed world persists as a matter of national urgency to reduce the deficit and ensure that it lives within its means as rapidly as possible.

While debtors, especially those servicing large debt piles, may welcome persistently low interest rates, they are a reflection of continued economic fragility rather than a clear sign of imminent economic recovery. Any sustainable economic recovery will require a path towards normal levels of credit pricing. After six and a half years of that emergency 0.5 per cent rate, businesses and individuals worryingly, if understandably, now begin to see this as some sort of new norm.

What should concern policymakers more than it evidently does at the moment is that it is difficult to imagine the circumstances in which the cost of credit might be raised without the economic roof falling in.

‡

Time to put that long-term economic plan into action, 21 June 2015

Not for nothing is economics hailed as the dismal science. Since the financial crash almost seven years ago, virtually every economic orthodoxy has been confounded by raw experience. The UK's deepest post-war recession should have heralded unprecedented levels of unemployment. By contrast, not only were the downturns of the early 1980s and early 1990s not replicated, but the coalition government oversaw a jobs miracle with employment levels today at an all-time high. The impact of £375 billion of quantitative easing and over six years of continuous near-zero emergency interest rates should by rights have resulted in runaway inflation. Yet the news from the *real* economy in May 2015 was the first dose of monthly *de*flation in sixty years. (Incidentally, discount much of the alarmist nonsense about this temporary drop in average prices – once last year's oil price collapse drops out and the wage rises of recent months are fed into the statistics, inflation will be back into positive territory.)

More worryingly, however, are two persistent deficits. As we know, for all the talk of 'reckless austerity', the past five years have seen the Treasury adopt a more pragmatic approach to social cohesion than its critics have credited, with the budget deficit still the second highest among developed nations at 5 per cent of GDP. It is the current account deficit, currently at some 5.5 per cent of GDP, which has also ebbed and flowed contrary to expectations. As sterling slumped in 2008, depreciating by over one-quarter, conventional wisdom anticipated an export boom. This did not come to pass. Meanwhile the 15 per cent rise in the UK's currency value over the past two years has thankfully not impacted even more adversely on that trade deficit.

Not that there is any cause for complacency. One of the central planks of the Treasury's economic plan in 2010 was to rebalance the economy by promoting savings, investment and exports. By any objective measure, five years on this is still very much work in progress. The UK's share of global exports has continued to contract – from 5.8 per cent at the turn of the century to 3.6 per cent in 2010, and down to just 3.3 per cent today. While the continued rise of China and India as global economic players clearly has a part to play in this, it is worth noting that Germany's export performance remains as robust today (an 8 per cent global share) as it was fifteen years ago. It is sobering to reflect that if we had been able to maintain our share of the fast-growing export growth markets, the current account deficit would have been wiped out over the past five years.

It is not for lack of initiatives. Many seasoned diplomatic watchers have been aghast as our own Foreign Office has rebranded itself almost exclusively in the direction of old-fashioned mercantilism and trade promotion. Let's hope UKTI's work starts to bear more tangible fruit soon. I know it is still achingly unfashionable to say it, but we are world leaders in financial, legal and business services, and global demand is returning in these spheres – so too in the bio-tech, pharmaceuticals and the creative industries, where the UK's comparative advantage remains clear.

Meanwhile, as we continue to spend beyond our means, we need to recognise that much of our current account deficit is funded by foreign direct investment. Ours is a proud global trading nation, and I am not suggesting we should shun Qatari, Chinese or even Russian investment in the UK economy. However, it is worth remember-ing that the income these assets (whether stocks or smart new office blocks) will produce in the decades ahead is liable to be exported from these shores. How will the next generation of UK pensioners be able to fund their retirement if the asset base of domestic pen-sion funds continues to be depleted in this way?

More urgent still, while the political risk of an anti-business Labour/SNP government has been put to bed, what if turmoil in the emerging or eurozone markets or a sharp correction in the UK commercial property market triggers a withdrawal of some of this foreign investment? The prospect of higher credit costs making the servicing of our burgeoning debt pile ever more difficult should not be ruled out. It makes it all the more important that we promote our long-term economic plan with renewed vigour.

More business investment should also help boost the UK's per-plexingly poor productivity record. Ironically, during the recent general election campaign Ed Balls' determination to play down Labour's 'tax, spend and borrow' image meant that he felt unable to propose a substantial boost to infrastructure investment. Historically low interest rates may now allow a Conservative government to take on this mantle. Borrowing to invest in infrastructure and our lam-entably lagging skills base potentially provides the best shot in the arm to reverse the UK's weak productivity record in many sectors.

In short, it is high time to ramp up that long-term economic plan!

‡

DfID – a practical rethink, 28 June 2015

The long-standing Conservative promise to commit 0.7 per cent of GDP to overseas aid had always been a difficult sell at a time when the message was one of austerity and belt-tightening across domestic spending departments and restraint at the Ministry of Defence and Foreign Office. I had been a long-time defender of the commitment, and set out in this article some ideas on how we might broaden public support for the Department for International Development as a crucial tool in projecting soft power.

TV quiz shows in Ethiopia, Facebook lessons in Laos and Hamlet productions in Ecuador – in the mind of the general public, I suspect none of these items counts as a worthy destination for British taxpayer cash. In the wake of press revelations this week detailing the recipients of overseas aid, the government seems inclined to agree, swiftly launching an investigation.

It is uncomfortable timing, as pressure mounts on the Department for International Development to justify its now legally guaranteed budget of 0.7 per cent GDP. As scores of migrants die weekly crossing the Mediterranean and others pitch up in Calais camps, Defence Secretary Michael Fallon has been pressing for aid money to be spent on preventing conflict in African nations. Sir Gerald Howarth's success in the Private Member's Bill ballot further turns the screws as he seeks to guarantee a 2 per cent GDP spend on the Ministry of Defence, in line with our NATO pledge. Meanwhile, £12 billion of welfare cuts are being sketched out that will sorely test the notion that nearly the same amount should be annually earmarked for overseas aid (up by over a third since 2010).

All this adds up to ever more critical attention being paid to DfID and its work. However, we should see this as an opportunity, rather than a threat.

I have long been a supporter of our overseas aid policy, but equally I believe the time has come for a broadening in the uses of the aid budget and a critical rethink of the way in which DfID operates. If the 0.7 per cent aid commitment is to command continued public support, we need to be wiser – and probably a little more candid and transparent – about how our money is being (and should be) spent.

Formally established as an independent department only in 1997, DfID was seen as a key component of the 'ethical foreign policy' set out by Robin Cook in the first ten days of the New Labour government. Overseas aid monies previously distributed from the Ministry of Defence and Foreign Office budgets were centralised, leaving little financial autonomy for either major department of state on key international projects. Instead, a new culture of 'programming' took hold in DfID that managed-out the potential for 'inappropriate' spending that could cause presentational problems to the government.

Cautious mandarins became more risk-averse. DfID project money was routinely awarded to known international bodies such as the World Bank or Unicef, rather than smaller, nimbler UK organisations and businesses. This helped dodge any accusation of conflicts of interest. The government would not be seen to promote corporate Britain abroad under the cloak of humanitarian assistance, but it also left those recognised brands to deal with any fall-out should questions be raised about the success of particular programmes. Indeed, these organisations' very respectability tended to mute testing questions about the effectiveness and impact of British aid money. This shift went hand-in-hand with the emergence of increasingly professional bidders who learned to speak the language of DfID programmers in order to win contracts. The result was often ponderous, expensive and wasteful programming that removed the ability of the UK to act quickly and effectively when specific needs arose.

Sadly, this culture remains today, with DfID programmers often overloaded with cash that is being increasingly bundled off to international bodies. That is not to suggest that the Department is not committed to providing good value or that our aid money is not typically spent effectively. However, DfID has become too process-driven, reducing our agility in the field and risking the benchmark of success for our development aid being the amount spent, rather than the added-value delivered. This approach also deters British organisations from being providers of assistance even when many overseas countries are keen for UK firms to be actively involved in development programmes.

This does not make the 0.7 per cent commitment to overseas aid wrong. In fact, the case for extending Britain's reach in this field gets stronger each year as we are confronted domestically with problems whose roots start thousands of miles away. However, I question whether large parts of DfID's budget should not now be devolved to the Foreign Office and Ministry of Defence. This would enable and authorise those on the ground (whether in overseas embassies or military bases) to spend sensibly, carefully and locally against agreed objectives rather than via DfID's programming process. The risk is that the degree of 'inappropriate spending' may rise as operatives test out ideas and providers, and then judge their practical impact on the job. But I reckon the costs of such seepage are likely to be more than compensated by wiping out the various layers of programming bureaucracy.

Finally, and most importantly, we must start encouraging the UK to be the provider of services and partnerships, particularly when it is the stated provider of choice for the recipient country. For instance, if a developing African nation wishes the London Stock Exchange to help partner in the establishment of proper financial markets, it should be directed to the City of London, not the World Bank.

Ironically, the one dog that did not bark during the recent general election campaign was the long-overdue debate on Britain's place in the world. Even Ed Miliband's brief and controversial foray at Chatham House on international affairs was overshadowed by his comments on the aftermath of the Libyan skirmish in 2011. In truth, some of our foreign aid monies are already being spent on global security and intelligence projects. We are paying more than lip-service to community-building and social cohesion in war-torn countries of the world alongside the more traditional aid programmes, centred on African as well as Asian and Caribbean Commonwealth nations.

However, I believe it is essential that we are more transparent, in this very dangerous and uncertain world, about the importance of integrating our foreign aid with military, diplomatic and trade commitments. Indeed, the time may soon be ripe for international security and social cohesion goals to be explicitly recognised by DfID funding in the years ahead. Few will have been unmoved by the appalling scenes in recent months on both the Mediterranean Sea and the Bay of Bengal, as thousands of refugees from Libya, Bangladesh and Burma risk literally everything for a better life. The solution to combating trafficking networks is both humanitarian and military, and where better than for the UK to take a lead?

It would be helpful if we were to communicate a broader range of benefits that come from our work abroad. In a globalised world, governments recognise that not all policy solutions are to be found at home. To prevent crime, to curb new waves of immigration, to stop the spread of disease, our efforts can be made more effective by concentrating on the source of an issue. Hunger relief and health programmes may be laudable in their own right, but British people want urgently to understand how DfID money benefits them personally. We should also, as a matter of course, communicate how strengthening our ties with developing countries will be of huge benefit in terms of our trade, energy and security interests.

During an era when UK defence expenditure, and with it our projection of 'hard power', is in decline, we should recognise that our taking a lead in provision of overseas aid brings the nation tangible 'soft power' benefits.

‡

Grexit may solve nothing, and cost Britain dearly, 10 July 2015

'Britain deserves a pay rise'

On 8 July, George Osborne delivered his second Budget of the year, but his first as Chancellor in a Conservative-majority government. At its heart was a promise to make the UK a 'low tax, high wage' economy, with a new National Living Wage for all workers aged over twenty-five, which by 2020 would stand at £9 per hour. Alongside this would be a squeeze on tax credits payments and a freeze on working-age benefits.

There would be £37 billion of further spending cuts by the end of the parliament, including shaving an additional £12 billion off the welfare budget and £20 billion from departmental budgets. Yet, spending overall would be £83.3 billion higher by 2020 than had been forecast in the March Budget. The Chancellor had well and truly broken from the austerity laid out in the unpopular 2014 Autumn Statement, but had sown the seeds of future discord among a batch of Tory backbenchers concerned about families in receipt of in-work benefits.

Other eye-catching measures included a gradual paring back of the bank levy; a commitment to spend 2 per cent of GDP on defence, in line with NATO requirements; further devolution of powers to cities; a new apprenticeship levy for large employers; and the abolition of the permanent non-dom status.

But chaos was once again erupting on the continent. In January, radical, anti-austerity party Syriza had swept to power in Greece on the promise to renegotiate the terms of the nation's EU/IMF bailout package. 'Greece is leaving behind destructive austerity, fear and authoritarianism,' declared new Prime Minister Alexis Tsipras. 'It is leaving behind five years of humiliation and pain.' Yet the pain was far from over. Tsipras and his flamboyant finance minister, Yanis Varoufakis, had managed to negotiate with Brussels an extension of Greece's loan agreement, shifting the deal's expiry date from February to June. However, they were only postponing the inevitable, and as June rolled around, Greece was thrown into turmoil once again when its leadership was given an ultimatum to impose a reform agenda or to face bankruptcy and likely ejection from the eurozone.

Rather than take the decision itself, the Syriza government passed the buck to the Greek people in a snap referendum on whether or not to accept the terms of the bailout package on 5 July. The result was a resounding 'No', with 61.5 per cent of voters rejecting the deal, but it made little difference. Only a few days later, Tsipras went cap-in-hand to Brussels to ask for a three-year bailout. I sketched out my thoughts on this rapidly developing situation in an article I wrote for ConservativeHome.

The utterly desperate situation in Greece is fast developing. As a consequence of these unprecedentedly momentous events, I appreciate any of my observations here risk being superseded rapidly.

However, in the aftermath of the unexpectedly clear rejection of the latest bailout deal, it is evident that the original 2010 Greek rescue package was way too heavily weighted towards preserving the interests of bondholders, banks (mainly German and French) and private sector creditors, rather than rebuilding an already shattered Greek economy.

The same, of course, applies to many of the bailouts secured by nations after the financial crash.

Nevertheless, the petulance of the Syriza government, first elected on an 'end to austerity' slogan in January, has done lasting damage to the Greek reputation for straight-dealing. The preposterous referendum last Sunday was merely the latest in a series of infuriatingly manipulative gestures in recent months.

Even the narcissistic, game theorist Finance Minister, Yanis Varoufakis, threw in the towel the day after that vote.

He doubtless recognised that the ECB, IMF and European Commission (the notorious Troika), not to mention the German government, realise that time is on *their* side – why be rushed into further meetings? Let Syriza and their supporters stew for a while before returning to the negotiating table.

The truth is that Alexis Tsipras, the Greek Prime Minister, is less the charismatic democrat he would like the world to believe and more a political fantasist.

His 'business as usual' approach flies in the face of the critical need for structural reform to the Greek economy, alongside a programme of living within its means, for once. Rather than levelling with its electorate, the Greek government has simply ramped up a culture of grievance and victimhood.

Tsipras would like to make the Greek people believe that the challenge facing them is to meet wholly unrealistic spending targets. What is really being asked of his administration, however, is the implementation of a credible programme of reform that modernises the Greek state and tackles head-on embedded crony-ism and corruption.

In the absence of delivery over recent years since the bailouts began, there has been the complete erosion of trust and a consequent, under-standable reluctance by other eurozone members to offer any broader debt relief or commit to the longer-term goal of transfer union.

While the world awaits the next moves in this increasingly ill-tempered negotiation, it is also clear that the Spanish, Italian, Portuguese, Slovenian and Slovakian governments (to name but five) are implacably hostile to any concessions being made to the Syriza government, whose antics compared unfavourably with the genuine efforts made by the people and rulers of all these nations to stabilise their own economies within the eurozone.

Giving ground now after a succession of Syriza stunts would only encourage opposition parties in all those other eurozone nations to 'play the system' and campaign to have their own debts written down. Granting Greece a free lunch would be contagious, and a recipe for chaotic economic irresponsibility.

However, exiting the euro may not prove the elixir that many in Greece fervently believe.

For the new drachma to be successful requires deep depreciation of the domestic currency. Yet this presupposes the structural reform in Greece that has been woefully lacking (successive governments have kicked this as well as the debt can down the road ever since Greece became a founder member of the euro), as well as a flexible labour market (which it does not have) to ensure that the boost of currency depreciation is not immediately offset by a rise in nominal wages.

Leaving the euro will only work if Greece can sustain an economy producing robust domestic goods and services rather than its never-ending reliance on imports. The truth is that Greece today desperately lacks that range of domestic expertise that can easily replace imports from the EU and beyond, especially in the energy and food sectors.

Without hard currency, Greek business will struggle to fund even the most basic raw materials. Falling out of the euro will make it even harder to avoid the economy grinding to a standstill.

What of the UK's position in all this? Well, if Greece were to be forced from the eurozone, its future economic and social travails would end up being funded by all twenty-eight fellow EU members.

While much Greek debt is indeed held by German and French banks, the interconnected nature of global finance means that many British banks will also be indirectly on the hook in the event of a Greek bankruptcy and large-scale debt write-off.

Moreover, such an outcome would probably result in speculators in the capital markets turning their attention to Spain, Italy and Portugal as the next 'weakest links' in the eurozone, potentially driving other nations out of the single currency, whose very integrity will have been dangerously undermined by Grexit.

The worst case scenario would be a further cycle of extreme turbulence in global financial services, a renewed credit crunch and, given the importance to the City and UK as a whole of the banking industry, the derailing of the domestic recovery.

‡

Universities are on the front line in the UK's battle against Islamic extremism (*City AM*), 22 July 2015

The conflict in Syria had started to take an increasingly personal turn for Britain when it became apparent that a number of UK citizens were travelling to the Middle East to live and fight in territories now held by ISIS. Among them was Mohammed Emwazi, an unassuming 26-year-old IT student from Westminster, who could now be seen in brutal propaganda videos beheading hostages. Better known by his tabloid pseudonym 'Jihadi John', Emwazi held a mirror to the growing numbers of radicalised young people in the UK and sparked a debate on what might turn them from lost teenagers to fundamentalist killers.

The radicalisation process was becoming increasingly swift and the tactics of terror groups increasingly nimble, with recruits groomed online and new terror cells able to appear quickly to wreak havoc before their existence could be uncovered by overworked Western security services.

On 26 June 2015, the tentacles of terror extended to Tunisia, when engineering student Seifeddine Rezgui picked up a gun in the coastal resort Sousse to massacre thirty-eight people on the beach, including thirty British holidaymakers.

Under pressure to find solutions to this adaptable and brutal threat, David Cameron gave a keynote speech on 20 July on how the government would defeat home-grown extremism. In this piece for City AM, *I explored how our five-year plan against Islamist fundamentalism might affect British universities.*

Mohammed Emwazi, Michael Adebolajo, Seifeddine Rezgui – by all accounts quiet, unassuming individuals until becoming ISIS's celebrity executioner, Lee Rigby's murderer and author of the Tunisian massacre respectively. Insofar as any common thread binds this grim trio and all too many other recent terrorists, it is not poverty, deprivation or social isolation but instead their youth, university education and rapid conversion to extremist Islamist ideology.

The Prime Minister's groundbreaking speech on Monday, detailing how government is to tackle such Islamist terrorism, was a clear recognition that this multi-headed hydra will be slain only once the ideology which nourishes it is confronted head-on, in much the same way that both fascism and communism were faced down in the last century.

While the government will be setting out a broader counter-extremism strategy in the autumn, the Prime Minister's speech was a uniquely personal collection of conclusions drawn from five years in high office dealing with this toughest of issues. This made it an especially comprehensive and powerful statement of intent that will see all parts of our community called upon in the fight. Universities will be granted no exceptions.

It is alarming to reflect that many of the highest profile Britons convicted of terrorist offences over the past decade or so have been graduates, whose radicalisation was triggered or developed by activism at university. As David Cameron observed, too many young Britons today feel a deep sense of conflict about their identity as they seek to reconcile the culture and ethnicity of their parents or grand-parents with the nation in which they have grown up. It is often at sixth form college or university that such Britons find themselves most susceptible to radical ideology, which offers bold, definitive and simplistic answers to that conflict, as well as active routes to express their inner discontent. Away from their families for the first time, students are not only more vulnerable to new influences, but harder to keep tabs on, particularly in the non-campus environ-ments of the London universities.

It is small wonder, therefore, that students have been targeted by extremist Islamist organisations wishing to extend their vision for a caliphate, all too often via infiltration of university Islamic soci-eties. Between the 1970s and the turn of the century, the growth and flourishing of Islamic societies on campus was typically funded by money from Saudi Arabian sources, generally supportive of the fundamentalist Wahhabi strain of Salafism. The default setting for most university authorities has been to turn a blind eye to the activi-ties of these groups – whose umbrella organisation has until recently had close ties to the Muslim Brotherhood – unless actual violence has been invoked. Meanwhile, radical preachers invited to speak at college events organised by Islamic societies seem apparently only to fall foul of university rules when views objectionable to women's or gay rights groups are espoused.

The government has expended a great deal of political capital removing some of the most notorious hate preachers from the UK and trying to expunge radicals from mosques. It should come as lit-tle surprise if our universities, especially here in the capital, now find themselves at the forefront of efforts to do the same on campus. The Prime Minister has underlined his commitment to free speech and the proud university tradition of encouraging open debate. But he equally exposed university authorities' passivity, challenging them to treat extremist Islamist preachers with the same distaste that might be reserved for neo-Nazi speakers on the extreme political right.

At the start of this year, plans to oblige higher education estab-lishments and student bodies to vet outside speakers for potentially extremist views were dropped amidst coalition tussles. However, emboldened by an overall Conservative majority, it may be that the government now returns to this proposal in the autumn. Not that obliging universities to take a sterner stance under the law will necessarily be the answer. Indeed, the internet risks neutering any new legislation designed to tackle radicalisation on campus. Fundamentalist Islamic preachers may in future be banned as a matter of course from our universities, but often their message of ideological purity, division or hate may have already radicalised young, impressionable minds online.

Virtually all UK immigrant communities instinctively appreciate the key importance of education to social mobility, aspiration and economic progress. This is in stark contrast to much of the rest of Europe, where immigration and lack of educational attainment go hand in hand. Paradoxically, the UK's relatively strong record of integration in education has spawned a new set of headaches for our already beleaguered university authorities. The government has given clear notice that it now expects them to administer a much more robust antidote.

‡

Some thoughts on the refugee crisis, 8 September 2015

Writing in 2011 about the conflict underway in Libya, I warned, 'The unrest has already led hundreds, maybe thousands, to flee across the Mediterranean and seek refuge in Italy and Malta, for example. I fear a prolonged conflict will turn this trickle into a flood.' I had not realised at the time that in the space of only a few years, refugees from north Africa would be joined by a wave of people fleeing conflict in Syria, alongside a band of economic migrants keen to take their chances in seeking a better life in Europe.

By summer 2015, the flow of people to European shores had turned into a full-blown crisis for the continent. Hundreds were dying in Mediterranean waters while those who made it to the mainland, heading mainly to Germany and Sweden, steadily overwhelmed the capacity of EU member states to assist. With thousands of migrants in Hungary waiting at the Austrian border to make their way to Germany, German Chancellor Angela Merkel suspended the Dublin protocol requiring asylum seekers to register in the first EU state they enter, and effectively issued an invitation to Germany for those seeking refuge. Merkel was widely praised for her bold humanitarianism, but as the numbers making the journey swelled, it was predicted that Germany could receive up to one million asylum claims in the course of the next year.

Domestically, David Cameron was under increasing pressure to provide a more robust response to the emotive scenes from the Mediterranean, and an argument broke out about the numbers of refugees the UK should seek to provide sanctuary to. While confirming that Britain would play its part in housing the most vulnerable, the Prime Minister emphasised that the UK's response would primarily focus on providing aid to Syria's neighbours, such as Jordan and Lebanon, where the most people could be helped.

Deeply seared in the collective German psyche is the memory of the nine million or so displaced ethnic German civilians as the Second World War drew to a close.

As the boundaries of post-Third Reich Germany were redrawn at the Potsdam Conference of 1945, so a tide of human refugees was forced westwards from modern day Poland, Russia, Lithuania and Ukraine. My own mother, as a five-year-old girl, was one of this vast number having been forced to leave a village outside Breslau (now Wroclaw) where my forefathers had lived since the 1720s.

To a great extent, this explains the decision of Angela Merkel's Grand Coalition unilaterally to welcome 800,000 refugees from the war in Syria to German shores. Chancellor Merkel's bold initiative was also designed as a safety valve, since it has become abundantly clear in recent months that the Italian and Greek governments have totally lost control of the unmanageably large numbers of people reaching their shores and claiming asylum.

While the Hungarian Premier Viktor Orban does not cut an

especially sympathetic figure at the best of times, it is difficult not to feel some sympathy for his nation's current plight. In recent months Hungary has been the recipient of vast numbers of Middle Eastern migrants who have been allowed through Greece, Macedonia and Serbia in flagrant breach of the Dublin Convention. Their numbers will now doubtless be swelled by the tantalising prospect of assurances of safe haven in Germany.

Mr Orban stands singly accused of racism, yet in the more far-flung corners of the European Union, such as Poland and the Baltic states, governments have already made it clear that they will give overwhelmingly strong preference to Christians fleeing Syria, Egypt and Iraq. He is also within his rights, at the very least, to question the legitimacy and providence of many of those turning up in Budapest and other central European cities. I fear it is not entirely fanciful to suggest that ISIS sympathisers might well be infiltrating this mass of refugee humanity with a view to obtaining asylum and becoming sleepers ready to agitate and foment terrorist activity in the West in the years ahead.

Meanwhile, we need to recognise that the German government's actions, while representing decisive leadership which has been so lacking in the EU over this issue, will also have collateral costs attached. The clear message has now been delivered to people traffickers and their hapless prospective clients that the Mediterranean waterways are open for business. Tragically, the direct consequence of giving a green light and a clear route towards successful asylum in the EU's largest economy is the acceleration of this appalling exploitation of some of the most desperate people.

It also poses a dilemma that our own government has wrestled with in the recent announcement that refugees will be taken *exclusively* from camps in countries adjacent to Syria. I fully support this decision. Migrants who pay people traffickers to ship them across the Mediterranean in order to engage themselves in the EU and international asylum bureaucracy are essentially trying to jump the queue using their financial resources – something which is utterly inequitable. Their plight is a dreadful one, but is surely no more desperate than those in Jordanian, Turkish, Tunisian or Lebanese refugee camps. If we want to end the evil trade of people trafficking, then we need to end the institutional incentives that our asylum rules provide for *all* those associated with this terrible trade in human misery.

I welcome the government's acceptance of our international, moral obligation to take additional refugees. However, I also believe the UK's global leadership in the sphere of international development is where our most lasting contribution to this crisis will shine through. It is clear that it will be several years before many fleeing war and conflict will be able to return to Syria or Libya. I trust that we shall use our expertise and financial clout to help rebuild communities in these war-torn regions. In the meantime, we should also lead the way encouraging global companies to open operations adjacent to refugee camps where displaced persons might be gainfully employed while we try to forge some sort of stability in their homelands to allow them to return.

‡

Corbyn's capital city effect, 12 September 2015

The resounding defeat of Labour at May's general election had led to the immediate resignation of Ed Miliband, kicking off a colourful contest to replace him as party leader. Liz Kendall, Andy Burnham and Yvette Cooper all made it onto the shortlist, alongside token left-wing candidate, Jeremy Corbyn, who had agreed with socialist bedfellows, John McDonnell and Diane Abbott, that it was his turn to 'broaden the debate'.

Neither he, nor anyone else, had counted on 'Corbynmania' sweeping the Labour ranks as a growing base of young activists got fired up by an anti-austerity message and the unassuming, authentic character promoting it. Indeed, Corbyn's genuine passion seemed in stark contrast to the apparently identikit political careerists also in contention, and his ideas on nuclear disarmament, renationalisation of the railways and wide-scale wealth redistribution seemed strangely fresh.

Clinching his remarkable ascent, however, were the new party vot-
ing rules that Ed Miliband had introduced in 2014 allowing anyone to
take part in Labour leadership ballots as an 'affiliated supporter' for a £3
charge. As the contest wound on, nearly 200,000 people took up the oppor-
tunity, with the Islington North MP securing 85 per cent of those votes.
Nonetheless, Corbyn was also to top the poll among trade unionists and
party members in what became a complete rout of Labour's mainstream
centrists. In the end, the 66-year-old Corbyn managed to secure 59.5 per
cent of votes cast in a jaw-dropping victory declared on 12 September.

With former Prime Minister Tony Blair warning that Mr Corbyn's
successful leadership bid would make the Labour Party virtually
unelectable, Conservatives had much to feel optimistic about. However,
I cautioned that, in London at least, Mr Corbyn's message might have
more cut-through.

It is perhaps with a sense of deserved satisfaction that many of
us Conservatives watched the unseemly civil war break out in the
Labour Party this summer. After all, we have had plenty of our own
moments of public soul-searching in the years that followed Tony
Blair's resounding 1997 victory. The neurotic (and ultimately unsuc-
cessful) attempts to kill off Jeremy Corbyn's bid for the Labour
leadership highlighted the extent of the uphill battle Labour has to
win back support in Scotland, tackle the threat from UKIP (which
came a surprisingly strong second in many northern parliamentary
seats in May) and appeal once again to Middle England at the same
time as uniting its parliamentary party and grassroots.

Nonetheless, as a London Conservative MP, I am a little less
sanguine about our chances against the new opposition leader.

Since 1951, it was unknown for a governing party not also to command a majority of seats in the capital, but that is precisely what
resulted from the 2010 and 2015 general elections. We may have
done a fantastic job in breaching the Liberal Democrat fortresses of
south-west London in May, but elsewhere we saw Angie Bray, Lee
Scott, Mary Macleod and Nick de Bois slide to defeat as Labour
increased its tally of London MPs to forty-five out of seventy-three

on the back of a 3.5 per cent swing to Ed Miliband's party. Today in the capital we stand nine points behind Labour – in 1992, we were eight points ahead. Yet the national Conservative lead in vote share and outcome for these two general elections, only twenty-three years apart, was almost identical.

As London Conservatives well know, Labour's campaigning machine in the capital is formidable. But we should not forget either that it was in London that Ed Miliband's retail offering had most res-onance, exploiting, as it did, growing unease about the city's wealth divide. It is precisely the message that Jeremy Corbyn – a central London MP himself – used to great effect in his leadership bid, and which motivated a broad coalition of Londoners to support him, particularly young urban and suburban dwellers struggling with high rents, student debt and suppressed wages.

The central idea underpinning Corbyn's policy programme – that once the rich have paid their 'fair share' then all our debt and deficit problems will be solved – seems faintly ludicrous beyond London, where there are simply not enough well-off voters to fund Labour's lavish redistribution plans. Yet in a city that is home to the global super-rich, where £25 million mansions accrue the same council tax bill as properties over twenty times less valuable, super cars race down Park Lane and 'Middle England' is a dwindling contingent, the prop-osition appears far less preposterous. It is London where many feel the rich should not only pay their share, but deserve to be penalised for the apparently distortive effects of their vast wealth, particularly when it comes to the property market. Anyone working the doorsteps of the capital during the campaign will have found that these sentiments extended far beyond socialist voters in Labour's London heartlands to formerly Tory-voting professionals in the leafier suburbs. It is very difficult to get cut-through with our message of aspiration when a family-sized home is quite literally a pipe dream to many, and own-ership of a mere studio flat an impossibly distant goal.

Meanwhile, in spite of the compelling story we have to tell on employment, the incomes of 22–30-year-olds remain almost 8 per cent down on 2007, before the financial crash. Today, a greater proportion of their salaries and wages is also devoted to living and housing costs. Indeed, housing has become such a toxic issue in the capital, that more and more Londoners are beginning to believe that nothing short of a major market intervention is required, and open their minds to the kind of radical policy prescriptions that Jeremy Corbyn actively promotes. In addition, for all its enterprise and trade, London still has a significant number of public sector workers in the civil service and local authorities. With 900,000 jobs axed in the public sector over the course of the last parliament, I was not surprised to meet a number of former public servants who felt that a vote for the Conservatives was directly contrary to their own interests.

It would be wrong to overstate the appeal of Labour in London under Jeremy Corbyn. After all, being a populist does not always make you popular and he still presents an enormous risk in isolating centre-ground voters, regardless of his authentic appeal. However, his message undeniably taps into a growing sense of scepticism towards the notion that hard work and talent translate into reward in modern day London. A focused Conservative government will hopefully spend the next five years addressing bubbling unease in the capital with a positive offering that involves infrastructure investment (with rapid decisions on Crossrail II and airport expansion), significantly more high-quality homes, the entrenchment of our education reforms and, above all, a dynamic economy that continues to offer exciting opportunities to ever more people.

But we must also wake up to the fact that, over the past decade, London's politics have been diverging ever more from the rest of the UK.

‡

The end game in Syria is still far from clear
(Cap X), 30 September 2015

Ever since Syria had descended into civil war, President Bashar al-Assad had maintained one ally on which he could reliably depend – Russia. With

Vladimir Putin's ongoing support of the dictator, it had been impossible to dislodge Assad and move Syria's people towards some kind of negotiated settlement that would bring an end to the bloodshed and refugee crisis.

By summer 2015, Assad's troubles were deepening as anti-regime forces gained ground. In response, Russia began a military build-up before launching airstrikes against opposition forces on 30 September in an intervention designed specifically to prevent Assad from being deposed. An already complex battleground was about to get even more dangerous.

In this article for Cap X, I sketched out how Western calculations might change in this new phase of the Syrian conflict.

By the time this year is out, Parliament will almost certainly be called upon to endorse military action in Syria. Many relatively disinterested observers may assume that in the seemingly endless diplomatic saga over our relations with Syria such a debate will be a rerun of the sensationally lost August 2013 vote. But it will be different in two key ways. Firstly, the regional refugee crisis, which has so dramatically spilt over into Europe, has added urgency to the West carving out a lasting solution in the travails of the region. Secondly, in direct contrast to the parliamentary motion of two years or so ago, the government will seek support for action to destroy opponents of the Assad regime. How has it come to this?

Unpalatable as it may seem, the key external player here is President Putin's Russia. If there is to be a United Nations solution to the Syrian calamity, the West will need – for now – to put aside our deep misgivings over events in Ukraine and the Baltic States, and work alongside Russia. The Russian President believes that Anglo-French humanitarian action in Libya four years ago was essentially a proxy for regime change; as a consequence, he has always opposed the UK government's admirably principled insistence that Assad must have no future role once a military and diplomatic deal can be brokered in Syria.

Russia also has strong strategic ties to Syria, which would likely be undermined if Assad were toppled. The Russian state has a naval facility at Tartus; Syria is its only loyal ally in the region and has consistently been a trusted trading partner, not least in military hardware. Then there is the simmering threat of Islamic fundamentalism on Russian soil, which means the elimination of ISIS (Assad's sworn enemies) is a key priority to Putin.

From its almost quaint beginnings in 2011 as an output of the so-called Arab Spring, the democratic uprising in Syria has developed into a bitter religious civil war. This involves Russian sponsorship of the Assad military regime, working alongside Iran's Lebanese allies, Hezbollah, to defeat the 'moderate' opposition forces. Meanwhile, ISIS's position has been enhanced by Saudi/Qatari funds, which has resulted in any secular opposition forces being utterly marginalised.

More recently still, the Free Syrian Army, sponsored by the US, has been fighting Assad, but the main dynamic force of recent months has been Sunni-backed rebel militia which, as well as claiming substantial territory in a war that had seemed close to stalemate, have also been responsible for attacking US-trained fighters. So it is not evident that even if the UN were able to muster the will and capacity to destroy ISIS within Syrian borders that this would assist in resolving the conflict there. Indeed, for all the apocalyptic claims made about ISIS, it is still the case that over two in three of the estimated 250,000 fatalities in Syria are down to the Assad regime, which has used chemical weapons and barrel bombs against its own population.

Back in 2013 there was consensus that Syria should remain intact. I have argued before that the unravelling of the Treaty of Sevres and the Sykes-Picot division of the Ottoman Empire in the Middle East following the First World War may prove to be the end game here. However, before parliament commits to escalating our role in Syria, we should have a clear idea of the desirability and impact of partition in the region. In particular, in ensuring that the Syrian Kurds become part of our coalition for action, what promises can safely – and deliverably – be made to them (and indeed their Iraqi Peshmerga friends) about their status in the post-conflict region?

Essentially, however, the key question that needs a clear answer is this: what is our primary objective in Syria – the destruction of ISIS or the removal of President Assad? Confusion has reigned at the highest counsels among Western allies over this. Meanwhile, the impact of the refugee and migrant crisis close to home coupled with the ever-looming threat to domestic national security of terrorist action on home soil, I suspect, has helped subtly shift British public sentiment in recent months from fatalistic resignation to a mood generally more supportive of the UK government joining in decisive action in Syria.

The fundamental disagreement over Assad's role in post-civil-war Syria was always a stumbling block between Russia and the Western Allies. Clearly it suits the Syrian President that the conflict in Syria is increasingly regarded by Western observers as a clash between Islamist jihadists and his regime. However, there must be a nagging doubt that continuing to prop up the Syrian Premier's discredited regime will act only to recruit more young men and women from the region and beyond to violent Islamist militancy. It is also unclear whether the continued presence of Assad at the helm in what may become of Syria will help solve the refugee crisis.

Nevertheless, of all world leaders, President Putin has shown himself passionately and strategically engaged in Syrian affairs. Working in tandem with Putin potentially opens the door to a legally watertight, wide-ranging UN solution to Syria's dreadful plight. This will apply especially in the areas of humanitarian aid, community rebuilding and the establishment of institutional structures for its future.

Diplomacy often requires painful compromise. As Foreign Secretary Philip Hammond and his US counterpart John Kerry have recently made clear, Assad's status might be the bargaining chip as part of the negotiations for settlement of this conflict.

Realpolitik of this sort rightly induces a certain queasiness. However, murderous dictators, like the rest of us, respond to incentives. If President Assad's only other option is as a defendant at the UN International Criminal Court at the Hague, we should not be surprised if he chooses the utter annihilation of what is left of his Syrian homeland.

If there is to be an effective regional strategy for the Middle East, we should recognise that the West will need to keep as many options open as possible.

‡

What now electorally for the Lib Dems?, 8 October 2015

If Labour had a bad night on 7 May, the Liberal Democrats arguably had a worse one. Taking his party from a parliamentary contingent of fifty-seven MPs before the election to a rump of only eight afterwards, Lib Dem leader and Deputy Prime Minister Nick Clegg had been dealt the exquisite cruelty of re-election for another five years in his own Sheffield Hallam seat while the majority of his troops dropped by the wayside. He had immediately stood down as leader of his party, making way for a damp squib of a leadership contest between mild-mannered left-winger Tim Farron and former Health Minister Norman Lamb.

Farron had won convincingly on 16 July, taking 56.5 per cent of the vote, but had struggled ever since to be noticed in a House of Commons in which he now led the UK parliament's equal fourth party with the same number of seats as the Democratic Unionists. In this article for ConservativeHome, I mused on the future electoral prospects of the Lib Dems.

The prolonged battle for the Labour Party's leadership and soul with its sensational outcome has occupied the limelight for most political commentators since May's general election.

Understandably the plight of the Liberal Democrats and their prospects of recovery since their own calamitous reckoning with the voters last spring attracted less rapt attention.

Yet the mood music from their Party Conference was unexpectedly upbeat. Tim Farron's plucky leadership speech reflected unexpected optimism, with over 500 new party members in attendance. The short-term challenge for the new fourth party of British politics is to harness this new energy and enthusiasm before disillusionment sets in. However, it is difficult to see any clear, rapid route towards sustainable electoral revival.

In the aftermath of Jeremy Corbyn's triumph, speculation abounded (encouraged by Tim Farron himself) that several Labour MPs were contemplating defection to the Liberal Democrats.

Frankly, this seems rather implausible. After all, those Blairite Labour MPs most hostile to, and refusing to serve under, Corbyn's leadership, generally have views on civil liberties, foreign policy and economics that are social democratic rather than liberal. Most have little love or respect for Tim Farron, and the wounds of the Lib Dems' five-year collaboration in the coalition remain too raw. By the same token, the prospects of an SDP-type breakaway from Corbyn's Labour remain remote – the current generation will be all too aware of the electoral frustrations that the centre party foundered upon in the 1980s. Moreover, the plight of both UKIP and the Greens at the most recent general election is a reminder of the harsh treatment that faces any fringe party under the current electoral system.

So what hope of the Liberal Democrats' electoral revival being driven at local government level? The party's current tally of councillors is a little over 1,800 nationwide, its lowest since 1982 and under half of its aggregate strength throughout the 1990s and 2000s. Historically, there has been a lag between achieving substantial local government representation and winning a parliamentary seat. Only in 1997 with the collapse of the national Tory vote was the party able to translate local strength into general election gains; to a lesser extent the decline in Labour's urban and suburban support as a result of the Iraq War gave the Lib Dems another breakthrough in 2005. It has been downhill ever since.

As it was, over three decades of painstakingly accumulated electoral progress was wiped out in exchange for a single five-year term of coalition office.

In contrast to the elections of the 1950s and the 1970 contest when the Liberal Party was reduced to six seats chartered in regional strongholds (Highland Scotland, rural Wales and far south-west of England), the eight survivors of the 2015 tsunami sit for a ragbag of non-adjacent seats. All six of their constituencies in England were won by the Conservatives as recently as 1992, an election whose outcome so closely mirrors that of 2015.

Only one current Lib Dem seat (Orkney and Shetland) has been consistently held for more than twenty years; fully half of their current constituencies were not even won by the party in 1997, while Tom Brake is their only sitting MP to have served in parliament in the last century.

In addition, the impact of the impending boundary changes may result in the notional loss of three or four of their current seats; presumably several of the current incumbents will also retire in 2020.

Early indications suggest that some degree of recovery at local government level may not be a fanciful possibility; nevertheless, next year's London and Scottish elections are unlikely to be especially fruitful. So if the energy of their new recruits is to be maintained, a high-profile victory or two in parliamentary by-elections will be desperately important. Naturally, much here depends upon vacancies arising in seats where the Lib Dems are competitive. Meanwhile, while their sights may be on many of the twenty-seven seats lost in May to the Conservatives, the importance of 'double incumbency' for first-time Tory defenders in 2010 should not be forgotten. It was clearly important in 2015 as first-time defenders held the line against anticipated gains.

It is evident that in the years ahead the Liberal Democrats will not be able to rely upon Labour's woes to kick-start their own recovery; indeed, many of the party's defectors from the Ashdown/Kennedy era will probably feel supremely comfortable in a Corbyn-led Labour Party. In truth, many psephological signs suggest that even the calamitous result in 2015 may *not* necessarily reflect the low point of the Liberal Democrats' parliamentary election fortunes.

‡

Thank goodness for political stability, 25 October 2015

'We are the builders'

Chancellor George Osborne had put in a robust and confident performance at our party's Manchester conference at the beginning of October. In a deliberate foray into Labour's freshly vacated centre-left territory, he

described how Conservatives were now the 'only true party of labour'.
He also set out a range of measures to boost the economy in the north
of England and invest in infrastructure across the country, including a
new local authority infrastructure fund and the appointment of Labour's
Lord Adonis as head of a National Infrastructure Commission. 'We are
the builders,' he triumphantly declared.

Back in parliament, the government sought to highlight Labour's con-
tinued economic irresponsibility by resurrecting the idea of a Charter
for Budget Responsibility, or fiscal charter, which would pass into law a
commitment for governments to run a budget surplus in 'normal' times.

Put to one side parliamentary frolics over signing up to Mr Osborne's
Charter for Budget Responsibility. Credible economic policy in the
UK is thankfully secure as a consequence of an election outcome
that confounded virtually everyone, pundits and participants alike.
Thank goodness – for amidst relentlessly positive news stories herald-
ing record-high levels of employment, rising investment, sustained
levels of overall growth and real wage increases, future economic
recovery cannot be taken for granted.

In truth, any incoming administration in May would have faced
an economic outlook almost as grisly as that inherited in 2010; the
real relief is that this sense of uncertainty has not extended to the
government's political survival.

With hindsight it becomes clearer that the novel demands of
peacetime coalition administration meant that too many economic
problems were parked rather than solved over the past five years.
Ultra-low interest rates, held at emergency levels now since March
2009, have also helped mask the true extent of the UK's debt mountain and ongoing deficit financing.

Anyone under the age of thirty has been lulled into the false sense
that these costs of borrowing are 'normal'. Few realise the distorting effect this is having on our economic recovery. In addition, the
electorate have shown signs of austerity fatigue without realising
that collectively we have barely begun to rebalance the UK economy away from reliance on consumption driven by rising property

values, towards investment, infrastructure programmes and export-led growth.

As a consequence, one unhelpful number that ought to be giving rise to major disquiet within the Treasury is our persistent current account deficit. In decades past, this monthly statistic enjoyed a near-mythical importance and general elections were regarded as being won and lost according to the calculation of this esoteric measure between what the UK spends overseas and what it earns.

Today, our current account deficit stands at 6.5 per cent of GDP, a historic high outside of wartime conditions. It is the most obvious indication that we are persistently living beyond our means.

One reason for this is that the UK's overseas liabilities now exceed our assets, which for decades until the financial crisis had been a reliable source of dividend income into our public coffers.

The continued importance of the UK's global reach in financial and professional services makes it all the more critical that a pragmatic UK Treasury continues to promote a credible policy framework that enjoys the confidence of the capital markets.

The price for any loss in confidence would be instant and devastating. This level of current account deficit requires the reassurance of those overseas investors lending to the UK. Any suggestion that the policy prescription of Messrs Corbyn and McDonnell might hold sway would almost certainly rapidly result in a severe balance of payments crisis, which would soon feed into sterling rates. But – as Chancellor Osborne will surely point out in his forthcoming Autumn Statement – we are by no means out of the woods. The subdued external demand in both China and a slew of emerging markets make for a potentially turbulent time ahead.

During this early period of majority government, the Chancellor rightly seeks to cut the deficit by means of sustained growth and further cuts in public spending. Substantial tax hikes will only be on the agenda if Plan A fails to have the desired impact on deficit reduction.

But remember this: there is no end in sight here in the UK to the era of emergency-level interest rates. Continuing global economic strife underlines the Bank of England's reluctance to raise rates, with emergency levels of credit having now been sustained for over six and a half years. By rights this should have set alarm bells ringing. But the flooding of capital into financial assets – and the enrichment of those holding bonds, stocks and especially real estate – means that there is a conspiracy of silence over exactly what is happening out there.

Let's face it – at a time when Barclays, RBS and others have been slapped with astronomical fines for rigging the markets in LIBOR and foreign exchange, we should not be blind to the fact that the most dangerous contemporary market rigging is being undertaken by *central* banks across the globe. Excessively loose monetary policy will eventually spark another financial crisis on a potentially more devastating scale. When all the normal market signals have disappeared under a mountain of cheap money, it remains nigh-on impossible to make a rational investment decision. Risk is being almost universally mispriced and before the world is very much older, there will surely come a reckoning...

But, as ever, the real question is when, precisely, this reckoning will come. All of which points towards renewed political impetus to promote growth via infrastructure – one of the many dogs that failed to bark during the recent general election campaign. Pity the Labour Party, whose gut instinct at the last election, as we now know, would surely have been to promise vastly higher borrowing to help patch up the UK's deteriorating infrastructure. However, Ed Miliband knew that even to suggest such action would have left Labour open to a tsunami of accusations that it was set on 'more borrowing and more debt'.

Watch the Chancellor step into the breach in the months ahead and quietly indicate a willingness to exploit the ultra-low cost of borrowing by a UK powerhouse programme on high-tech infrastructure, roads, railways and perhaps even, following a final decision on the Davies Commission's report, airport capacity...

‡

Britain is a force for good in the EU
(Cap X), 28 October 2015

With the eurozone and migrant crises dominating the political agenda at international summits, the Prime Minister's renegotiation of Britain's membership of the European Union had at times seemed a distant priority to EU leaders. Behind closed doors, the government had been urging France and Germany to speed up the renegotiation in time for a deal to be struck at the European Council meeting in December, hoping that a referendum might be held as early as May or June 2016.

Downing Street promised to share its list of negotiation demands by November, with reform based around four key goals: a promise to exempt the UK from 'ever-closer union'; a red card system that would allow groups of national parliaments to prevent unwanted EU legislation being imposed on them; protections for non-eurozone members; and exemption from the euro, with the explicit recognition that the EU is a 'multi-currency' union.

It was a fascinating time for me personally, since my new role as party vice-chairman was taking me across Europe to speak to sister parties in countries such as Sweden, Italy and Germany. Discussing the renegotiation at length with our continental allies helped crystallise in my own mind why I believed our remaining in the European Union was so important. I shared some of these views in the following essay I wrote for Cap X.

The European Union is not working – or so its detractors claim. No one can deny the extent of the strains that give weight to their argument. The perennially shambolic conduct of eurozone business threatens to undermine the Union's claim to create prosperity and respect democracy. Meanwhile, the refugee and migrant crisis that has spread so rapidly through the Schengen area challenges one of the EU's founding principles in its suggestion that free movement of labour and secure borders may indeed be mutually exclusive.

The UK government's commitment to hold a referendum on continued EU membership by the end of 2017 surely comes at the best possible time for the 'Outers', who will make the case for Brexit with renewed vigour as the gap of time narrows between each wave of continental calamity. Britain is neither a member of the eurozone nor party to Schengen, but that will not prevent both crises being used to whip up toxic and emotive responses to the question of our membership.

Naturally, it is the instinct of both Remain and Leave camps to condense their analysis of our EU membership into black and white. But Britons do not need to be panicked or lured into their ultimate decision with wild predictions on job losses or gains, scaremongering about corporate exodus or misty-eyed visions of a rejuvenated Commonwealth and secure borders. A more successful tactic would be to accept that the UK's national interest lies in our having a mature, sober and honest debate about the pros and cons of membership, and then to trust Britons to come to their own mix of rational and emotional judgement. The truth is that life will go on whether we remain an EU member or not. Which path we now choose will for many be a finely balanced call that takes into account the merits and flaws of each route.

The Prime Minister's renegotiation attempt recognises that truth by implicitly acknowledging the EU as neither an unalloyed good nor a power-grabbing superstate, but an international forum in desperate need of greater flexibility and reform. A Europe which cannot bend will break, so the renegotiation needs to result not just in a retail package of specific reforms to present to voters pre-referendum, but a clear demonstration that the EU is capable of maintaining the pace of change needed to address today's realities and tomorrow's challenges. Whatever the Prime Minister negotiates must be seen as a down-payment for future reform, the start of an ongoing process that seeks to benefit all EU members, not simply secure further UK exceptionalism. If he manages to pull it off, it will be yet another example of the critical role Britain plays when it actively engages with European allies.

It is abundantly clear that the European Union is a flawed institution that struggles to deal nimbly with the challenges thrown at it by the modern world. It was designed to provide peace to a continent in the aftermath of two catastrophic wars in the first half of the last century, an acknowledgement that prescriptive cooperation was preferable to conflict. Indeed, we Britons consistently underestimate just how much our European partners value the EU as a vehicle for seven decades of lasting peace, to the extent that their dedication to the institution seems sometimes to defy logic. But we also underestimate how successfully the UK has itself shaped the EU and the opportunities it continues to provide our own citizens.

It took some Swedish counterparts to remind me recently just how crucial Britain's role in the EU is to fellow members who believe in the Anglo-Saxon values of free trade and competition, and share our desire to resist 'ever-closer union'. The notion of Brexit is terrifying to northern European allies who look to the UK as an essential bridge between the EU and the English-speaking world, a critical counterweight to the Franco-German axis and the asker of awkward but essential questions over reform. They see an EU which Britain has been instrumental in shaping, citing the expansion eastwards into pro-Western countries like Poland, the promotion of the Single Market, open competition for goods and services, new trade deals and English as the dominant language. Their view of the UK as an influential EU player is quite removed from the view of commentators here, who tend to portray the EU as an alien institution imposed from afar while overlooking the tangible membership benefits that we have ourselves helped bring about.

Let us not forget, for instance, that the Single Market provides one of the finest examples of international cooperation in global economic history. This vast economic zone is larger than the combined GDPs of the US and Japan, and provides a level playing field in which UK businesses can trade. This has allowed the City of London, in my constituency, to develop a role as Europe's offshore–onshore financial centre, supplying legal, financial and professional services with ease to our European neighbours, while providing a base to foreign firms seeking access to the continent. It has been a recipe for enormous success as the biggest market around for UK exports of financial services, responsible for a third of the UK's surplus in financial services in 2012. But it has been sustainable only because the UK has also vigorously fought to shape the rules of the market to its advantage, despite its safe haven outside the eurozone.

It means too, for example, that UK start-ups are able to access markets swiftly without complying with twenty-seven different sets of regulations. British car manufacturers have been able to enjoy a resurgence with the investment that has flowed from foreign firms seeking a base from which to access the continent. Consumers are able to obtain a much wider choice of products at a cheaper price and, through the Open Skies policy, Britons have been able to fly at low cost across the continent. It is via the European Union too that the Transatlantic Trade and Investment Partnership (TTIP) is being negotiated that could bring enormous benefits to British consumers and businesses.

Post-Brexit, my working assumption would be that the UK would seek to continue its well established trading relationship with the EU rather than follow the 'Swiss model' of countless bilateral agreements. However, that would see us facing a tough choice between access to a Single Market over whose rules we would have no influence or regulatory autonomy with tariffs galore. When I recently explained to a Norwegian parliamentarian the enthusiasm of some Brexit advocates to mimic Norway, Liechtenstein and Iceland in their trading relationships with the EU, she implored the UK not to go down that route. 'We have all of the rules,' she explained, 'but none of the influence.' Indeed, EU officials might be inclined to make market access even tougher for the UK, lest other countries be tempted to follow suit and exit the EU themselves.

Meanwhile, I am unconvinced that our standing apart from the EU makes it easier to face the international and domestic challenges ahead. On freedom of movement, to give one example, I suspect French border police would be virtually incentivised to relax Calais controls if the UK were no longer a member of the EU, making the migrant crisis far harder to handle. I also fail to see how the anti-immigration message that will likely form a key pillar of the Leave campaign marries up with the idea of the UK as an open, global trading nation.

Britons would be forgiven for worrying that too much European energy is now being expended on solving the problems in the eurozone, to the detriment of measures that might improve Britain's future wellbeing. However, the Single Market is far from finished, and there remains much more that we can achieve in close alliance. Work is well underway, for example, towards an ambitious digital Single Market where individuals and businesses can access and exercise online activities under conditions of fair competition and a high level of consumer and personal data protection.

Politics is a messy business that can be slow to deliver results. The EU is not a commercial entity which can implement solutions quickly and without regard for detractors. Equally, for the EU to demonstrate intransigence during the Prime Minister's renegotiation will play straight into the hands of those who portray it as an organisation unfit to govern in the modern world. It is vital not just for the confidence of the UK but the twenty-seven other member states that the EU shows itself open to reform.

Once the renegotiation process is over, however, it is for Britons to ask themselves – in participating in this imperfect enterprise, what is our return and what compromises are we willing to accept as the price? No matter the attempts of the Remain and Leave campaigns, for most voters the answer will not be clear cut and therefore the outcome of the UK's renegotiation will be crucial in helping them weigh up the value fellow member states place on Britain's contribution and the extent to which the EU is willing and able to adapt.

I am optimistic that the Prime Minister's renegotiation of our relationship with the EU can prove the opening salvo in a process of European reform. In this way, our nation will be at the forefront, advancing a free trade and competitiveness agenda that promotes growth, jobs, security and stability long after the referendum. If he is successful, it will be the latest in a long line of British achievements at European level, ultimately helping the EU accept change and challenge at a time when its very survival depends on flexibility.

‡

Data protection – can UK exceptionalism hold?,
3 November 2015

From 2010 to 2015, I had sat on parliament's Intelligence and Security Committee, scrutinising the work of our security services at a time when they had suddenly been unwillingly shifted into the public spotlight.

In May 2013, Edward Snowden, a young IT contractor for the US National Security Agency, had boarded a flight to Hong Kong, from where he shared with journalists countless classified documents that revealed the extensive global surveillance programmes of Western security agencies. The sheer scale of the programmes and the close cooperation between communications providers and governments shocked the public and enraged privacy campaigners, sparking a broader debate about where to draw the line between security and privacy in the matter of state surveillance.

In response, the government published in November draft legislation to give new surveillance powers to the police and security services to hold everyone's internet connection records for twelve months. The legislation also introduced safeguards on the use of interception and a raft of other oversight measures including the creation of a new post of Investigatory Powers Commissioner. I previewed the legislation in the following article for ConservativeHome.

At the heart of the political and ethical tensions over the government's draft Investigatory Powers legislation to be published later this week is the issue of judicial authorisation.

In a democracy, who should decide the extent of operational powers exercised by our intelligence services in pursuit of national security? Historically, the UK has regarded this as an issue of ministerial prerogative with specialist judges having only post-event oversight of such decisions. This has increasingly put us at odds with other Western intelligence partners, and the pace may soon be set by the demands of global communication service providers (CSP), whose cooperation is so critical in counterterrorism initiatives.

In the aftermath of the Edward Snowden revelations, battle lines have been drawn more clearly between privacy campaigners and the securocrats. The former argue that the industrial-level bulk collection of communications data and methodology for its retention and analysis, the extent of which was revealed by the rogue NSA contractor's disclosures to *The Guardian* in 2013, amounts to unprecedented state surveillance – inadequately authorised or overseen.

Meanwhile, the clock ticks relentlessly towards December 2016 when the UK's emergency data retention legislation expires. So decision time will soon be upon the Home Office. Yet the CSPs, acutely aware that the Snowden disclosures have exposed an arguably over-cosy relationship between the multinational internet giants and US security agencies, are now reportedly demanding global surveillance protocols. The days of UK exceptionalism in the surveillance sphere may be numbered. We should not underestimate the implications this may have on the capabilities, yet alone public reputation, of our intelligence services at a time of heightened national security concerns.

In the final year of the coalition administration, the government commissioned our erstwhile ambassador to Washington, Sir Nigel Sheinwald, to report on security oversight. Predictably, the fact that his conclusions have *not* been made public has led to a storm of controversy; clearly these are sensitive matters, but I should hope that at the very least the Intelligence and Security Committee will be granted access to his important contribution to this active debate. The speculation is that Sir Nigel's deliberations with the global CSPs have resulted in his proposing international standards aligning the British, US and European surveillance regimes. If adopted, such a proposal would have the potential to disrupt the capabilities of GCHQ and MI6 profoundly, since it would almost certainly herald judge-led authorisation of surveillance of the internet, email and related communications for subjects of interest.

The speculation is that a compromise may now be on the cards, resulting in a two-stage approvals process. The Home or Foreign Secretary, especially in emergency, time-critical cases, will make the surveillance decision, but judicial consent will need to follow within a short, prescribed period. For this purpose, a small, highly specialist cadre of senior judges (Court of Appeal or Supreme Court) with specific security clearance would be appointed. This would probably satisfy all but the most privacy-obsessed libertarians.

Nevertheless, it has been the leading international tech companies who have felt the heat since their role in gathering up, filtering and assisting government in the analysis of communications data became clear. On these shores, beyond an alliance of the libertarian right and old left, most Britons were rather disinterested at the fuss created by the Snowden revelations. The reaction elsewhere to the unexpected extent of digital espionage was anything but relaxed. In the US, the instinctive mistrust of government was compounded by a new hostility towards CSPs playing fast and loose with individual rights. While the French are instinctively less agitated at the prospect of centralised surveillance techniques, their government recognises that the sheer scale of US technology companies has helped provide their home nation with a terrific competitive advantage in this sphere. Clearly US government and corporations know full well that this capacity to control the tech infrastructure across the globe might one day be used *against* its national interests and security.

The German government has felt compromised by its own historical legacy of the Gestapo and Stasi (never forget that Angela Merkel spent the first twenty-five years of her life living in communist East Germany) at a time when it has also sought to cooperate with the US security agencies on a range of counterterrorism surveillance operations.

The Snowden affair sparked off a new wave of anti-Americanism in Germany, and even now the revelations as to the antics of internet giants threaten to stall talks over the Transatlantic Trade and Investment Partnership (TTIP). Part of the problem, as we have seen, is that currently, the global technology market is so manifestly dominated by US-based companies. The perception that they have been able wilfully to ignore European sensibilities over privacy in the collection and storage of bulk data has led the CSPs to push for global standards – the protection of individual rights irrespective of the public interest, with warrants issued by judges being at its heart.

For European governments, the impending terror threat means that, for all the indignation, reaching an acceptable deal is imperative.

Here in the UK, critical decisions central to that ever-delicate balance between security and liberty may, despite a Home Office rear-guard action, be about to be taken out of politicians' hands. Nevertheless, a regime of judicial consent, rather than authorisation or oversight, would still see our arrangements at odds with many of our Western intelligence partners.

‡

Are we really so wise to rely upon foreign investors to sustain our deficit?, 22 November 2015

Since entering government in 2010, both David Cameron and George Osborne had tirelessly promoted Britain across the world in the hope of boosting UK exports, but also to attract inward investment at a time of public spending constraint.

In September, the Chancellor had signed off on a landmark deal to make London a major hub for the trading of the Chinese renminbi. At the same time, a China–UK Infrastructure Alliance was announced to make way for Chinese funding of flagship projects such as the new HS2 rail link. These announcements were intended as a preview to the carefully choreographed State Visit to the UK by President Xi Jinping, who had assumed leadership of the Chinese Communist Party in March 2013. The lavish visit included a welcome pageant on Horse Guards Parade, a state banquet at Buckingham Palace and formal address to parliament, while behind the scenes the government furiously worked to unlock £30 billion of commercial deals. While I supported the push to secure such wide-ranging investment, I also sounded a note of caution about the long-term effects of diminishing domestic ownership of our underlying asset base.

October's state visit by Chinese President Xi was, according to taste, either a triumph of traditional British mercantilism or a humiliating kowtowing to a ruthless emerging superpower. Ties of Empire and

Commonwealth ensured that the trip, hot on its heels, by Indian Prime Minister Modi, attracted less controversy, but both were surrounded by the fanfare of multi-billion pound trade contracts.

Enticing foreign money to these shores is scarcely novel. However, the attraction of government bonds – whether denominated by the UK or countless other 'First World' nations, is not what it was.

Perhaps it would be wiser to examine more closely the implications of allowing free movement of capital, whether from Middle Eastern or Chinese sovereign wealth funds or the global oligarchical super-rich of the former Soviet Union and beyond.

We welcome open investment in cosmopolitan residential and commercial property; in corporations, especially those rich in intellectual property; in an array of commodities, not least as a hedge against Western currencies whose underlying value cannot for ever be immune to the effects of colossal central bank money-printing.

The impact upon the London and Home Counties property markets of international inflows has persuaded many even from the free market centre-right of the political spectrum to contemplate more stringent taxation arrangements for overseas investors, especially those neither domiciled nor resident in the UK. The Swiss or Singaporean models bear some scrutiny, not least as their implementation has not noticeably diminished the appeal as global financial centres of either jurisdiction.

More generally, as we continue to spend beyond our means, the UK political class needs to grasp that much of our structural and current account deficit is funded by foreign direct investment. Free movement of capital has enjoyed widespread support in recent decades, but it is timely to recall that the income derived in dividends, rents and capital gains from assets owned by overseas corporates and individuals – such as smart new office blocks and substantial shareholdings in public companies – is liable to be exported from these shores in the decades ahead. How will future generations of UK pensioners be able adequately to fund their retirement if the underlying asset base of domestic pension funds continues to be systematically depleted in this way?

Meanwhile, the Bank of England continues to issue bonds on a scale unprecedented outside wartime, simply to plug the gap between government spending and income. Lest we forget, seven years – a full biblical economic cycle – have now passed since the financial crash, yet the public finances (here and in much of the West) remain so precariously (un)balanced.

Much is made of the fact that our central bank has mopped up about a third of the bonds issued during this period, thereby helping enable the emergency interest rate of 0.5 per cent to sustain as it has since March 2009. Potentially, however, the greater distortion is that over 40 per cent of our gilts are held by foreigners. In this uncertain economic environment where the UK's performance clearly outshines many of our G7, let alone G20, counterparts, overseas creditors clearly see the UK as a relatively safe haven. However, while accepting artificially low returns on their bonds (granted better 'value' is not easily obtainable elsewhere) the impact of currency risk may have more serious implications. To date, despite a succession of record-high current account deficits, market sentiment towards sterling remains strong. As we know well, confidence is a fragile commodity, and if there were to be even a short-term run on the pound, those sterling-denominated gilts in the hands of foreign investors and sovereign wealth funds would rapidly lose their value.

All of which is a timely reminder that the UK's vastly expanded debt pile over the past decade needs the urgent, drastic, determined action that the new Conservative administration has promised. The period in which markets regard debt benignly may well be running out – the government must be supported in all its plans for rapid deficit reduction.

Even the UK economy's welcome return to growth since 2012 has been largely funded from borrowing – all that has shifted has been that the typical borrower has been the state, rather than the individual, with a huge programme of asset sales at its centrepiece. As was widely documented during the Chinese state visit, even before the most recent multi-billion investment in the UK nuclear industry, Chinese sovereign wealth had been on a spending spree on these shores. The China

Investment Corporation (CIC) owns 9 per cent of Thames Water, 10 per cent of Heathrow Airport and continues to make less high-profile investments in the oil and gas exploration and property sectors. The Chinese state-owned food manufacturer bought a 60 per cent stake in Weetabix in 2012; China's second largest insurance group now owns the iconic Lloyd's of London building while last year, House of Fraser and Pizza Express were snapped up by Chinese private equity players.

The returns on these UK-based assets and the now Qatari and UAE-owned equivalents will no longer find their way back, via domestic pension funds, into the retirement income of Britons in the decades ahead.

Thirty years ago this month, in November 1985, Harold Macmillan famously spoke of Mrs Thatcher's privatisation programme as 'selling the family silver'. Yet virtually all of the shares sold off then found their way into the hands of individual investors or, in time, pension funds, and the assets continued to be sweated for domestic gain. Potentially, today's ongoing disposal of public and private assets to overseas buyers has far more serious implications.

‡

Autumn Statement: the verdict, 25 November 2015

The run-up to the Autumn Statement had seen the Chancellor's summer Budget plans on tax credits come under fire. While promising to hike the minimum wage to £9 by 2020 and increasing the personal allowance and free childcare, he had also frozen benefits for four years, lowered the income threshold at which tax credits would be lost and limited child tax credit to the first two children. If the opposition to the plans from Labour quarters had been predictable, the disquiet on the Tory benches was less so. Trouble came also from the Lords, where peers controversially broke from convention to vote down the tax credits cuts.

Under pressure to rethink his plans, the Chancellor used the Autumn Statement to carry out a surprise U-turn, funded by a recalculation of the public finances by the OBR that suggested the UK was likely to be

£27 billion better off by 2020 than previously thought. Also announced were the results of the Comprehensive Spending Review that saw the policing, health, defence, education and aid budgets all protected, while £20 billion of savings were made to other departmental spending.

I was asked to provide my initial reaction to the afternoon's announcements as part of a ConservativeHome panel.

At the general election in May, Chancellor George Osborne needed to portray an economy both firmly on the road to recovery, but in a perilous enough condition to require another five years of his medicine. In securing a Conservative majority, he triumphantly pulled off this balancing act. However the relentless focus by the media on polls over policy meant that our economic position was endorsed without being fully scrutinised.

This has created two difficulties for the Chancellor going forward. Firstly, nobody is quite clear on the extent of his mandate, which is why policy needs to be tentatively tested out until it meets fierce enough opposition to provoke a retreat. Secondly, we allowed the electorate to believe we were, perhaps, three quarters of the way to recovery, when the reality is that we are barely halfway. There are some pretty heroic assumptions within the OBR's growth projections if we are truly to finish this parliament in surplus. This makes it hard to convince voters that they should grin and bear economic pain rather than push against unpalatable decisions.

As a result, today's Autumn Statement had rather a surreal feel to it. Our back was against the wall on tax credits, but with one bound the Chancellor is apparently free. The OBR has unilaterally changed its methodology, allowing for the sudden unearthing of an additional £27 billion to play with. Essentially every Budget and Autumn Statement is an exercise in cascading figures, and the truth is, for so long as a Chancellor enjoys the confidence of the capital markets, this does not matter. Retaining this confidence has been George Osborne's single biggest achievement.

I am instinctively uneasy, however, that there may be some unravelling still to come. I wholeheartedly endorse bold moves towards the greater devolution of power. However, it is clear that many of the most difficult future decisions on spending will have to be made by local authorities rather than Whitehall. By 2018/19, the cumulative impact of cuts on local councils (many of which may no longer be Conservative-controlled) will really be bearing down on service levels. Meanwhile, the private sector has been asked to plug the gap on housing, apprenticeships and wages.

Nonetheless, it was a bravura performance from the Chancellor, and in projecting certainty and the broad strokes of a long-term plan, he will retain the trust of the markets. He presented ambitious projections on growth for 2018 and beyond. I sincerely hope they come to pass.

‡

Debate on military action in Syria, 2 December 2015

On 13 November, a coordinated series of attacks by suicide bombers and gunmen gripped Paris in a vice of terror and tragedy. One hundred and thirty people lost their lives as the band of terrorists visited venues ranging from the Stade de France to the Bataclan theatre to kill Parisians enjoying a Friday night out. Responsibility for the attacks was claimed by ISIS and it was later revealed that the majority of the attackers were young French and Belgian men, although two of the suicide bombers were thought to have slipped into Europe on one of the migrant routes from Syria.

It was the second calamity to hit the City of Light in 2015, the first being a vicious attack in January on a Jewish supermarket and the offices of satirical magazine Charlie Hebdo, *which had been condemned by Islamists for its cartoon portrayal of the prophet Mohammed. Seventeen innocent people had been slaughtered.*

France fell into mourning, with President Francois Hollande declaring a state of emergency and ordering further bombing raids on ISIS targets in Syria. With an international coalition forming against ISIS that was willing to extend military operations to expunge the terror group from the region, it seemed unthinkable that the UK would not also play a broader military role of some kind. The RAF was already engaged in operations to bomb ISIS-held areas of northern Iraq at the request of the Iraqi government. Inevitably, the question on whether now to extend those operations across the border into Syria returned to parliament. It was a deeply contentious issue and I was inundated with correspondence from constituents on both sides of the argument. I sent them the following reply.

As you might imagine, the UK's potential involvement in military action in Syria is a subject that elicits strong feelings, and I have received hundreds of messages in the past few days alone. This reply is lengthy, but this is an important issue and I wish to set out the context of the vote and my position on it.

When the House was first asked to consider military action against the Assad regime back in August 2013, I was very reluctant to support it. If you recall, the move towards military intervention at that time came on the back of President Assad's use of chemical weapons against his own people. I was deeply fearful that the notion of a swift, surgical strike against the Syrian dictator risked the worst of all worlds – highly unlikely to dislodge him or bring hostilities to a more rapid conclusion, it would simply draw in the UK as an additional player in a complex bunfight of interests underway, without any clear goal or exit strategy.

Sensing disquiet among MPs, the government tabled a watered-down motion that took into account the serious concerns that I and other parliamentary colleagues had expressed, and included, absolutely crucially, the assurance that there would be a second vote in parliament before any military action was taken and an emphasis on securing consensus through the UN – two things I had asked for. On that basis, I voted in favour of the motion, but told the whips I would not support military action, particularly without a UN resolution. As it happened, the government was not able to get even this initial motion through the Commons.

Two further years have passed and the Syrian conflict rages on, bloodier and more brutal than before and with ever more tragic consequences. President Assad remains in place, while the moderate forces fighting him have been drowned out by the death cult of ISIS, which seeks to spread a barbaric way of life that condemns anyone failing to conform to its bizarre ideals on ethnicity, sexuality and religion. Meanwhile, thousands of innocent civilians have been killed or forced to live in refugee camps, while others have tried their luck in building new lives in Europe, creating a crisis of confidence in the European Union as it deals with huge numbers arriving at its door. ISIS-sponsored terrorists have murdered our own citizens in Tunisia and Paris, while the citizens of other nations die every day at their hands. In short, any notion that inaction comes without its own cost is also misguided. Without a more comprehensive response from the international community, it is quite possible that things will get worse, and certainly the terror threat to us here in the UK now exists whether we get further involved in a Syrian solution or not. So the question is, what do we do?

Some people are willing to tolerate the costs of inaction. Others believe that this can be solved through diplomacy alone. Some agree that a military solution is right, but that an aerial bombing campaign is not enough. Others prefer to see our allies deal with the problem without our support.

It is clear that diplomatic efforts have failed so far to bring matters to a head, though they have been and continue to be vigorously pursued in Vienna and at the UN in New York. Our own government is the second biggest contributor of aid to the region, but that too is not enough. Some European governments have opened the door to limitless numbers of Syrian refugees while we have agreed to take 20,000 of the most vulnerable, yet either approach is a sticking plaster. Our intelligence services are already doing all that they can to prevent attacks and undermine ISIS economically.

Sadly, there are no neat, clean solutions to this issue, so the Prime Minister is left to consider whether military action should form a greater component of any British response. Today, I stand more convinced of his argument that UK armed forces should play a greater role in Syria. First, he has listened to what many of my colleagues and I have been asking for and delivered a United Nations Security Council resolution, embracing both China and Russia, that provides a legal basis and political unity in taking action against ISIS. Second, he accepts that military action is only a component of our response, one part of a multi-dimensional strategy that must include diplomacy, aid and post-conflict planning.

Finally, I am convinced that one of the reasons we have failed to make a breakthrough on Syria is the absence of political will among the international community to get involved. It is faintly ludicrous to suggest that the Prime Minister is 'rushing us to war'. Given the scars left on us all by the Iraq vote in 2003 and the lack of popular support for further British involvement in the Middle East, no government readily contemplates military action in the region. That sentiment has been shared across the Western world. But, as I have said, that inaction, that absence of will to help resolve the Syrian crisis, has left it as a running sore with far-reaching consequences.

One of the reasons I shall be supporting tonight's motion is not just to give the Prime Minister the green light to further military action (we are already engaged in operations in Iraq) but to display to the Syrians and our allies that the UK stands united with those countries which have the political will to find a lasting and comprehensive solution to this terrible humanitarian tragedy. It is worth noting that yesterday the German cabinet backed the use of their armed forces in the fight against ISIS. What military action will also assist with is altering the current balance of power on the ground such that we have a greater chance of being able to work out a political settlement that does not involve ISIS, and may help build an understanding among the international coalition that President Assad's rule must before long also come to a close.

Taking military action is not without risk, but neither is doing nothing. While scepticism over our long-term strategy is understandable in light of conflicts like Iraq, United Nations involvement in this particular instance means that whatever we do is done multilaterally as part of an international coalition. It may also be worth mentioning that the authority to put our armed forces into action is in truth constitutionally an Executive power. I am unconvinced that the precedent set in 2003 by Tony Blair in putting these matters before the legislature in the House of Commons is one that we should continue, as it undermines our ability to respond nimbly and effectively to threats.

I appreciate that my answer will be one that disappoints a number of my constituents who have written to me, but this is not a decision I have taken lightly.

‡

The UK needs to insure itself better against the cyber-terrorism threat (*City AM*), 3 December 2015

At the heart of the government's dilemma about online security, as shown by the Snowden files, was how to ensure security agents could monitor the online activities of terrorists without the self-same terrorists being able to exploit any weaknesses or 'backdoors' in IT systems to wreak their own brand of havoc.

Understandably, after the Paris attacks, the focus of security services and media was firmly on how to prevent relatively small-scale, sporadic gun and bomb attacks. However, it was becoming ever-clearer that the risk of cyber-attack was growing too, not just from terror groups but from state actors. For several years, discussions had been underway between the City, big business and government about how to protect the UK's IT infrastructure, but there was yet little clarity about how the economic consequences of any wide-ranging attack might be handled.

In a speech at GCHQ on 17 November, the Chancellor announced that he would be doubling UK funding to fight cyber-crime to £1.9 billion over five years and launching a National Cyber Centre. In this article for City AM, *I suggested that we look too at creating a cyber-reinsurance vehicle to protect businesses from substantial economic damage in the event of online attack. This would be along the lines of Pool Re, the institution set up in the wake of the IRA attacks on the City in the 1990s that compensates businesses for physical losses as a result of terror.*

In the week after the devastating atrocities in Paris, the Chancellor of the Exchequer announced that infiltration of our online infrastructure ranks alongside 'guns, bombs and knives' as a terrorist threat against which the UK needs urgently to defend itself. Elevating cyber-terrorism in such a public manner, backed up with commendably generous financial resources for our security services, is a critical first step in tackling the evolving dangers to Britain's national security. But how capable are our major institutions and the broader economy of withstanding damage from a cyber-onslaught?

So concerned is the Bank of England about the systemic risk posed to the financial system of a targeted cyber-attack, that for almost two years now it has worked hand in glove with GCHQ to test resilience in the Square Mile. This work recognises the potential financial impact of a cyber-attack on businesses and citizens, and implicitly concedes that our institutions are not currently adequate to handle the physical impacts of the cyber-terrorist threat.

In October, telecommunications firm TalkTalk was hacked by two teenage schoolboys who leaked millions of people's bank details online, costing the company around £35 million. Meanwhile, the Federation of Small Businesses claims that September's tube strike came with a price tag of £600 million in economic disruption. A terrorist cyber-attack would likely seek to replicate both of these events, albeit on a much larger scale. With UK cities becoming ever-'smarter' and more reliant on sophisticated computer software, it is vital that we have the confidence that these systems can be backed up, protected or swiftly rebuilt in the event of a catastrophic breach.

Unfortunately, however, there is serious concern about whether the existing insurance cover for such events is robust enough. This is where a reinsurance vehicle, which effectively guarantees insurers and governments against heavy losses, stands to play a crucial role. The IRA bombing of the Baltic Exchange in my constituency in 1992 proved a seminal moment in the Square Mile's centuries-old insurance industry. The scale of damage was so colossal that reinsurers began to withdraw cover for terrorism in double-quick time.

It swiftly became clear that the gap could only be plugged if the insurance industry and government worked together. The result was Pool Re, a partnership between the UK Treasury and Britain's insurers which – for the first time ever – made the government insurer of last resort. Following the 9/11 attacks, its coverage was extended to include incidents of chemical, biological, radiological, and nuclear terrorism. Just as the terrorists have evolved, so have we.

With the threat now more dispersed but no less deadly, the question for the insurance industry is how to calculate and manage that unpredictability. One area where surely we require better cover before a major incident occurs is cyber-terrorism. This is not wholly unfamiliar territory for this government. A similar insurance gap was recently identified following the serious floods of 2013, with the insurance industry and government stepping in to create Flood Re to ensure that those domestic properties in the UK at the highest risk of flooding could receive affordable cover. Now that the cyber threat is so clearly tied up with terrorism, the time may be ripe for the UK government to create a new, standalone reinsurance fund – 'Cyber Re' – to ensure that major British businesses and institutions are covered in the event of cyber-attack.

This made it all the more curious when, as recently as March, the erstwhile coalition government declared that there was no need for state intervention in this area. Despite all the emerging evidence and vocal campaigning from security experts and academics, as well as insurance underwriting insiders, the Cabinet Office (the government department with chief responsibility for cyber issues) concluded that the insurance industry could handle known risks without the need for a Pool Re type structure.

I accept that a Cyber Re proposition is not without difficulties, particularly when it comes to defining what constitutes a 'terror attack' – it can be tricky to assign responsibility in the online world, sorting industrial espionage from security threat. However, the importance of financial, professional and business services to the UK economy as a whole should now incentivise government into taking a lead alongside our world-leading insurance sector to withstand one of the greatest systemic risks that UK Plc currently faces. As we all know, in the insurance business, providing the right cover – at the right cost – relies on our ability accurately to predict the probability and severity of future losses. But as the Baltic Exchange and the Twin Towers showed to such devastating effect, single events can turn assumptions on their head in a flash.

While I am a free marketeer, bringing all these perils under one roof might ensure a much more resilient economy in the face of threats otherwise difficult to insure. It could give the insurance industry the confidence it needs to expose its balance sheet in the knowledge that it has a safety net, simply because the potential losses at stake cannot be handled by the private sector alone.

So the Chancellor is right to raise the issue of cyber-terrorism. As nations prepare themselves against bomb plots, gun attacks and airline hijackings, so terrorists will adapt, finding new weaknesses to exploit. The provision of insurance and reinsurance for such threats will become an increasing factor in the government's fight against terrorists and their criminal gang cohorts. We must face facts: in the event of a catastrophic cyber-attack, it will *only* be reinsurance that will collectively enable us to get back on our feet.

‡

London tech city (*House Magazine*), 11 December 2015

I was asked by the House Magazine *to contribute to their end-of-year special on economic issues by outlining some of the challenges facing London as a hub for technology and IT firms. I took the opportunity to raise some of the issues appearing most consistently in my postbag, particularly the rollout of superfast broadband in urban areas – a problem I had been campaigning to fix for many months.*

The transformation from the mid-noughties of an unloved district around Old Street into a swinging Silicon Roundabout was a timely reminder of what can happen when enterprise is left to its own devices. It was the low rents of the City fringe that first began to attract a cluster of small technology firms – a process accelerated in the aftermath of 2008's financial crisis. When shaken together, the creative influences of Shoreditch and Soho, the money men of Canary Wharf and the Square Mile, and the brains of London's top university graduates and global workforce, transformed that small cluster into what is, today, Europe's biggest hub for IT start-ups. London has once again proven itself to be the perfect canvas for the cross-pollination of new ideas, innovations, skills and resources.

As with any freshly rooted phenomenon, however, Tech City remains vulnerable to change in the delicate ecosystem from which it grew. Thankfully, it already has influential PR to attract government interest in its fate. The handwringing in the aftermath of 2008's financial crisis about London's over-reliance on financial services, and anxiety over how we might 'rebalance' and diversify the capital's economy, mean that government is desperately keen to see Silicon Roundabout succeed. Nevertheless, there are questions hanging over its future. How will it now retain the low-cost office space so critical to start-ups as the increasing popularity of the area drives up rents? How will it continue to attract innovative, highly skilled and competitively priced labour when London's housing costs are so high and immigration rules are tightening? How can it retain a competitive edge over rival tech clusters when London's broadband infrastructure is still so creaky?

Alive to concerns that several of us local MPs have raised about IT skills shortages, government has introduced a Tech Nation Visa Scheme to attract talented tech entrepreneurs. But concerns remain about the availability of developers, and we must ensure that Tier 2 visas for those with more general skills are opened up if the skills shortage continues. Fantastic work is being done in schools and universities to encourage students to code and open their eyes up to the employment opportunities in the tech sector; however, that will only bear fruit in the next five to ten years. Employers need skilled labour now.

Shared work spaces, rented desks and incubator hubs are springing up across the city to cater for new businesses in need of cheap space. The Innovation Warehouse, for instance, brings together entrepreneurs, investors and the City of London Corporation to support early-stage tech firms, and the provision of low-cost space is becoming a requirement in a number of planning applications in the area. The housing nut is proving harder to crack, and the cost of living is now ranking as one of the key worries for Tech City employers who are finding it harder to attract good people to their businesses.

Perversely, superfast broadband continues to be an enormous headache here in central London. BT's Openreach brand has a near monopoly on the lines leading from local telephone exchanges to individual buildings, which then must be leased by rival broadband providers. Arguably, the time is ripe formally to split Openreach from BT and start sharing their mapping on precisely where superfast gaps exist so that other providers can assiduously target those areas currently not being catered for. To give them their due, Openreach have agreed to invest more heavily in inner London after a fierce cross-party lobbying campaign. They also have to contend with reluctance by TfL and local authorities to allow more roadworks to lay necessary cables. But rollout is simply not fast enough, so no potential solution should be ruled out.

The financial technology sector alone is now generating £20 billion of GDP for the UK economy, directly employing 135,000 people. This is no new dot.com bubble – technology is a rich vein for an advanced economy like the UK's to tap. The appointment at the Summer Budget of a Special Envoy for financial technology and the launch of the Upscale programme to help start-ups grow are just two of many targeted initiatives to keep the wheels of Tech City turning. The trick for the future is to ensure that the very fluidity and dynamism that first got the engine going is not snuffed out as the first wave of digital entrepreneurs mature and become part of the commercial establishment.

‡

Time for radicalism to address London's housing affordability crisis? (*City AM*), 18 December 2015

The affordability of housing, even to people in high-paying jobs, had rocketed up the ladder as a political issue. Since 2010, the average UK house price had increased by 15 per cent, and buyers now required more than five times average earnings to purchase a property. The problem was particularly acute in London, where houses were priced more than three times the average UK home. Renting was no better, with the capital's private sector rents increasing by 34 per cent over the decade to 2015.

Chancellor George Osborne had responded with a range of measures at the 2015 Autumn Statement, including doubling the housing budget, further reform of the planning system and an additional £7 billion to boost the supply of affordable homes by 400,000. In this article for City AM, *I suggested we also look at ideas on how to deter overseas buyers from purchasing homes as 'buy to leave' investments.*

As MP since 2001 for the most central London constituency, I cannot recall a time when housing issues have not dominated my postbag. No surprise, perhaps, when UK buyers compete for a limited supply of homes with a global citizenry seeking its own slice of prime London. But I have also witnessed how the polarisation characterising my own constituency has spread to far-flung suburbia. Today, the cheapest 10 per cent of London's homes are affordable only to the highest-earning quarter of workers.

There was a time not so long ago when the media and politicians saw rising London house prices as an unalloyed good. But as ever more Londoners find themselves excluded from the property bonanza, so the negative economic effects have grown. When rent costs gobble most of one's monthly income, less can be saved to start up or invest in a business. As the capital loses its lustre as a place to raise a family, employers have to spend more to attract and retain the best people. Meanwhile, productivity suffers as more time is wasted commuting, and buyers pushing the boundaries of mortgage affordability make London's property market ever more vulnerable to interest rate rises.

When the sky-high cost of London's housing comes at such a fearsome economic price, even free-market capitalists like me wonder whether it is time for more radical solutions. It is perilous for any politician to talk of morality, but it seems wrong for hardworking, aspirational people to be so completely priced out of their own property market. It is precisely these Londoners who, in previous generations, would maintain, build and pass on our city's social capital to the next generation – social capital that is a crucial part of London's appeal in the first place. What I mean here is the rule of law, a lack of corruption, protected property rights, respected emergency services, personal freedoms, academic and industrial excellence, and so on. That capital cannot simply be created out of thin air, but instead evolves over centuries.

Increasing supply has to be the first step in addressing our housing crisis, and efforts are underway to loosen planning blockages, free up public land, and incentivise development. Nonetheless, our ability to build is undermined by shortages of skilled labour and basic supplies – one developer lamented that the lead-in time for bricks alone is forty weeks – so it will take time for new homes to materialise. We need urgently, therefore, to look also at who is buying up that new supply.

It is no secret that, in recent years, unimaginably vast sums of foreign money have flooded London's housing market in search of yield and a safe haven. Last year, a Civitas report revealed that 85 per cent of prime London property purchases in 2012 had been made with overseas money, with two thirds of those purchases made not for owner-occupation but as an investment. Overseas buyers are purchasing not just at the top end, but less expensive new builds too. Since unoccupied property in the crowded metropolis is one of the factors pushing up the cost of living for other city dwellers, Civitas suggested imposing curbs on foreign ownership.

There has been an understandable reluctance to do anything that might risk London's attractiveness as a global city. However, competitor nations like Switzerland, Singapore, the United States and Australia – open, free-trading capitalist states – have all taken action to restrict or deter foreign ownership of residential property. In Switzerland, only citizens and permanent residents can own property. Most Singaporeans live in Housing and Development Board (HDB) properties which citizens alone can own, while foreigners may buy non-HDB homes, but will be taxed heavily if they sell within four years. Any foreign non-resident or short-term visa holder has to apply to buy property in Australia through the Foreign Investment Review Board, a body whose rules state that an investment can only go ahead if it leads to an increase in available homes. In New York, there is an annual property tax of up to 19 per cent of the assessed value for homes not occupied by people on the electoral roll.

By contrast, the UK government has hiked stamp duty at the top end of the market – and at the most recent Autumn Statement, on buy-to-lets. These levies hit domestic buyers hard and risk landlords passing costs to tenants. The time may now be ripe, therefore, to consider instead having residential developments which are only open for purchase to UK citizens and permanent residents. Additional levies on speculative ownership and 'buy to leave empty' purchases might be considered alongside a potential system for higher non-resident council tax.

Alternatively, we might consider a 'community contribution' of, say, 15 per cent of the last sold value of properties not occupied by voters. Unlike a mansion tax, it would not sweep up those UK residents who have been in their homes many years. Indeed, such a change would positively encourage foreign owners with empty properties to rent them out to Londoners, boosting supply and helping to suppress rents.

Some of these proposals may prove impracticable, and the impact of foreign cash is, of course, just one part of the bigger housing picture. I am trying instead to provoke debate. We must not lose sight of either the wider economic damage being done by high house prices or the foundations on which high property prices in London are built – the priceless value of social capital created in the past by generations of Londoners.

‡

Still alive, but is the Greek economy kicking?, 20 December 2015

With 2015 drawing to a close – a year that had been domestically triumphant and internationally tumultuous – I reflected once again on the state of the eurozone. My July article about the ongoing Greek crisis had been followed by yet more dramatics from the Syriza government. Having dragged the Greek people to the polling booths to respond to a referendum on the latest terms of a bailout deal, Greek parliamentarians had gone on to approve a third bailout anyway. Prime Minister Alexis Tsipras duly resigned and called a snap election, claiming he had a moral duty to go to the polls after agreeing to bailout terms that included extensive pension reforms and significant cuts to public expenditure. 'I want to be honest with you,' Tsipras confessed. 'We did not achieve the agreement we expected before the January elections.'

Syriza was nonetheless returned to power on 20 September, with Tsipras retaining the prime ministership after a convincing victory. But it made little difference to Greece's problems, and I suggested in this article for ConservativeHome that the same issues would only resurface in July 2016 when the next ECB repayments were due. The Greek experience had only highlighted the increasing irrelevance of voters' voices in the face of creditors' demands. It was becoming clear that in the battle to keep the euro show on the road, democracy might have to be sidelined.

On 4 October, only a fortnight after the Greek election, fellow eurozone member Portugal held parliamentary elections which saw the ruling centre-right coalition of Prime Minister Pedro Passos Coelho win 37 per cent of the vote, but fail to command a parliamentary majority following unexpected gains by radical leftists. Nonetheless, Portugal's constitutional President, Anibal Cavaco Silva, first invited Mr Passos Coelho to form a government. Silva explained that it was too risky to let any leftist coalition into power given that some of their number had vowed to smash the austerity programme imposed on Portugal by the IMF and EU.

President Silva's intervention enraged the opposition, who interpreted it as a sidelining of democracy to appease foreign investors and Brussels. After only eleven days of power, the Passos Coelho minority government was toppled as the Socialist, Communist, Left Bloc and Green parties formed their own governing coalition with Antonio Costa, leader of the Socialist Party, as the new Prime Minister.

Casual observers of the eurozone scene might be forgiven for believing that the worst of Greece's economic woes are behind it. Sadly, nothing could be further from the truth, as recent events in Portugal and Spain remind us.

Excitable commentary in June suggested that finally, but finally Grexit was upon us. However, while Greece had seemingly exhausted all options (not to mention the patience and cash of its eurozone partners) at the eleventh hour, yet another deal was cobbled together to kick the can further down the road. Newly re-elected Prime Minister Alexis Tsipras ended up agreeing to a third bailout on even more stringent terms than he had rejected before calling a near farcical referendum, which had itself firmly endorsed that stance. The Greek Syriza movement's radicalism has been snuffed out under the weight of eurozone orthodoxy. The ugly constitutional stand-off following October's Portuguese election shows that no avowedly anti-austerity governing coalition will smoothly assume office, or be permitted to implement its programme regardless of the voters' wishes, until the institutional apparatus of the single currency is established.

As ever, the wheels of EU/eurozone bureaucracy seem set to meander slowly onwards, taking all too little account of the realities on the ground. Spain's general election takes place today, but as with its Iberian neighbour, many voters there have little cause to believe the ECB propaganda that its financial crisis is over and that the Spanish economy will remain on the road to recovery simply by sticking to the austerity script. What remains painfully lacking is *sustainable* economic growth – stagnation at a time of high historic debt, and the prospect of deflationary forces, represents a toxic mix that threatens democracy as well as the European economy.

A myth has taken root that such growth will come once eurozone members get their public finances in order and undertake reforms towards creating leaner, more dynamic states. What should worry us all, however, is that growth remains elusive for the one eurozone economy that has *already* ticked those boxes. Finland sits at the very top of world league tables for competitiveness, education, commercial legal rights and innovation. If Greece wears the dunce hat, Finland is the eurozone's model student. Nonetheless, demand is growing from Finns for a national referendum on withdrawal from the single currency – so-called 'Fixit' – after three years of economic contraction. The euro was sold to Finns as the ultimate defence against its looming Russian neighbour, but the Finnish economy has been performing worse than any other eurozone nation, contracting 6 per cent since 2008, while its Swedish neighbour (sitting comfortably outside the currency zone) can boast of 8 per cent growth in the same period. No amount of reform, according to the new Finnish coalition government, can apparently make up for the damage inflicted on exports by high labour costs and a fixed exchange rate.

Then there is Italy, still by some margin the EU's fourth largest economy. The dynamic economy and constitution-reforming centre-left premiership of Matteo Renzi had at first won over the confidence of Italy's business leaders and financial community, and by mid-year there were clear signs of recovery, especially in its more liberalised employment market. The direct impact of the migration crisis on its southern shores and the emboldening of the left wing of Mr Renzi's party at the populist anti-austerity revolts elsewhere in the eurozone now threaten to push him off course.

With such widespread uncertainty abound, it would probably be unwise to predict with any conviction just how the Greek situation will play out. Remarkably, an albeit diminished Mr Tsipras remains at the helm and just possibly all is not lost. However, Greece's creditors, whose patience was at breaking point and many of whom had probably discounted their losses as the farcical referendum played out in June, will need to be convinced that Syriza #2 is serious about governing for the long haul. Only then will recapitalisation of Greece's beleaguered banks be guaranteed along with inclusion in the ECB's quantitative easing programme and a restructuring of the country's debts, allowing markedly longer repayment terms.

How will the Greek government use the breathing space it has been granted? There is no necessity for large-scale repayments of the latest bailout until July 2016, which should until then at least silence talk of a Grexit. Austerity will continue, interest groups (of the elderly and its rural communities to name but two) will draw new battle lines, and crisis fatigue may also set in.

Commentators have continued to struggle to explain why the Greek economy has been such an acutely unique problem. One view, favoured by economists and bankers, is that Greece was always a special case – it should never have been allowed to join the EU as early as 1981, especially with the Cyprus issue unresolved (as it is to this day, despite all the recent hopeful signs of progress) and an utterly unreformed economy. Its then leaders, rather like those in Romania and Bulgaria in the run-up to their accession in 2007, saw linking up with Brussels as the road to salvation to 'save Greece from itself'. Unlike every other country requiring a bailout, no Greek government has ever properly accepted the urgent need for internal reform.

The alternative interpretation, favoured by left-leaning journalists and Eurosceptic commentators, is that Greece's recent travails are the fault of outsiders. In particular, the loathed troika – the ECB, European Commission and the IMF – who imposed a grotesquely unfair straitjacket upon the Greek economy and subsequently *pour encourager les autres* have insisted that austerity be prolonged irrespective of the utter misery to millions of Greek citizens. Regardless of the Greek people's democratic wishes, the Frankfurt and Brussels elite were determined to show that Greece's euro membership was incompatible with the anti-austerity message of the twice-elected Syriza party.

The one key feature that these two interpretations have in common is that they ignore any responsibility that the Greek people had, or should have had, for their own fate. In truth, a succession of Greek political leaders has failed to display the statesmanship of levelling with the electorates and persuading its population of the need for reform in the modern, outward-looking globalised institutional world to which Greece aspires to belong.

EPILOGUE
2016

Since rounding off *The Best of Times* at the end of 2015, the first quarter of 2016 has been spent busily tying this book together with historical context amidst contemporary events that are both politically and economically explosive.

The New Year kicked off with tumult on the Chinese stock market, where trading was halted on the opening day after a shock 7 per cent fall in the value of shares on the CSI 300 and Shanghai Composite. With panic rife that the slump in share value was indicative of China's economic slowdown, volatility quickly spread to other markets with precipitate dips on the Dow Jones, FTSE 100, Dax and Nikkei.

A fall in Chinese demand for commodities means that there is much to be written about the drop in oil price that occurred during the period covered in *The Best of Times*, a phenomenon which it has perhaps been remiss of me not to have analysed in detail. Were this to continue into the future, it would doubtless have a profound impact on the balance sheets of nations such as Venezuela, Nigeria and, critically, Saudi Arabia, and be seen as a defining characteristic of change during the years covered in this book.

Markets were spooked too by the rapid ratcheting of tensions between Saudi Arabia and Iran as the execution of Nimr al-Nimr, a prominent Shia cleric, by the Kingdom, and reactive protests at the Saudi embassy in Tehran led to the breaking-off of diplomatic relations. Ongoing conflicts in Yemen (an issue only tangentially touched upon in this book) and Syria raged on, with all the consequent human tragedy. Six weeks into the New Year and more refugees and migrants had reached Europe than in the first six months of 2015, leading to the ad hoc resurrection of border controls across the European Union and the brokering of a controversial deal between the EU and Turkey to deport those arriving in Greece illegally.

In March, President Putin announced a surprise partial withdrawal of Russian troops from Syria in a new push towards UN-mediated peace talks, once again dictating the terms of a conflict that had shown up the absence of US leadership in the Middle East. Barack Obama had instead chosen to use his final year as US President defrosting relations with Cuba, concluding a historic visit to Havana to meet Cuban President Raul Castro just before Easter. Meanwhile, the battle to secure the Republican and Democratic Presidential nominations pushed on. By the end of March, only Ted Cruz, Donald Trump and John Kasich were left in the Republican race. With the controversial Trump well out in front, only the prospect of a brokered Convention in Cleveland in July seemed to leave open the possibility of his being beaten by a potentially brand new, alternative candidate. A plucky challenge from Senator Bernie Sanders for the Democratic nomination looked sure to be seen off by establishment candidate Hillary Clinton.

David Cameron was eventually to get his renegotiation deal signed off at an EU summit in Brussels in February, extracting a series of concessions on Britain's EU membership. The UK would be explicitly exempt from ever-closer union and any prospect of signing up to the euro; there would be new protections for the City of London as a financial centre outside the eurozone; and a limit to the access EU migrants would have to in-work benefits. After calling a Leave/Remain referendum for 23 June, London Mayor Boris Johnson, Justice Secretary Michael Gove, and Work and Pensions Secretary Iain Duncan Smith all declared themselves in favour of Leave. A later disagreement with Chancellor George Osborne over cuts to Personal Independence Payments led to the shock resignation of former Conservative leader Duncan Smith, and threatened to derail the government's deficit reduction plans and destabilise the Conservative leadership.

Sadly, the terror threat did not abate, intensifying fears over the spread of violent Islamic extremism. The sense of widespread unease and panic permeated through into perceptions towards newly arrived migrants in Europe. This translated into an upsurge in political support for anti-refugee party Alternative für Deutschland in German regional elections, delivering a blow to Chancellor Angela Merkel's authority. In Spain, there was still no new government three months after December's inconclusive general election result.

With an overriding sense of the world in 2016 being a dangerous and unpredictable place, it was hard to tell how the year might play out. But the extraordinary and unthinkable did not seem beyond possibility.

ABOUT THE AUTHOR

Rt Hon. Mark Field MP

First elected in June 2001, Mark Field is a fourth-term Conservative MP representing the Cities of London & Westminster, a central London constituency that incorporates in the West End, Whitehall and City of London respectively the capital's prime cultural, political and financial districts.

Educated at Reading School (a direct grant grammar school), Mark later read Law at St Edmund Hall, Oxford. During his undergraduate days, he set up his first business, specialising in publishing career handbooks.

Upon qualifying as a solicitor in 1990, Mark joined leading international law firm Freshfields as a corporate lawyer. He went on to set up his second business, Kellyfield Consulting, in 1994. A recruitment organisation serving the legal profession, it quickly acquired an enviable reputation in niche search/selection, and as one of two directors, Mark built this start-up enterprise into a company of twelve full-time staff with a turnover of £1.8 million.

Bringing business, legal and political experience to his role as a Member of Parliament, Mark has served on the front bench under three party leaders, including spells as shadow Financial Secretary to the Treasury and shadow Minister for London.

Throughout the 2010–15 coalition parliament, he served on the prestigious Intelligence and Security Committee. In recognition of his work in this demanding, sensitive area, Mark was sworn of the Privy Council in March 2015. Following the general election of that year, he was appointed vice-chairman (International) of the Conservative Party, and chairman of its International and Outreach Office.

The Best of Times is Mark's second book, and follows on from 2013's *Between the Crashes*, which provided an account of the financial crisis and its aftermath from his perspective as the City's MP. Over the past decade, Mark has become a prominent broadcaster and writer, appearing frequently on political television and radio programmes, and writing regular columns for newspapers including the *Daily Telegraph* and *City AM*.

Julia Dockerill

Mark wrote *The Best of Times* with his Chief of Staff, Julia Dockerill. Julia is a graduate in Social and Political Sciences from Queens' College, Cambridge, and attended the comprehensive Herts and Essex High School. In 2014 she was elected to the London Borough of Tower Hamlets as one of five Conservative councillors, representing St Katharine's & Wapping, a ward that includes the Tower of London within its boundaries.

Julia also assisted Mark in writing his first book, *Between the Crashes*, and is slowly researching her own, *London in the Noughties*, in her spare time. She is a trustee of education charity Inspire Malawi.